TREASURES OF
THE NEW YORK
PUBLIC
LIBRARY

TREASURES OF THE NEW YORK
PUBLIC
LIB

MARSHALL B. DAVIDSON

IN COLLABORATION WITH
BERNARD McTigue
CURATOR, THE ARENTS COLLECTIONS

AND KEEPER OF RARE BOOKS

ORIGINAL PHOTOGRAPHY BY
JONATHAN WALLEN

RARY

HARRY N. ABRAMS, INC.,
PUBLISHERS, NEW YORK

THIS BOOK IS DEDICATED TO THE LIBRARIANS AND CURATORS,
PAST AND PRESENT, OF THE NEW YORK PUBLIC LIBRARY.

Editor: Mark D. Greenberg
Designer: Bob McKee

Library of Congress Cataloging-in-Publication Data

ISBN 0-8109-1354-2
1. New York Public Library.   2. Library resources—New York (N.Y.)
3. Rare books—New York (N.Y.)   4. Manuscripts—New York (N.Y.)
5. Printed ephemera—New York (N.Y.)   I. Davidson, Marshall B.
II. McTigue, Bernard.   III. Title.
Z733.N63N45 1988
027.4747′1—dc19   88-3323   CIP
Illustrations copyright © 1988 The New York Public Library,
Astor, Lenox and Tilden Foundations
Text copyright © 1988 Harry N. Abrams, Inc.
Published in 1988 by Harry N. Abrams, Incorporated, New York

A Times Mirror Company
Printed and bound in Japan

CONTENTS

ACKNOWLEDGMENTS

The authors wish to acknowledge and thank those members of the staff of The New York Public Library who shared their knowledge and time with them in the preparation of this book: Donald Anderle, Jean Bowen, Lisa Browar, Susan Davis, Howard Dodson, Paul Fasana, Leonard Gold, Mihai Handrea, Edwin Holmgren, Alice Hudson, Glenderlyn Jackson, Richard Jackson, Edward Kasinec, Dorothy Lourdou, Francis Mattson, Robert Morris, Angeline Moscatt, Rodney Phillips, Robert Rainwater, Lola Szladits, Julia Van Haaften, and Roberta Waddell.

We are particularly grateful to Donald Anderle and Gloria Deák, whose 1985 exhibition, Treasures from The New York Public Library, provided us with inspiration and with information about many of the works included in this book.

Richard Newman, William Coakley, and Lawrence Murphy of the Library's Publications Office gave us much needed support.

Edith Pavese and Mark Greenberg, senior editors at Harry N. Abrams, Inc., were heroic in their patience and efforts on our behalf. Jonathan Wallen's photographs and Bob McKee's design ensured a beautiful book.

Any errors of fact or judgment that may appear in this book are the result of our own limitations and have been made in spite of the assistance of those named above.

Marshall B. Davidson
Bernard McTigue

FOREWORD

Every great library has its treasure trove, its carefully preserved rare and valuable books and manuscripts, often well protected from public view and use. At The New York Public Library we have dazzling jewels—the Tickhill Psalter, the Hunt-Lenox Globe, the Bay Psalm Book, the first Gutenberg Bible brought to the New World, Thomas Jefferson's handwritten copy of the Declaration of Independence, George Washington's draft of his Farewell Address, and richest of all, perhaps, our beautiful and beautifully restored treasure house itself. You will see many examples of our great wealth displayed in this book.

But objects are rare for being overlooked as much as for being sought after. One of the great strengths of The New York Public Library has been, and continues to be, the vision of curators and librarians who see beyond convention, high culture, and sometimes even good taste in order to acquire the seemingly insignificant, the unfashionable, or the offensive. History, too, these days, takes less interest in the trappings of importance, the pomp and circumstance, and shows more curiosity about the daily round of seemingly unimportant lives.

Let us celebrate the treasures of The New York Public Library, then, by broadening the definition of what "treasure" is.

Along with T. S. Eliot's manuscript copy of *The Waste Land*—with Ezra Pound's comments!—and Virginia Woolf's diaries, we have dime novels and penny dreadfuls. Along with the banquet menu from the tsar's coronation in 1899, we have the bill of fare of steerage passengers to Texas in 1835. Along with the family genealogies of the wellborn, we have plantation maps that help descendants of slaves trace their roots. Along with Columbus's letter announcing his discovery, we have the safe-conduct pass of a member of the International Brigade in the Spanish Civil War. Along with a score in Bach's hand, we have sheet music from the Jazz Age.

And these are treasures all, for each is capable of bringing a flash of recognition or insight or knowledge to one of the thousands of readers and researchers who come to the Library every day to consult our books, manuscripts, prints, ephemera, and now, computers.

Democratic historiography has enlarged the definition of cultural treasure to include much that is seemingly prosaic or trivial. Indeed, we can be certain that most of what now is not considered a "treasure" will be to future generations. It is my deep conviction that the Library is truly a democratic institution because we collect both the gems of human culture and that which represents the everyday. We cherish all of it because it is all essential to our discovery and rediscovery of who and what we are, were, and will be.

The Library's mission is profoundly democratic, offering free and equal access to all of its holdings. It is a pleasure to share them with a public that may be unaware of its patrimony, for the Library does not truly possess these works, great and small, it is their custodian. For our present public and for generations yet unborn, we preserve the best of the past to inspire and inform the future.

Vartan Gregorian,
President, The New York Public Library

INTRODUCTION

The New York Public Library is a precocious young giant among the scant handful of the largest and most important libraries in the world. When this library was conceived less than a century ago, the British Museum in London and the Bibliothèque Nationale in Paris had already amassed formidable collections largely through royal and princely patronage. In this country, the collections at Harvard University had deep roots in the fertile intellectual soil of New England, and the Library of Congress had made large strides toward the greatness it would soon achieve. Yet today, The New York Public Library ranks as an indisputable peer of these institutions—and it continues to grow.

It embraces the seventh largest research library in the world and the fourth largest in this country. Its branch system is the largest in the world. The Research Libraries contain over eight million volumes, twenty-three million manuscripts, and five hundred thousand recordings. The branches have nine million items at their disposal. The overall budget is in excess of $100 million. There is a staff of 2,951 full-time employees serving 1,063,000 visitors to the Central Research Library and nearly one million cardholders who borrow 9,800,000 items a year. The Library has grown up, along with the city and nation it serves.

Although The New York Public Library ranks with the greatest institutional collections of the world, because of its unique character, it is also set apart from them. Unlike other great libraries, it is based upon a commitment of service to the general public as much as to the community of scholars, and it owes its birth as well as much of its continuing support to private generosity rather than government or alumni support. If a library may be termed the mind and memory of a free society, then none better suits the definition than this one.

When they think of The New York Public Library, many people think only of the magnificent structure on Fifth Avenue, but that building is only the flagship of a system that numbers eighty-one branches (including the Mid-Manhattan Library) the Performing Arts Research Center, the Schomburg Center for Research in Black Culture, and the Library at Forty-third Street (the old "Annex"). This vast network of learning and diversion provides the people of the city, the state, and the country with services from childhood to old age.

THE ASTOR LIBRARY

The New York Public Library may be said to have been born in 1848 when John Jacob Astor, a German immigrant who had become the wealthiest American of his time, pledged $400,000 ($7 or $8 million in today's money) in his will for the establishment of a reference library in New York. He had been urged to do this by Joseph Green Cogswell, whom a contemporary referred to as "Astor's trainbearer and prime minister" and upon whose advice and close association Astor depended. Indeed, so heavy was that dependence that when Washington Irv-

ing, recently appointed minister to Spain (and later to be the first president of
the Astor Library), proposed that Cogswell accompany him as the well-paid secretary of the legation, the aged and anxious Astor bribed Cogswell to remain where
he so sorely needed him—at home with a permanent salary as superintendent of the
great public library he had been encouraging Astor to build and endow.

This "trainbearer" had been educated at Harvard and the University of Göt-
tingen, a teacher and librarian at the former institution, and a widely traveled
scholar. He became fired with an inspired mission to build, with Astor's money,
an incomparable reference library. In his turn, Astor loved literature and enjoyed
the company of such literary figures as Washington Irving, the poet Fitz-Greene
Halleck, and other eminent contemporaries.

THE LENOX LIBRARY

In 1876, the great private library that had been amassed by the wealthy New
York collector, James Lenox, was opened to the public, on the site of what is now
the Frick Collection. Lenox was consumed with a passion for collecting; he would
fill up rooms in his house with books until they could hold no more, then he would
close them off and start on the next room. His primary interest was Americana,
books documenting the discovery and exploration of North and South America and
the establishment of the Republic. Being a good, stern Presbyterian, he also
collected Bibles and editions of John Bunyan's Puritan classic, *The Pilgrim's Progress*. The library he opened to the public was a research facility intended primarily
for scholars and bibliophiles. He was also fond of eighteenth- and nineteenth-
century English and American paintings and sculpture, examples of which were
contained in the art gallery that he included in his library building.

THE TILDEN TRUST

These two great nineteenth-century institutions—the Astor and Lenox libraries—
provided the core of the collections and established the tradition of private philanthropy on which the present Library is founded. The legacy of Samuel Jones
Tilden provided the third major unit of what was to become The New York Public
Library.

Tilden, one-time governor of New York and unsuccessful candidate for the
presidency (he won the popular vote but lost in the Electoral College), had died
in New York in 1886, leaving an estate valued at $5 million. He never married and
left a will in which he bequeathed the bulk of his estate "to found a free library
and reading room in the City of New York."

This did not sit at all well with his nephew, George Tilden, who immediately
contested the will. His suit dragged on for six years, until, in 1892, the courts is-

John Jacob Astor

James Lenox

sued a "decree of partition," splitting the estate between Tilden's relatives and the Tilden Trust, which was left with $2.4 million.

By the 1890s, the original endowments of the Astor and Lenox libraries had so declined and their collections had so expanded that it had become necessary for them to reconsider their mission. Largely through the efforts and imagination of a New York attorney, John Bigelow (a Tilden trustee), a plan was devised whereby the Astor and Lenox foundations would be joined with the Tilden Trust in a legal entity to be known as The New York Public Library. The City of New York would build a new library, which the city would own, to house the collections, and the combined private foundations would continue to own the collections themselves. This marriage of public good and private largesse took place in 1895.

CONSTRUCTION OF THE NEW YORK PUBLIC LIBRARY

The site chosen for this library was that of the defunct city reservoir, a picturesque building in the "Egyptian" style, the necessary demolition of which was bemoaned by many faithful admirers of that exotic pile. The site was, however, admirably chosen. At the heart of Manhattan, facing Fifth Avenue, extending from Forty-second to Fortieth streets and reaching back to Bryant Park toward the west, it was excellently positioned for an institution designed to serve the ever-growing metropolitan area.

As a result of an open competition among scores of the city's most prominent architects, the firm of Carrère and Hastings was finally selected to design and construct the new building. The cornerstone was laid in May 1902. When, after nine years of meticulous planning and construction, and an expenditure of $9 million, its doors were opened, the public, the press, and professional architects generally agreed that this great marble building was, inside and out, one of the city's most gracious architectural ornaments and, according to the prestigious magazine *Architectural Record,* "the most important public building erected in the city during several generations." It contained more marble than any other building in the United States—marble that had been brought by horse cart from Vermont and by ship from Italy, France, and Belgium.

This was an era when great public buildings in the classical revival style known as the "Beaux Arts" were going up all around the United States. These buildings were the embodiment of civic pride and national confidence and reflected in their style the mood of national expansionism that gripped the country in the latter part of the nineteenth century. As America flexed its political and military muscles, it sought to erect monuments to its power and prosperity.

The mind-boggling wealth that was being accumulated by individuals received its outward manifestation not only in huge mansions and vast art collections, but also in philanthropic foundations, which reflected both the donor's resources and his concern for humanity.

Not only was the Library architecturally distinguished, but it had been admirably designed to house the multitude of vital functions it would be called upon to serve over the years to come, a happy marriage of beauty and utility. To achieve this, the architects had the invaluable counsel of John Shaw Billings, the Library's first director, who has been termed the mastermind of the whole very complicated operation. It takes a great librarian to make and maintain a great library, and under Billings's inspired leadership, the new, consolidated library became, almost overnight, an illustrious institution.

A plaque mounted in the entrance hall declares: "The City of New York has erected this building to be maintained forever as a free library for the use of the people." As Billings remarked, everything in the collections would be accessible

Overleaf:

Above left
The city reservoir demolished to make way for The New York Public Library

Below left
Craftsmen carving the marble detailing for the Library building

Right
Construction of the Library's facade in 1902

Nov. 1ˢᵗ 1902

4

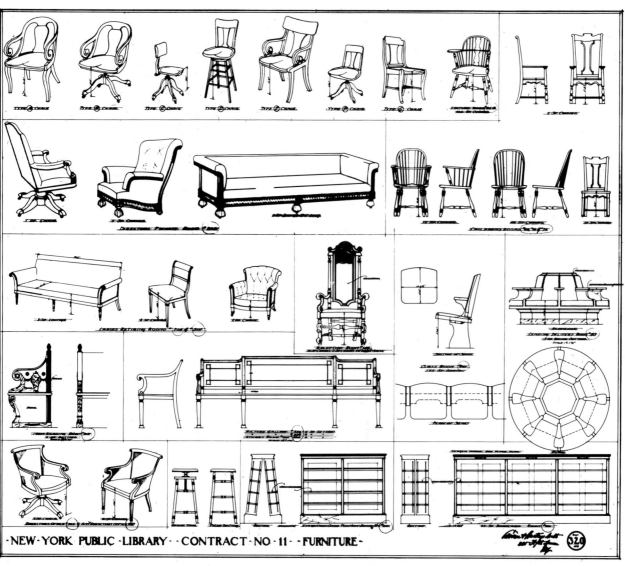

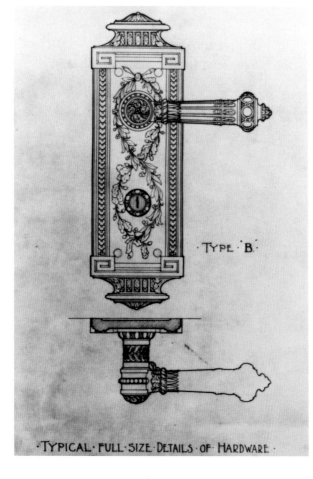

TYPE · B ·

· TYPICAL · FULL · SIZE · DETAILS · OF · HARDWARE ·

Carrère and Hastings not only designed the Library building itself but also the furniture, hardware, and even, as pictured on the next page, the wastebaskets!

to everyone. The public was quick to respond to this "open house" invitation. On the first day, May 24, 1911, from thirty to fifty thousand visitors streamed through the building from 9 A.M. until closing time!

Wanting to be the first to put in a call slip, Mr. C. A. Montgomery requested a copy of Delia Bacon's *Philosophy of the Plays of Shakespeare Unfolded*. To its embarrassment, the Library did not own a copy, but since Montgomery did, he returned with it as a gift. (Apparently, he had known that the Library could not produce the book and had planned this ploy to publicize the theory of Bacon's authorship of Shakespeare's plays.) Another among the first comers asked for a copy of N. Y. Grot's *Nravstennyye ideally nashevo vremeni* (*Moral Ideas of Our Time by Friedrich Nietzche and Leo Tolstoi*). He filed his slip at 9:08 A.M. and received the book six minutes later! The staff has sought to maintain this prompt response ever since, and in spite of the millions of additional titles that now fill some ninety miles of stacks, it has succeeded in doing so—a feat rarely performed in any other large library in the world. One has to imagine the distances covered daily as the pages incessantly journey from stack to book elevators and back to the stacks. Indeed, a legend has arisen that sometimes they use roller skates to speed their way. (There was once an interruption to that very tight schedule: a new lighting system was being installed in the stacks, and the pages had to rely on miners' lamps attached to their caps.) At the moment of this writing, the Library is planning to add more stacks under the west terrace of the main building, the first major expansion of these facilities since the opening of the Library.

Most city structures from the turn of the century have long since been demolished. When he wrote his exhaustive history of the Library in 1923, Harry Miller Lydenberg, its sometime director, poignantly mused, "How long the building will last is unwise to predict in this restless, changing New York, but surely as long as it stands it will remain a monument to civic pride and to those responsible for its planning and completion."

A cross-sectional rendering of a portion of the Library's ninety miles of stacks

An early photograph of the completed Library building

REVITALIZATION

It does still stand, and with undiminished—or rather renewed—distinction, a result of the same combination of public and private activity that gave birth to the institution in the first place. Under the leadership of Mrs. Vincent Astor and board chairmen Richard Salomon and Andrew Heiskell, both the physical and financial structures of the Library have been refreshed and renewed and strengthened. With the active and enthusiastic participation of the mayor of the City of New York, Edward Koch, who is also an ex-officio member of the Library's board, this handsome landmark has been cleaned and restored to its original appearance. Its marble facades with sculptures by Frederick William MacMonnies, George Grey Barnard, and Paul W. Bartlett—among the most distinguished American artists of their time—now appear as they were originally intended to be seen. And the amiable lions fashioned by Edward C. Potter that guard the Fifth Avenue entrance (affectionately dubbed "Lady Astor and Lord Lenox"), with unblinking eyes, keep their never-resting vigil over the passing crowds on the thoroughfare they face. Inside, we can now once again admire the walls of marble, the Philippine teak floors, and the French walnut paneling. We can see with our own eyes why this building is considered the finest example of Beaux-Arts architecture in the nation.

In addition to revitalizing the Library's physical presence, now efforts have also been made to bring new life to those activities that are never seen by the public but that are crucial to the Library's function as a major repository of the world's knowledge. One may say that this giant, old-fashioned computer has been entirely reprogrammed in the last decade.

OPERATION

Someone once claimed that the total of the world's knowledge has been doubling about every ten years; it has probably since been reduced to five years. The Library has the formidable responsibility of keeping abreast of that rising tide. "We're acquiring more than we can process," one Library official recently reported, "and, yet, we're not acquiring enough." In rooms closed to the public, the indispensable functions associated with selecting, cataloguing, and conserving acquisitions are carried out by a staff of 220 people.

What books and other documents to acquire is decided by divisional selection officers who keep a constant watch over publishers' catalogues and dealers' listings from this country and others around the world. In the process, around ten thousand

Mrs. Vincent Astor, whose efforts have helped immeasurably in the current renovation and revitalization of The New York Public Library

This page and opposite
The refurbished Astor Hall, the main entrance into the Library

items in dozens of languages are acquired by the Library each week. When a selection officer decides that an item should be acquired by the Library, it is then ordered by the Acquisition Division, which enters the order in the Library's computerized acquisition files. The acquisitions process does not, however, come to an end here.

Acquisition at the Library does not merely mean sending out a computer-printed slip, it also means tracking those orders and generating reminders to suppliers of material not received within a reasonable time period. It also means paying the bills, and making sure that what has been paid for has actually been received. With five hundred thousand items coming in each year and several thousand peri-

odical subscriptions coming up for annual renewal, that is no simple task. But that is only the beginning.

This new material must go back through the acquisition and then through the cataloguing and the conservation divisions for processing before it reaches the stacks. These "back-office" operations demand skillful, detailed, and scholarly attention, and they can also be time-consuming. But, in effect, a library book exists only when it can be found in a catalogue, and to determine the most helpful classification can often try a good scholar's erudition and imagination.

As a hypothetical example, under what heading would one look for a book on the economic history of the medieval Church in Provence? This is the sort

of question that a cataloguer must ask himself or herself each time a new book or periodical comes across the desk. Should it be listed under the history of France or under the history of the Roman Catholic Church? What about putting it under Provence? What will best serve the needs of the public, i.e., what is the quickest means of getting the book into the hands of the reader who needs it? In this case, the cataloguer would opt for the specific subject: Economic history–France, before 1500. In terms of the hours spent in such preparations, the processing of a book can be four times as costly as its purchase price!

Just as it is crucial to make a book accessible in a wisely organized catalogue, so it is essential that the catalogue itself be comprehensive and widely available. About twenty years ago, it became clear that the main card catalogue, a file of

This page and opposite Gottesman Hall, the Library's principal exhibition space, restored to its original state

the Library's holdings that embraced some nine million entries, was deteriorating rapidly through use. Rather than attempt the herculean task of rehabilitating the entire card file, it was decided to repair the major damage and reproduce the cards photographically in book form. The result is an eight-hundred-volume set that documents the Library's holdings through 1972. This monumental task was performed by a staff of twenty-six over a three-year period. The catalogue has been purchased—at $34,000 a set—by the Bibliothèque Nationale, the British Library, and other major research libraries, thereby making the Library's holdings more conveniently available to a national and international audience than ever before.

As the task of salvaging the old catalogue was proceeding, a new computerized catalogue was devised to deal with post-1972 acquisitions. At first, this data base was produced only for use at the institution itself, creating the anomalous situation wherein the old card-based technology was accessible throughout the world, while the new technology was accessible only locally. As the cost of this new catalogue began to get out of hand, the Library looked for ways of cooperating with other institutions to share the expense of devising records for new acquisitions. Out of this exploration grew the Research Libraries Information Network (RLIN), which was incorporated in 1974 and which now embraces some thirty-two American libraries. This network enables the Library to reduce its processing

This page and opposite
The Celeste Bartos Forum, the most recently renovated room in the Library

costs through shared cataloguing information, and the public can conveniently discover the location of materials that the Library does not own and have them brought into Forty-second Street. Such interdependent exchanges help to avoid unnecessary duplication in purchasing and at the same time enlarge the facilities of each sharing library. In sum, the Library now houses one of the largest bibliographies in the world.

Access to this enormous bibliographic data base is quite simple and direct. Once a librarian has verified that the catalogues have been properly searched for an item needed by a reader and has determined that it is not owned by the Library, then the reader is referred to the Cooperative Services desk in the catalogue room. There a librarian will search the RLIN data base to determine if the item has been acquired by a member library. If it is available, then a message is sent via electronic mail requesting the work itself or a photocopy for use at Forty-second Street. There is no charge to the reader for this service, although the Library pays a considerable sum each year in dues to RLIN. In this case, the Library once again demonstrates its faithfulness to the great tradition of making information available without charge to the public.

Conservation

Learning not preserved is learning lost. The Library is engaged in an incessant, never-ending campaign to maintain the physical integrity of its holdings. For more than a century now, paper used in bookmaking (and just about everything else made of paper) has contained acids that will inevitably destroy the material itself—on contact with the air, the acid oxidizes the paper's fiber. It is ironic that books produced five hundred years ago, when printing was invented in the West, are in magnificent condition, their paper as white and flexible as it was when it was placed in the press by Gutenberg and his heirs, while those produced over the last hundred years are severely deteriorating. Progress, clearly, has built into the explosion of knowledge a kind of Malthusian pressure-release valve: as knowledge expands and is published, work previously published self-destructs, presumably to avoid an overpopulation of books.

In order to combat this bookish Malthusianism, The Research Libraries spend more than $1 million a year on the conservation and rehabilitation of the collections. It is a giant task, and even while books wait their turn for treatment (or for conversion into microfilm), their deterioration continues. There is good reason for considering this danger to the physical well-being of books and manuscripts one of the most serious problems afflicting not only libraries but civilization itself.

Specialized Libraries

Just as the Library's conservation and cataloguing procedures had to be rescued from obsolescence, the great marble palace on Fifth Avenue could not accommodate the growth of the collections and their audience. New buildings were constructed and old ones remodeled in different locations in Manhattan to provide more efficiently new and special services to a growing number of users. The Library's superb Performing Arts Research Center (commonly referred to by the acronym PARC) at Lincoln Center opened in 1965, and almost overnight it won worldwide esteem for the wealth of its resources and for facilities that ensure their usefulness. So, too, a spacious new building in Harlem was constructed to contain the library and archives of the Schomburg Center for Research in Black Culture, known around the world for its uniquely important resources in this field of rapidly mounting interest.

Branch System

The revitalization of the Research Libraries in the last five years is only part
of the story of The New York Public Library. For the Library is not just the magnificent research facilities, it is also the branch system with its network of eighty-
one libraries located throughout Manhattan, The Bronx, and Staten Island. Brooklyn and Queens have their own independent systems, a result of the one-time
autonomy of these two boroughs.

The headquarters of The Branch Libraries is located in the Mid-Manhattan
Library at Fortieth Street and Fifth Avenue, catercorner from the Central Research
Library. This library, opened in 1972, is housed in the former Arnold Constable
department store and contains a collection of one million volumes, both for lending
and reference use. It is the "neighborhood" library for Manhattan's Midtown section, one of the most populous neighborhoods in the world. As such, it reflects those
smaller libraries located in every corner of the city, which provide instruction
and diversion, at no cost, to the citizens of New York.

This branch system, the largest in the world, owes its origin, as do The Research
Libraries, to private philanthropy in combination with civic action.

In 1901, the Scottish immigrant Andrew Carnegie sold his steel company to
J. P. Morgan. Shortly afterward, he offered $5,200,000 to the City of New York
to build sixty-four library branches, on the condition that the city agree to provide
the sites and maintain their future operations. This was just one application of
a gigantic philanthropic program Carnegie undertook based on his conviction that
men of great wealth were merely custodians of their riches, which they held in
trust for the public benefit. The very hint of this munificent proposal was enough
to move the city's politicians to immediate action. One newspaper reported that
"every statesman in the wigwam [Tammany Hall] was fairly grinning with a love
of books and libraries." Carnegie himself was immensely amused when one staunch
advocate of free public circulating libraries remarked that if librarians ever had
a saint's day, it would surely be St. Andrew's Day.

These branch libraries—many of them handsome structures designed by the
distinguished architectural firm of McKim, Mead & White—are the embodiment
of the Founding Fathers' conviction that only a literate, well-informed public
can be the trusted guardians of their own liberty. From its beginnings, the branch
system has performed the broad social purpose of helping to teach the common
language and habits necessary for participating effectively and fully in American
life.

Among its earliest beneficiaries were recently arrived immigrants for whom
libraries provided contact with the literature and history of their new country.
But this was not done at the expense of the heritage these people brought with them,
for the branches have always been sensitive to and appreciative of the cultural
diversity that is one of New York City's proudest features. Early in this century,
for example, branch libraries made a point of celebrating ethnic holidays for children, thereby providing them with a sense of welcome and continuity in a city
that must have seemed foreign and forbidding.

In the last decade, there has been a new flood of immigrants, and now more
than a million New Yorkers are of foreign birth. Once again, the branches have
recognized their responsibility to help with the new arrivals' real and pressing
problems of orientation to the facts of life in the United States.

The branch libraries have become community centers of a sort, involved in
all kinds of local activities. Promoting an interest in reading among children
has always been a primary concern of the Library; each year several hundred
thousand children attend more than twelve thousand programs arranged for them

by the Office of Children's Services. Young adults are provided with materials that enrich their education and assist them in their school work. Adults are provided with recreational and professional reading matter. And the elderly, when they find themselves unable to travel to the library, are provided with books delivered by volunteers.

In addition to providing printed matter, the libraries also lend audio and video cassettes, records, films, and other materials. A special library for the blind and physically disabled provides materials in Braille and on records or tapes. People looking for work are guided to sources of employment information, and they are lent recreational reading.

The entrance and interior of the Public Catalog Room

MAIN LIBRARY

When the multitude of services offered by the branch system is exhausted, readers and researchers can turn to the imposing collections of The Research Libraries to continue their work. Like a neighborhood library, the great building on Fifth Avenue and its satellites make most of their holdings accessible to everyone (although there are restrictions, of course, on rare and fragile materials).

It is impossible to estimate the variety of needs this library may serve for the millions of visitors who come here each year to tap its resources. A sizable number who use the Main Reading Room arrive quietly and depart just as quietly without divulging the purpose of their visit. The staff respects their wish for anonymity and asks no questions, although it may answer several!

It is not just the size of the collections or the scholarly nature of its users that makes for a great research library. It is the variety and quality of the materials held by the Library that make it a mine of information for the ingenious user. For example, the Library stores some ten thousand telephone directories from many foreign countries as well as from the United States. Carefully read, they can reveal information that most of us would not think of looking for in their pages. In fact, in planning the invasion of North Africa, Allied military strategists relied heavily on the Moroccan and Algerian directories. More recently, the phone number of a secluded girls' school in Lebanon enabled a lovelorn young man to keep his romance alive!

One measure of a library's usefulness is the number of languages in which it collects. Some years ago, a visiting English journalist reported that polyglot New York might best demonstrate how successfully America has lifted the curse of the Tower of Babel. The truth of that observation is abundantly evident in The New York Public Library, which has been collecting works in practically every tongue spoken since mankind first learned to write.

Visitors from all corners of the earth come here to find answers to questions that may not always be found in their homelands. The confusion of tongues that was imposed on mankind at the time of the Tower of Babel can usually be brought to some purposeful order by reference to the Library's holdings with the assistance of an understanding staff member who can unravel some linguistic snarl.

The Library collects printed matter in all its forms. In its various files may be found millions of pamphlets, broadsides, journals, playbills, scrapbooks, postcards, and similar material known as "ephemera" (from the Greek word meaning "short-lived"). These unpretentious castoffs of yesterday, usually discarded almost as soon as they were produced, can prove to be invaluable research tools today. Their peculiar importance was underlined by Harry Miller Lydenberg, the Library's director shortly after America's entry into World War II. It then seemed possible that German bombers might attack New York, and like other repositories of important records in the city, the Library was obliged to plan for the evacuation of its most important holdings. The staff drew up a list of what they considered the most highly prized masterpieces in the collections, including the Gutenberg Bible, the manuscript of Washington's Farewell Address, the First Folios of Shakespeare, and so on. After reviewing these carefully considered suggestions, Lydenberg is said to have remarked, "But first I think we should evacuate all the pamphlets," implying that there were, after all, copies of many of these treasures somewhere in the world but that many of the pamphlets were unique and irreplaceable.

Among the Library's other impressive holdings is its cartological material—more than three hundred thousand maps and some eleven thousand atlases, resources sufficient to answer practically all the demands made on the Map Division.

During World War II, military intelligence used the Library extensively for researching the coastlines of countries in the theaters of combat.

Scientists working on the Manhattan Project, which resulted in the successful splitting of the atom and thus the atom bomb, did their early work at the Science and Technology Research Center. It was with the help of resources in this division that the problem of dehydrating food was solved by government chemists, and it was here that preliminary research was carried out for such significant inventions as the Polaroid camera and the Xerox photocopying machine.

Clearly, the impact of the Library is felt far beyond the confines of New York or even the United States. Scholars come from around the nation and the globe to explore the unique holdings of literary manuscripts in the Berg Collection of English and American Literature, Manuscripts and Archives, and the Pforzheimer Collection of Shelley and His Circle. They wonder at the riches of the Japanese manuscripts in the Spencer Collection or the magnificent holdings of nineteenth-century French prints in the Print Collection. They may look in on the Arents Tobacco Collection, the largest assemblage of its type in the world.

One could go on for some time enumerating the uses and wonders of the collections and still never quite communicate how valuable a treasure the Library represents. For the true greatness of this institution lies not only in its many rare or unique items but in the way in which those items and the collections in which they are contained interlock to present a panorama of human thought, communication, and artistic activity from the time of ancient Sumer until today.

The Special Collections

In this book we shall try to present this panorama by focusing on several hundred items that are not only compelling and attractive in themselves but that also suggest the relationships between apparently discrete fields of learning. They have been chosen from a number of the Library's divisions and reflect the channels through which learning and understanding of different times and places have contributed to our contemporary view of the world. It is not only books and manuscripts that bring us this message, but prints, drawings, maps, and photographs. Most of you who turn these pages will be viewing these materials for the first time, since, by their very nature, these objects are only occasionally displayed in the public areas of the buildings in which they are customarily housed.

So great is the wealth of material in the Library that from it a selection such as this can be made while still leaving possibilities for several more large volumes. And it is important to recall that this vast storehouse is a private institution totally devoted to the public weal—the only large institution of its kind in the world. One must not forget, when embarking on this survey of its treasures, that the Library's vast holdings of current materials are a resource constantly used by scholars, businessmen, artists, and the general public.

The growth and quality of these collections have always depended upon the generosity of its friends, and the future of these collections is likewise in their hands. Here is a conspicuous example of elitist excellence fused with democratic ideals. As one appreciative observer has concluded, The New York Public Library is one of the fairest monuments America has raised.

The massive piers in the Library's main entrance, Astor Hall, list the names of over 120 major donors who have participated in making this institution a great treasure house. These are only the most prominent names from among the thousands of people who have contributed money and materials over the years. Some of these contributions have been so extraordinary that special rooms have been named after them. These names will appear with a certain frequency throughout

*A conservator at work on pre-
serving a Polish theater poster*

this book, so we would like to introduce you to them here, in the hope that this will provide you with some of the flavor of an institution where once-private collections have become available for use by a public audience.

In the Central Research Library these names adorn rooms ranged mostly around the third floor. A tour of them might begin with Room 324, the Arents Collections, which house the gift of George Arents, a New Yorker prominent in the tobacco trade in the first half of this century. His collections are devoted to the history of tobacco and to books published in parts. Both of these are the largest of their kind anywhere. The most outstanding treasure they contain is the manuscript of two acts of the four-act version of Oscar Wilde's *The Importance of Being Earnest*.

Further along the corridor in Room 320, we find the Berg Collection of English and American Literature, which was the gift of a New York physician, Dr. Albert A. Berg. It is almost impossible to single out one item from this assemblage, but if one must choose, then the typescript of T. S. Eliot's *The Waste Land*, with manuscript corrections by the author and Ezra Pound, might serve to give some sense of the collection's riches.

Across the hall, in Room 319, is the Pforzheimer Collection of Shelley and His Circle, containing rare books and manuscripts documenting the Romantic period of English literature. This was given in 1986 by the Carl and Lily Pforzheimer Foundation. Here we find, in addition to a lock of Mary Shelley's hair, a manuscript notebook of Shelley's poems that the poet presented to his first wife.

Passing through the central McGraw Rotunda, we come to Rooms 308 and 313, the Miriam and Ira D. Wallach Division of Art, Prints and Photographs. Here we find a print collection, much enriched by Samuel Putnam Avery with a collection of nineteenth-century French prints unmatched by any other library or museum in this country. This is also the room in which materials from the William Augustus Spencer Collection are used. This is a collection of illustrated books, illuminated manuscripts, and fine bindings from throughout the world. The collection's splendors include medieval European and Japanese manuscripts, bindings from the Renaissance to the present day, and books illustrated by artists from Dürer to Donald Sultan.

Rounding the corner we come to a halt at Room 303, the Rare Book Room, at whose core is the collection of James Lenox, rich in early printed books of voyages and travels. The star of this room's holdings would have to be the copy of the Gutenberg Bible bought by Lenox in the mid-nineteenth century. This was the first copy to cross the Atlantic of the first book printed in Europe.

If we had the time to extend our tour to other floors in the Central Research Library, we might visit some of the many divisions to whose holdings we have only briefly alluded in this book. We should visit the Slavonic Division in Room 216, which was founded in 1898, and whose holdings number some 300,000 volumes. The division's rarities include a volume edited by the seventeenth-century mystic Johann Amos Comenius, entitled *Lux in Tenebris*, dated 1657; Georg Matthaei's 1721 Serbian grammar, *Wendische Grammatica*; a first edition of G. F. Stender's Latvian *Lettisches Lexicon* (1789–1791); and several unique files of Bulgarian periodicals, including *Mirozreniye* (1850–1851) and *Zornitsa* (1874–1881). The division has substantial holdings of early Cyrillic printed books. Among the Slavonic Division's resources for Czech history is a collection of 188 documents called *Artickel des allemeinen Landtag*, printed in Prague from 1567 to 1823. The division has more than 2,600 volumes from the personal libraries of the Russian royal family dating back to the eighteenth century. The late nineteenth- and early twentieth-century treasures to be noted are the George Kennan collection re-

lating to the Tsarist penal system, the John Reed collection of posters of the Russian Revolution, and the numerous photographs assembled by the American journalist Bessie Beatty during the early years of the Soviet regime.

On the ground floor, in Room 84, we find the Jewish Division, whose more than 125,000 volumes and 550 manuscripts comprise one of the most important research collections devoted to the Jewish people in a public institution in this country. Its collection of early printed books includes a copy of the *Hamisha Humshe Torah* (the Pentateuch) printed on vellum in Bologna in 1482; it is the first printed edition of the Hebrew Pentateuch. The manuscripts that grace this division number among them a group of *Mahzors*, or festival prayer books. The most striking of these is the one perhaps written in the Rhine Valley in the fourteenth century, with its charming representations of animals dressed up as humans.

Our tour might continue, were we permitted the rare privilege of visiting the stacks that descend stories beneath the Main Reading Room, with a view of the hundreds of smaller, discrete collections housed there. My personal favorite is the collection of old French and German children's books acquired by the Library from Walter Schatzki in 1932.

Such a tour would take hours and at its end the exhausted participants would still have done little but scratch the surface of the Central Research Library's holdings. Days would be involved in attempting a complete survey of the whole library system. More than one lifetime would be required to fully comprehend its glories.

In this book, we have tried to offer a glimpse of this library, a brief tour of some of its varied collections with a hint at the riches they contain. But we will not only be seeing a place, we will be seeing an idea; for, broadly speaking, the acquisition of recorded knowledge is what the Library is truly all about. It is not so much a place as it is the embodiment of an ideal. These records take on many forms, and we hope that their variety will astonish and delight you and reinforce in your mind the idea of the central role played by The New York Public Library in our cultural life.

Opposite
The loan desk in the Public Catalog Room

CHAPTER ONE

WRITING

Most of us take for granted the basic features of the books we read—the shape of the letters, for example, the paper, the format. These are things we see, of course, but do not really notice; indeed, we see *through* them for the information they convey. But, in fact, books and the elements of which they are composed have a fascinating history, and it is one of the Library's primary, if often unrecognized, functions to document that history, to serve as a museum of communication. Unlike art museums, however, which have permanent displays of their holdings, the Library cannot keep its masterpieces always on exhibit because the materials of which they are made are too fragile and are particularly sensitive to light.

The Library's temporary and ever-changing exhibitions give the visitor certain information about the history of communication in a variety of fields, but they do not have the ability to offer the visitor a sustained picture of that history or a complete sense of the Library's role in documenting it. In this chapter, we shall attempt to make up for that by offering a history of written communication as seen in a fairly breathless tour of the Library's holdings in that field.

It is important to keep in mind that the origins of writing are not clear and fixed. We do not know when, where, or how human beings first attempted to make a permanent record of experience or information. The available evidence indicates that writing is a relatively recent invention; while people have been around for a million years or so, the earliest writing we have is only about five thousand years old and comes from ancient Sumer (present-day Iraq). It is called "cuneiform" because of the wedge shape of its letters, which were impressed into damp clay that was then baked, thus creating a record far more permanent than much of the paper on which we write today.

The Library has an important collection of these clay tablets, which were origi-nally gathered and presented to the Library by Wilberforce Eames, who, for many years in the early part of this century, was the Library's "bibliographer." Eames was a man of wide and varied interests in the field of books and manu-scripts. Perhaps "interest" is too mild a word to fully describe Eames's devotion to books and the Library, which were his life; he lived alone in a house in Brooklyn filled with books, so many, in fact, that they were piled on the floor as well as on shelves lining the walls. Eventually, they left no room for any furniture, and so Eames slung a hammock over the stacks of books—as an alternative, no doubt, to actually making his bed among them.

With Eames's gift, the Library came into possession of 624 clay tablets, which were found at Abu Jamous in Iraq, and which appear to be the record of inventories or financial transactions. For example, one tablet (ca. 2300 B.C.) records the sale of a slave named Puzur-Hani for a sum of silver and some sheep. It was signed by witnesses to the transaction. The origin of writing, therefore, would seem to be prosaic, in the literal sense as it were. We have, in our collections, no cuneiform literature or personal letters.

Since the Library does not own any original Egyptian papyri or Greek or Roman manuscripts from the pre-Christian period, we must make a three-thousand-year leap from the ancient Near East to Carolingian France for our next major document in the history of writing. Rome is present in spirit, though, in a Gospel "lectionary" (readings from the Gospels) dating from around A.D. 900. Housed in the Library's Rare Books and Manuscripts Division, the Gospel lectionary known as Astor 1 (since it was given by John Jacob Astor III in 1884) reflects a number of trends that had developed in the Early Christian period (A.D. 200–500) and embodies many of the characteristics of books as we now know them.

Sometime in the fourth century A.D., the material of which books were made and the shape of the books themselves changed. Papyrus had been the material on which books were written in ancient Greece and Rome, as well as in Egypt. And these papyri were prepared as scrolls, single sheets of the plant-based material pasted together in long strips that were then rolled up around a stick. We retain a memory of this early book form in our word "volume," which comes from the same root as "revolve."

In the early years of the fourth century, papyrus was replaced by parchment (goatskin) or vellum (calfskin); books assumed the "codex" form with which we are still familiar today: sheets or pages grouped, sewn together, and bound. We do not know for sure why this change occurred when it did. It has been suggested that Christianity, which was then the relatively new but official religion of the Roman Empire, had a great deal to do with the change in the appearance of books, at least in part as a conscious effort to emphasize the distinctiveness of its sacred texts from those of pagans.

Whatever the reasons, the book we know took shape in the fourth century, and the Library's lectionary reflects this revolutionary development. It also reflects changes that occurred in the ninth century at the palace school of Emperor Charlemagne at Aachen. This had to do with the script used in writing books. At the beginning of the Christian era, the Roman alphabet consisted only of capital letters. As inscribed in stone on public monuments, such lettering has a restrained and sophisticated elegance that still affects contemporary letterforms, whether in typography or stone carving. These angular capitals evolved into forms that could be written more easily and rapidly by hand, the "uncial." Their smaller letters (what we now call, in typographers' terminology, "lower case") or "minuscules" came into use as the pace of writing quickened, responding to the increasing need for biblical and liturgical works in the growing number of Christian monasteries that were spreading out over the European continent and the British Isles.

The minuscule was the product of scribes working under Alcuin, an English monk whom Charlemagne had recruited to head his palace school. More than a local academy, this was like the Holy Roman Empire's education department, whose work in standardizing the texts and styles of manuscripts reflected Charlemagne's attempts to bring order and unity, on the model of ancient Rome, to the disparate and still nearly "barbaric" elements of his empire. The impact of this standardization can be felt even today in the page you are now reading, whose letterforms have a pedigree that can be traced back eleven centuries to the Carolingian minuscule.

The lectionary called Astor 1 was the first illuminated medieval manuscript of real importance to reach these shores, and it remains one of the finest books of its date and kind in any American institution. The headings of this treasure are written in Roman capitals (majuscules), the subheadings in uncials, and the text in minuscules. Many of its leaves are written in gold on a purple ground,

1–1. Cuneiform Tablets. Sumerian, ca. 2300 B.C. Baked clay. Rare Books and Manuscripts Division

The most ancient specimens of writing in the Library, these tablets record commercial and agricultural inventories and financial transactions.

in emulation of Roman codices (bound manuscripts) of the fifth century. The overall effect of this work is one of power and majesty, intended to inspire awe in the viewer. In these sacred pages, one sees echoes of the profane world in which they were created, a world in which sacred and secular majesty were united in the person of the emperor, who was crowned by the pope and granted the titles "holy" and "Roman."

With the collapse of Charlemagne's empire (which a nineteenth-century historian called "neither holy, nor Roman, nor an empire") were formed the various kingdoms and duchies that eventually became the bases of our modern European nation-states. In the slow process by which a national identity is established, localization of artistic activity—or the development of a national style of art—

plays a part, and we can see the origins of German medieval art in a manuscript of ca. 1220 in the Spencer Collection. It was produced at the Benedictine abbey of Weingarten in southern Germany when a certain Berthold (Bartholdus) was abbot. In his way, Berthold was a patron of the arts who worked diligently and wisely to add prestige to the abbey by providing it with fine books and other works of art. A number of these treasures remained there for almost six hundred years, until the abbey was secularized.

One of these has found a permanent home in the Library's Spencer Collection. Its major interest lies in the thirty-one illuminations that adorn it, six representing minor prophets, the others, saints, interspersed in the text, which is written in very large minuscule script with illuminated initials. Each of the prophets is com-

1–2. Lectionarium Evangeliorum. France, ca. A.D. 900. Illuminated manuscript on vellum. Rare Books and Manuscripts Division

The sumptuous pages of this manuscript, with its liberal use of purple and gold, hark back to late antique Roman models and reflect the ambition of the Carolingian revival to establish a new Roman Empire.

1–3. Prophetae Minores.
Germany, ca. A.D. 1220.
Illuminated manuscript on
vellum. Spencer Collection

*This manuscript was written
and illuminated at the Benedictine Abbey of Weingarten in
southern Germany. Its glowing
and austere portraits of prophets
and saints call to mind the hieratic imagery of Byzantine art,
which strongly influenced the
Romanesque style in Europe.*

pressed within an initial letter. The figure is drawn in the archaic, dynamic style
typical of pre-Gothic Romanesque art. There is a tense and hieratic quality about
the image of these prophets that calls to mind the Byzantine influence, still strong
in the Romanesque period.

The table of contents of an illuminated manuscript produced in northern France
in about 1300 states in Gothic lettering that it was "extracted from the histories
of the Old and New Testament"; that it recounts the lives and miracles of the apos-
tles, saints, and martyrs; and that it is illustrated by 1,034 figures, all "explained
in writing." Of these pictures, 846 have survived the incidents and accidents
of the past 700 years. They were obviously drawn by a number of different artists
and, at their best, are graceful and expressive examples of early French Gothic
miniature painting—and they are delightful reminders of how vividly people of the
time visualized their Christian heritage.

It reminds us, too, of the centrality of France's role in the development of the
Gothic style and in the production of medieval manuscripts, particularly Bibles.
With the foundation of the University of Paris in the thirteenth century, there

arose a veritable book industry in Paris, where manuscripts were mass produced by laymen, for a profit. Thousands of them, chiefly Bibles and books of hours, were produced in this period, with a decorative vocabulary ranging from simple red-and-blue pen-work lines to full-page gilded illuminations.

England, too, developed its own schools of art, and the Spencer Collection houses a psalter that is one of the most celebrated manuscripts produced in England in the fourteenth century. This precious document is beyond question one of the richest surviving examples of English Gothic illumination, and a rarity of exceptional beauty. By chance, more than 200 of the psalter's 482 illuminations remain unfinished—by good chance, it can be said, for those uncompleted leaves provide an unusual opportunity to trace the successive states of the medieval illustrator's procedure, from the first rough sketch to the finished picture.

The manuscript was produced about 1310 at Worksop (now Radnor), an Augustinian monastery near Nottingham in central England. John Tickhill was confirmed as its prior in November 1303, and was removed from that office by a visiting archbishop some eleven years later for "incompetence and delapidation." The psalter was given his name because it was long believed that he had both written and illustrated the manuscript. Although he may well have written the text, the illuminations were the work of an itinerant group of lay artists, a group that produced other manuscripts at about the same time for prominent, interrelated families associated with Nottinghamshire.

The figures of the Old and New Testament characters that appear in the manuscript are rendered in the elongated and willowy style we associate with the High Gothic. The borders are filled with scenes from nature and the rural life, evoking that image of the unity of medieval culture—of art and life, religion and daily activity—that so beguiled the nineteenth century's Gothic revivalists.

All the figures intended by the book's designer are not there, however, since the manuscript was only a little more than half finished. As such, it is highly instructive to pick it up and turn the soft vellum leaves from back to front. One sees sheets of plain white skin, followed by sheets with faint rules drawn on them to guide the scribe. Then come leaves with plain text, followed by leaves with a bit of uncolored decoration. One proceeds to colored decoration and then to gilt decoration. Not only a medieval book, but a whole genre is thereby revealed to the viewer.

So far our survey has dealt with the decorative content of books and not with their texts, since these are essentially well-known biblical stories. But there was another sort of manuscript of a devotional nature produced in medieval times, and the Library's Spencer Collection has a splendid example of this type. It is an English manuscript known as the "Grace Dieu," or "The Pilgrimage of the Soul," and dates from about 1430. It still has its original binding of white doeskin over oaken boards. The manuscript belongs to what medievalists refer to as "vision literature." The text was originally composed in French about the middle of the fourteenth century, and it was followed, over subsequent years, by English translations. A colophon of the Library's version states: "Here endeth the dreme of the pilgrimage of the soule translated out of the Franssh in to Englisshe the year of our lord M CCCC XIIJ."

Few other books of this period so clearly picture the state of contemporary religious feeling, with regard to death and prayer for the dead. The illuminations, sometimes grotesque images, outline the story of the episodes of the soul's perilous and solemn journey to the afterlife, starting from the author in bed dreaming of what is to come. His soul is first led to judgment between Satan and his guardian angel, then weighed by Justice, Truth, and Reason in a balance against Satan's

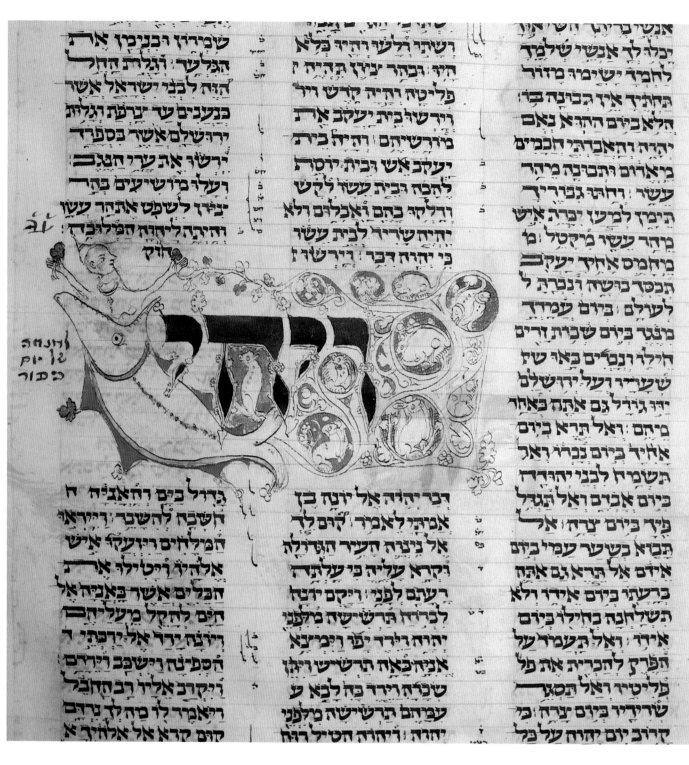

1–4. Old Testament. *Germany, 1294. Manuscript on vellum, calligraphed by Joseph of Xanten. Spencer Collection*

This manuscript on vellum of the entire Hebrew Bible was completed on Monday, the twenty-first day of the Hebrew month of Sivan "in the year 5054 of the creation of the world" by Joseph of Xanten.

The Hebrew text is arranged three columns to the page, with scattered historiated initials and miniatures throughout. Accompanying the text is the Masorah, the body of notes related to the accurate presentation of the text. Volume II, pictured above, is opened to a miniature of Jonah and the Great Fish.

This page and overleaf
1–5. Bible Historiée et Vie des
Saints. *France, ca. 1300. Illuminated manuscript on
vellum. Spencer Collection*

*This manuscript of stories
from the Bible and the lives of
the saints is illustrated with
846 miniatures. Originally designed to have 1,034 miniatures, this massive work is
typical of the great "picture
books" that gained a certain
measure of popularity in medieval France.*

1–5. Bible Historiée et Vie des
Saints. *France, ca. 1300. Il-*
luminated manuscript on
vellum. Spencer Collection
(see previous page)

1–7. Maḥzor [Festival Prayer Book]. Rhine Valley (?), 14th c. Manuscript on vellum, calligraphed by David bar Pesah. Jewish Division

This handwritten copy on vellum of the Maḥzor, containing prayers and hymns for daily use, including Sabbaths and fast and festive days, is open to Kol Nidre, the solemn declaration chanted three times at the opening of the Yom Kippur (Day of Atonement) service.

1–8. Grace-Dieu ("Pilgrimage of the Soul"). England, ca. 1430. Illuminated manuscript on vellum. Spencer Collection

An English translation of a French devotional work written in the middle of the fourteenth century, this manuscript is a prime example of late medieval vernacular religious literature.

flamboyant Medici family and other princely patrons of the arts were for a time reluctant to admit printed books into their libraries—so well stocked were they with the finest manuscripts money could buy that they did not wish them to be degraded by cheaper, mechanically contrived substitutes or additions.

In such circles, the luxury industry of producing fine manuscripts persisted into the sixteenth century. However practical and well conceived, the types cast for the new invention could not, in the eyes of some patrons, rival the elegance of the work created by first-rate scribes and skilled illuminators. A superb witness to the survival of the manuscripts is found in the Library's *Lectionarium Evangeliorum*, produced in Italy about 1540 for Cardinal Alessandro Farnese, later Pope Paul III. This manuscript is sometimes referred to as the "Townley Lectionary,"

124

1–9. RUDOLF VON EMS. Weltchronik. *Germany, 1402. Illuminated manuscript on paper. Spencer Collection*

Less familiar than the sumptuous medieval manuscripts written on vellum are those made with paper, which did not come into common use in Europe until well into the fifteenth century. The combination of this relatively new material, together with watercolor illustrations and a vernacular text written in a distinctively Germanic hand, signify the great changes that were afoot in both the art of the book and in religion in the late medieval period. Von Ems's Weltchronik, *or World History, is a retelling of world history based on Old Testament sources. The text was originally written in the early thirteenth century.*

1–10. Breviarium. *Germany, 1454. Illuminated manuscript on paper. Spencer Collection*

This manuscript, written by Friar Sebaldus in the Benedictine monastery of Kastle near Nuremberg, is noteworthy chiefly for its binding. This was made so that this tiny book (about 4 × 3 inches) could be hung from a monk's belt (or "girdle," from which it takes its generic name of "girdle book") while he worked. When the appointed time came for prayer, his book would always be close at hand.

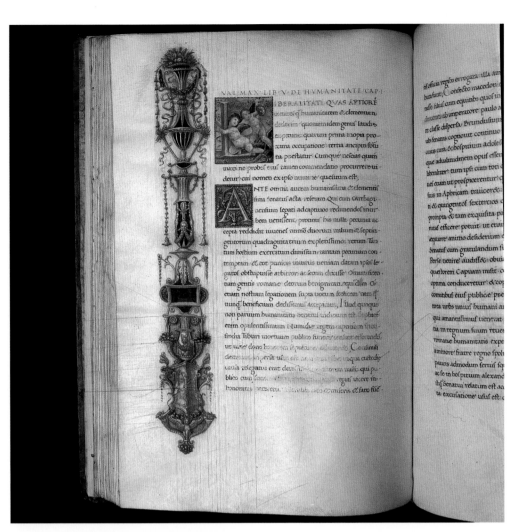

1–11. VALERIUS MAXIMUS. Opera. *Italy, ca. 1475. Illuminated manuscript on vellum. Spencer Collection*

Commissioned by King Ferdinand I of Naples, this manuscript epitomizes the taste in books of a Renaissance bibliophile, both in its classical text and in its classicizing decoration.

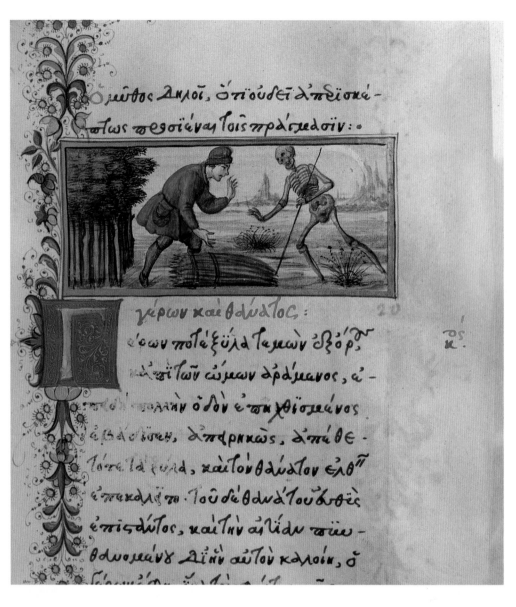

after the English connoisseur, Charles Townley, who owned it in the nineteenth century. Its miniatures were magnificently created by Giulio Clovio (born Clovic, in present-day Yugoslavia), a precocious artist who was trained in the school of Raphael and has been termed "the Raphael of miniatures." This work ranks very high among the truly great miniatures of all time. As Raphael brought Renaissance art to a summary statement in his oil paintings and frescoes, so Clovio was among those who brought the old art of the miniature to a splendid climax.

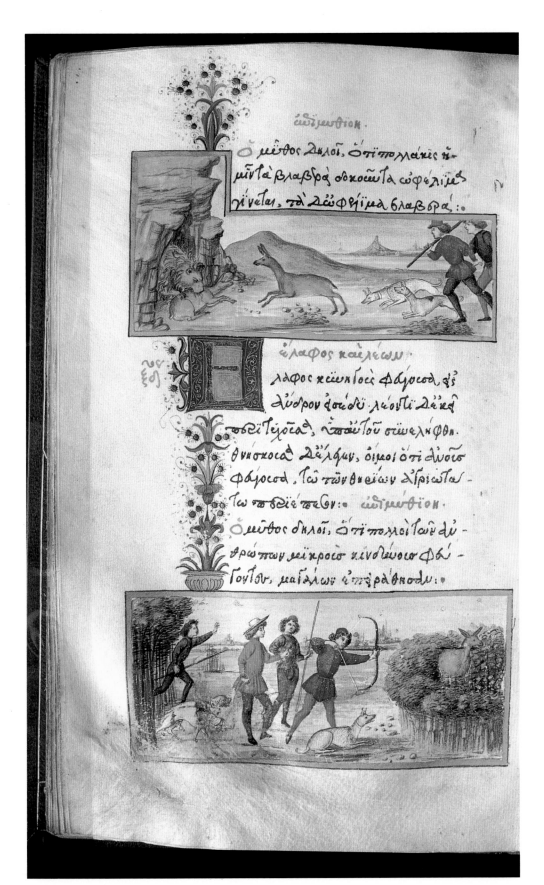

This page and opposite
1–12. A E S O P. Fables, *in Greek. Italy, ca. 1500. Illuminated manuscript on vellum. Spencer Collection*

This manuscript's decoration reflects two separate artistic traditions. Its layout—miniatures always preceding the text without regard for the symmetry of the page—recalls the Byzantine models on which it was no doubt based. The miniatures themselves are reminiscent of Florentine quattrocento cassone paintings.

This page
1–13. PETRARCH. *Trionfi.*
Italy, ca. 1500. Illuminated
manuscript on vellum. Rare
Books and Manuscripts Division
    It was not only the works of
the Greek and Latin classical
canon that were produced in
lavish manuscript copies. Ver-
nacular literature — in Italy pri-
marily the works of Petrarch —
was also occasionally accorded
this gesture of esteem and
veneration.

Opposite
1–14. HORACE. *Opera. Italy,*
ca. 1480. Illuminated manu-
script on vellum. Spencer
Collection
    The chief interest of this
manuscript lies in its calligra-
phy, which represents the work
of two of the most accomplished
Paduan writing masters of the
fifteenth century, Bartolomeo
Sanvito and Antonio Sinibaldi.

Q. HORATII FLAC CI VENVSINI CAR MINVM LIBER·I· AD MECAENATEM·

HOMINVM SCRIBIT OFFICIA·
PRACMATICE MONOCOLOS·

MECAENAS ATAVIS EDITE REGIBVs·

O ET PRAESIDIVM DVLCE DECVS MEVM·
Sunt quos curriculo puluerem olympicum
Collegiſſe iuuat: metáq; feruidis
Euitata rotis: palmáq; nobilis
Terrarꝝ Dominos euehit ad Deos.
Hunc si nobilium Turba quiritum
Certat Tergeminis tollere honoribus.
Illum si proprio condidit horreo
Quicquid de libycis uerritur areis

The manuscript arts of calligraphy and illumination have never really been completely extinguished, and indeed, our own century has seen a renewed interest in these arts, particularly calligraphy. But the printed book attained real prominence in the sixteenth century. When we speak of manuscripts now, we speak most often of literary manuscripts, objects cherished not for the magnificence of their handwriting or the elaborate use of gold in their decoration, but for their texts. Literary manuscripts have, for many of us, some of the same qualities that liturgical manuscripts had for medieval man: they are talismanic, magical things, for they show us a work of art as close to the author's act of creation as anyone outside his mind can get.

Of these literary treasures, the Library has a vast store, for it is one of the greatest repositories of English and American literary manuscripts in the world.

This page and opposite
1–15. Lectionarium Evangeliorum (The "Townley Lectionary"). Italy (Rome), ca. 1540. Illuminated manuscript on vellum. Rare Books and Manuscripts Division

Commissioned by Cardinal Alessandro Farnese, the paintings in this manuscript are by Giulio Clovio, the greatest illuminator of the Italian Renaissance.

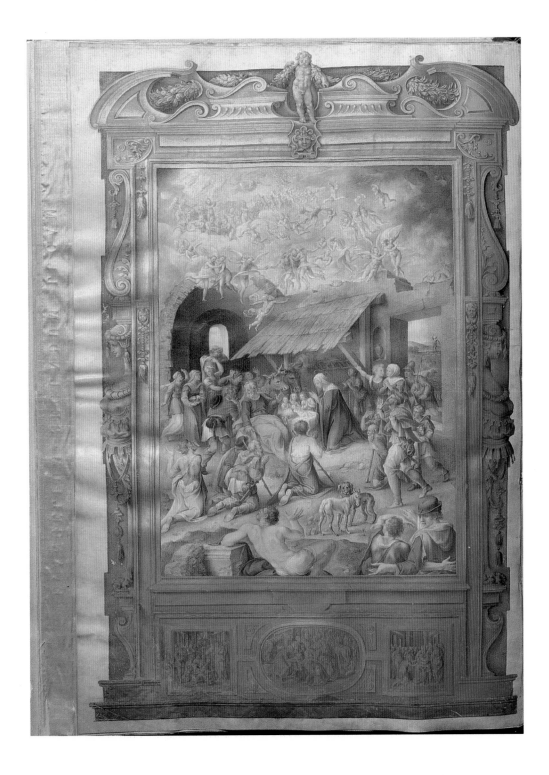

Lodged in the Library's Special Collections, they evoke for us the long and distinguished line of writers who have enriched our language. The depth of these collections is extraordinary, filling hundreds of feet of shelves in various divisions,
so that we may scarcely even hint at the glories of our literature that the Library
is preserving for us and for our posterity.

Perhaps the earliest English literary manuscript (ca. 1598) in the Library
is "The Poor Labouring Bee," a poem by Robert Devereux, earl of Essex, the
particular friend, for a time, of Queen Elizabeth I. It begins:

> It was a tyme when sillie bees could speak,
> And (in that tyme) I was a sillie bee,
> who fed on tyme until my heart did break.

1–16. ROBERT
DEVEREUX, EARL OF
ESSEX. The Poor Labouring
Bee. *Manuscript on paper, ca.
1600. Arents Collections*
   This is an autograph copy of
the poem in which the earl of
Essex laments his apparent mis-
treatment at the court of Eliz-
abeth I.

1–17. JOHN DONNE. Poems.
*Manuscript on paper, ca. 1620.
Arents Collections*
   John Cave, an Oxford divine,
prepared this manuscript of
Donne's Poems *for circulation
among his friends.*

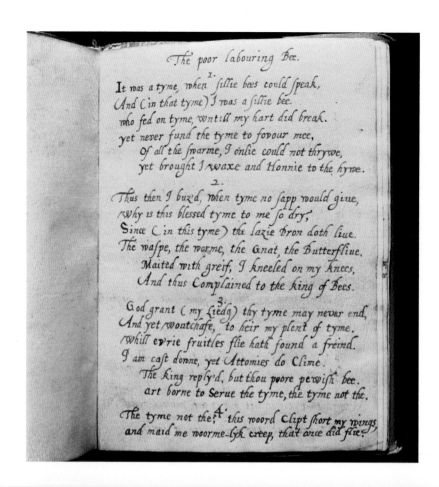

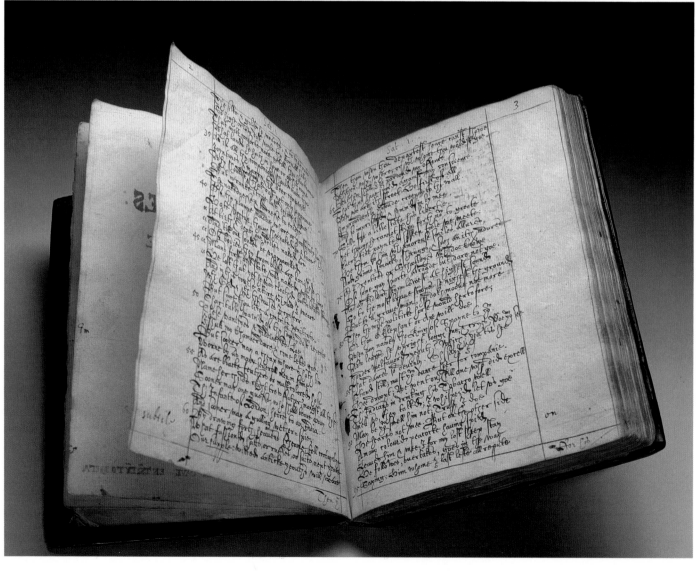

Yet never f[o]und the tyme to favour mee,
Of all the swarme, I onlie could not thryve,
   yet brought I waxe and Honnie to the hyve.

These lines (and the thirteen stanzas that follow) were evidently written by the
earl after a quarrel with his patroness over the appointment of a Lord Deputy
for Ireland, a quarrel that culminated in the queen's boxing his ears. Essex retreated from this battle to his country house and there composed this lament
for his ill treatment, which strikes a chord echoed by many English courtier poets
of the time: the sense of being treated unjustly by the monarch he so fervently
and successfully served. The poem ends with the lines:

Waking I found hye hop[e]s and all maid vaine,
   it was not tobacco, stupified my braine.

Because of this mention of tobacco, the manuscript is to be found in the Library's
Arents Collections, part of which is devoted to documenting the history of tobacco
in all its manifestations: literary, botanical, and medicinal, among others.
   The Arents Collections also contain a contemporary manuscript notebook
(ca. 1620) of the poems of John Donne written out by a certain John Cave. In
its 160 pages of rather crabbed script, we can read the works of this great Renaissance poet in the manner in which his friends first saw them. His poems were
not printed until 1633, but they were circulated in manuscript form, as was the
earl of Essex's poem mentioned above. This is another interesting survival from
the age before the printing press, for just as the illuminated manuscript survived
the appearance of the new technology, so also did the tradition of making multiple
copies of literary manuscripts as "reading" copies. Although, in the case of the
latter, it was the text pure (or, at times, not so pure) and simple that mattered and
not its "production values."
   You may by now be wondering what John Donne's poetry has to do with tobacco.
Well, in his first "Satire," he describes a walk through London with a fashionable
gentleman of the day. Among the many types encountered was a tobacco smoker
who evidently did not make a good impression on the poet:

. . . we went on; till one who did excell
Th' Indians in drinking his Tobacco well
Mett us, they talk'd: I whisper'd let us goe
Maybe you smell h'm not; truly I doe.

In seventeenth-century England, "drinking" tobacco was the term used for smok-
ing—otherwise, the poet's opinion strikes a rather modern note.
   The Arents Donne manuscript is one of two in the Library, the other being
in the Berg Collection of English and American Literature. Like Arents, Berg
started out as the private collection of an individual, or in this case, two individuals, Albert Ashton Berg and Henry Woolfe Berg, New Yorkers and brothers
whose joint collection of some three thousand items was given to the Library by
Albert Berg as a memorial to his brother, who died in 1938. This collection has
now grown to contain more than twenty thousand printed books and a hundred
thousand manuscripts. If the Library's only collection of literary materials consisted of the Berg Collection, it would still be a major international research center.
Combining Berg with the literary treasures of the Arents Collections, the
Pforzheimer Collection of Shelley and His Circle, and the Rare Books and Manu-

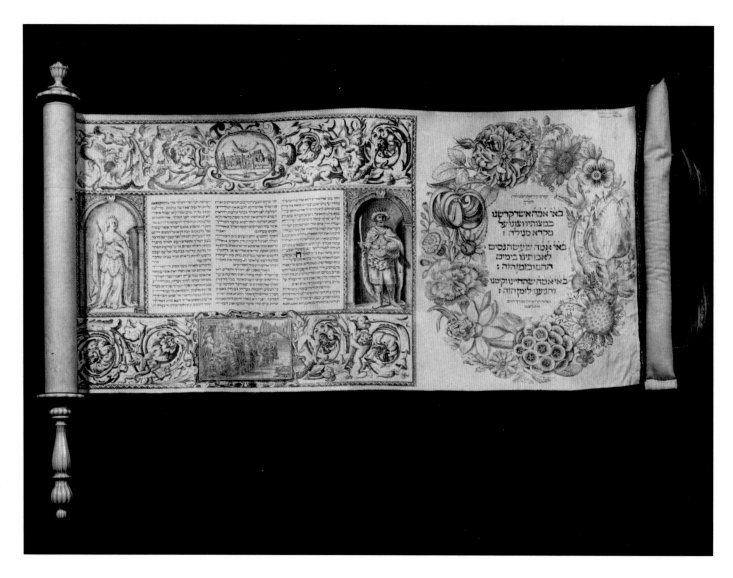

1–18. The Book of Esther. Holland, dated 5446 (i.e., 1685 or 1686). Manuscript on scroll, copied and illustrated by Raphael Montalto. Spencer Collection

Purim celebrates the deliverance of the Jewish community of Persia. The most prominent feature of the celebration is the reading of the Book of Esther, in which the Purim story is related, from a special scroll (Megillah) in the synagogue. Raphael Montalto was the son of Dr. Elijah Montalto, physician at the court of Marie de' Medici and Louis XIII.

scripts Division gives The New York Public Library a place in the front rank of literary research centers. Offering an even vaguely coherent vantage point from which to contemplate this wealth of documents presents a bit of a problem. There is the temptation to rattle off an enormous list of names and titles—like the census of the Tribes of Israel in the Bible—which leaves one impressed with its size, but still ignorant of what it may mean or why it is important that these manuscripts be protected and preserved for study.

There are many reasons for preserving literary manuscripts, and not least among them is the opportunity they afford scholars to establish an "authoritative" text—one as close as possible to what the author intended, and not, as so often happens, merely what a confused publisher has printed. Manuscripts also provide critics a glimpse into the working methods of writers, containing, as they often do, the multiple revisions in phrasing and organization that indicate both the way in which a particular writer has gone about his work and his real intent in writing what he did. Manuscripts bring all of us as close as possible to an author in the act of creating, and here, perhaps, we see the common characteristic of literary manuscripts and our chief motive in collecting and preserving them: the personal presence these documents reveal. We saw this in the Essex and Donne manuscripts discussed above. In the medieval period, works were rarely signed, and texts were rarely personal—at least those that have survived. But beginning in the Renaissance, writers like the earl of Essex and John Donne began to speak directly to the reader, searching for sympathy or a chuckle, and when we have the written document before us, this discourse takes on a sense of immediacy that no printed work can even begin to approximate.

Irony was not the strong suit of the Romantic writers, who flourished in the early nineteenth century. Keats, Shelley, Byron, and their circle prized an intense sincerity of the sort in which hearts (and often other anatomical parts) were always worn on sleeves. The Library stands at the front rank of those institutions whose collections document the Romantic phenomenon. This is due to the generosity of the Carl and Lily Pforzheimer Foundation, which, in 1986, presented Pforzheimer's unrivaled collection, now known as the Carl H. Pforzheimer Collection of Shelley and His Circle. This collection is housed in its own rooms on the second and third floors of the Central Research Library. As with the Berg Collection, it could stand by itself as a major hoard of the treasures of our literature. Added to Berg and the other Special Collections, it adds yet another jewel to the crown.

In pursuit of the personal, we find in the Shelley and His Circle Collection a manuscript, known as the "Esdaile Notebook," which was presented by Percy Bysshe Shelley to his first wife, Harriet Westbrook. It contains fifty-seven of the poet's poems, among them one he wrote to his wife, "To Harriet," which sums up the emotionalism and bravado of romanticism in the lines:

> Honor, and wealth and life it spurns,
> But thy love is a prize it is sure to gain,
> And the heart that with love and virtue burns
> Will never repine at evil or pain.

If one had to choose from among the hundreds of thousands of items in the Library's collections of rare books and manuscripts one object that epitomizes the real value of these relics, it would be this notebook. For here we have a great poet writing to the woman he then loved a poem contained in a volume that she and her descendants then treasured.

While the Romantics have their own rooms at the Library, there is no space set aside exclusively for rare books and manuscripts of American history and literature. This is in part due to the fact that, in a sense, the documentation and embodiment of the American experience is what the entire Library is about. There is no real need for setting aside a space for Americana, for it is present in the Library's many divisions, and these divisions all interlock smoothly. But it is also because the great cache of American manuscripts is housed — along with a great deal more besides — in the Rare Books and Manuscripts Division. Here among twenty-three million items documenting the careers of bankers, sociologists, and politicians are the manuscripts of Washington Irving, friend of John Jacob Astor, the first president of the Astor Library. Here we find the Gansevoort–Lansing collection of Melville family papers and the Oscar Lion collection of Walt Whitman books and manuscripts. These collections, particularly those of Herman Melville and Walt Whitman, shed light on the works of American artists at a time when the country was growing into a world power and developing, for the first time, a literature strong enough to stand on its own. Melville's great novels and Whitman's original poems are not merely works of high art, they are also the beginnings of a truly national literary voice, one that is not just an echo of English or Continental originals.

The Melville papers tell us not only about the artist, but also about the man. In 1984, among newly discovered papers of the family, the Library acquired a letter from the writer to his brother Allan in which he reports the birth of his

1–19. CHARLOTTE
BRONTE. Traveling desk,
"Saul," and *Jane Eyre. Berg
Collection of English and Amer-
ican Literature*

Among those objects associated with a writer none is more
evocative than the desk at
which he or she wrote. This is
the desk at which Charlotte
Bronte wrote when she traveled.
It is shown along with a portion of the manuscript of her
poem "Saul" (1834) and a copy
of the first three-volume edition
of Jane Eyre (1847).

1–20. JOHN KEATS. The
Poetical Works and "Ode on
Melancholy." *Berg Collection*

One of the three greatest English Romantic poets, John
Keats is represented here by an
autograph manuscript of Stanza
3 of his "Ode on Melancholy"
and a copy of the first edition
of his Poetical Works (1841).

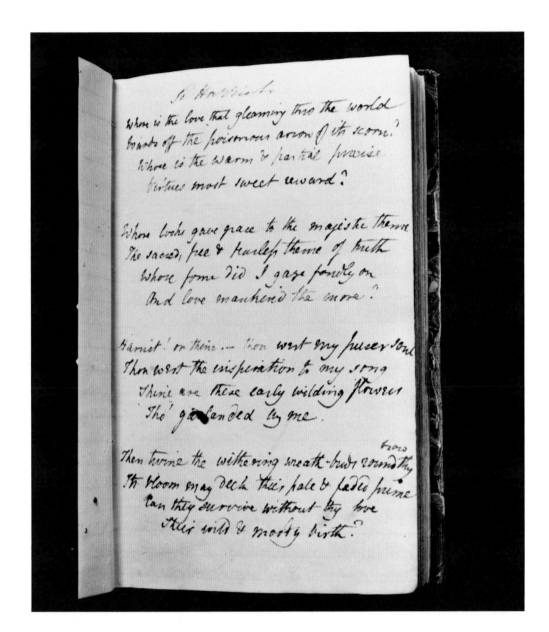

1–21. PERCY BYSSHE SHELLEY. "To Harriet," in the "Esdaille Notebook." *Manuscript, ca. 1810–1815. Pforzheimer Collection of Shelley and His Circle*

The "Harriet" of this poem was Shelley's first wife, Harriet Westbrook. The notebook in which it is written contains fifty-seven poems from Shelley's earliest creative period.

son, whom he referred to as "our little phenomenon." With great good humor and with exaggeration forgivable in a new father, he wrote that to celebrate this portentous event, "Stocks rose and brandy fell. Of course the news was sent by telegraph to Washington and New Orleans—when Old Zack [President-elect Zachary Taylor] heard of it—Mark me: that boy will be President of the United States before he dies." To cap the hyperbole, he added that the bells of all his town's churches were clanging, causing such pandemonium that "all the engines came out, thinking the State-House was on fire." The writer and the proud father are fully present here, speaking to us in a sprightly, inventive language of feelings that are shared universally.

Whitman was also concerned with feeling, with the sensations of existence and particularly with those of the dynamic new nation that was bursting out all around him. His growth as a poet is amply documented in the Oscar Lion Walt Whitman collection in the Rare Books and Manuscripts Division. The great star of this collection is what has come to be known as the "Blue Book," a copy of the third edition (1860) of *Leaves of Grass*, which was first published in 1855. The poet wrote over, pinned notes to, and otherwise revised the "Blue Book" in preparing the fourth edition of the work. It was this "work in progress" that cost Whitman his job at the Department of the Interior. Secretary Harlan found it in Whitman's desk as he routed about for contraband and, glancing at it, thought the book so offensive that he dismissed the author.

The bleak vision characteristic of literature of the twentieth century is echoed in the works of the American writer Truman Capote, whose estate presented the Library with his manuscripts after his death. Housed in the Rare Books and Manuscripts Division, they speak to us of the writer's obsession with violence and violent acts, an obsession that saw its culmination in Capote's "nonfiction novel," *In Cold Blood* (1965). The book opens simply and directly, in the way a good journalistic piece might: "The village of Holcomb stands on the high wheat plains of western Kansas, a lonesome area that other Kansans call 'out there.'" It gives no hint, in style or content, of the gruesome story of senseless murder in a bucolic setting that will follow.

This simplicity and directness was a hallmark of Capote's mature style. But the basis of that simplicity was not merely a natural fluency but also a strong commitment to the writer's craft, to hard work, in short. Just how hard Capote worked is evident in the portion of the Capote archive that pertains to *In Cold Blood*. Here we find the press clippings recounting the murder, the interviews conducted with witnesses, copies of the victims' death certificates, notes, diagrams, outlines, the notebooks in which the story was written down, and finally, the corrected galleys from *The New Yorker* magazine, in which the book was serialized. Through all this we can see the writer's mind at work and the growth of a book from concept to printed page, with every step laid out for us. We can also get a sense of the writer behind the work, for Capote's obsession with details of the murder and the personalities of the murderers suggests that he was trying not only to understand a single, isolated act of violence but also to come to terms with a personal demon; it is almost as if he were recounting a crime that he might have committed himself.

With Capote's masterwork we come to the conclusion of our survey of written communication over the last five thousand years, and we cannot help but wonder what someone reading this a hundred years from now will make of it. For the advent of the computer, and its accomplice, the word processor, has already made inroads into the way we write. We can now revise our manuscripts on a screen and drop the revised data from the machine's memory. We leave no trace of our thought processes or the evolution of ideas in a machine. We leave no trace of ourselves on a disc. Will the person reading this a hundred years from now think that such thoughts are merely romantic gushing, or will they feel a sense of loss?

1–22. HERMAN MELVILLE. *Letter to Allan Melville. February 20, 1849. Rare Books and Manuscripts Division*

The author of Moby Dick *is revealed in this letter to his brother as the very model of the "proud papa." He describes his newborn son as "the phenomenon" and "a perfect prodigy."*

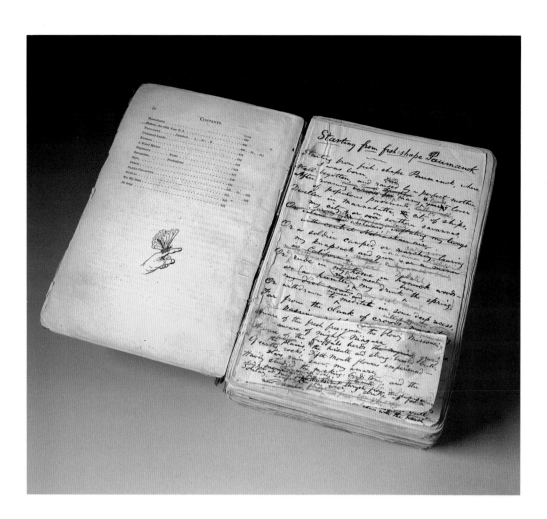

1–23. WALT WHITMAN. Leaves of Grass, *3d ed. ("The Blue Book"). Boston, 1860. Oscar Lion Collection, Rare Books and Manuscripts Division*

The great American poet is shown at work in this copy of his poems. He used it to revise the texts in preparation for the fourth edition. It is the very book that caused Whitman's dismissal from the Department of the Interior, when his "immoral" writings were discovered by his superior.

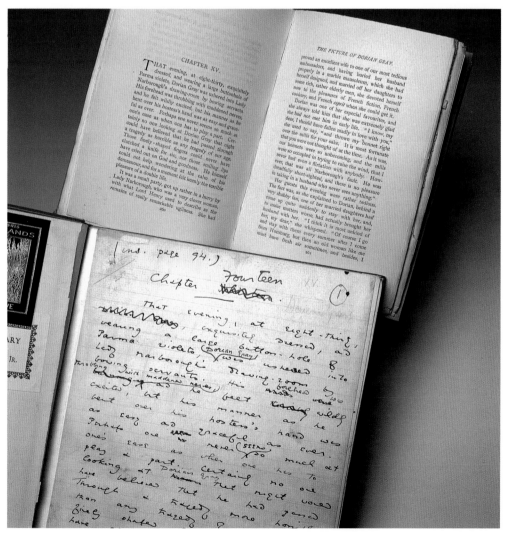

1–24. OSCAR WILDE. The Picture of Dorian Gray. *London, 1891. Berg Collection*

The first edition of Wilde's novel is shown here with a portion of the autograph manuscript of Chapter Fourteen of the work.

CHAPTER TWO

THE PRINTED BOOK

In all probability, the book you are now holding does not seem like an unusual article. True, its text and illustrations are different from any you may have encountered, but the package in which they are contained is quite familiar. This familiarity with printed things, be they books, newspapers, or just junk mail, almost makes us forget that 560 years ago no such thing was possible.

Printing was invented in Europe by Johann Gutenberg of Mainz, Germany, around 1450, and his invention ranks with those epochal achievements of humankind that change the course of history. Before Gutenberg, there were few books, and the transmission of information was a cumbersome and inefficient process. After Gutenberg, information became gradually easier and faster to transmit, and with that ease and speed came an explosion of intellectual and cultural activity.

In spite of its historical significance, we know little about how the invention was achieved or, indeed, about Gutenberg, who is credited with creating the process by which books could be relatively speedily produced by movable, metal type on a mechanical press. Centuries earlier, the Chinese had experimented with movable type and had learned the secrets of making paper and ink of good quality, without which type would have been pointless. But there is no evidence to suggest that Gutenberg knew of the Chinese invention.

His first book, the great Bible (sometimes known as the "Forty-Two-Line" or "Mazarin" Bible), which is undated but thought to have been printed about 1450, is represented in the Library by a splendid copy—the first one brought to America. It was purchased by James Lenox as the centerpiece of his collection of Bibles in 1847. His agent in London, Henry Stevens, had alerted him to the fact that a copy was coming up for auction that year, and he urged Lenox to put in a strong bid for it. Through a mix-up in communications, the Bible was bought for Lenox at the auction for the price of £500, more than twice the sum previously paid for a copy. The price was so high that the London newspapers characterized it as "mad." Lenox was not pleased, and so, when the book got to customs at New York, he refused at first to accept it. After some heart searching, however, he gave in to his collector's instincts and accepted the book.

As we gaze on the book today in the Library's Salomon Room, we cannot help but marvel. For looking at it gives no hint of the trial and error that must have gone into its creation; it looks to be brand-new and perfect. Gutenberg, it seems, got it right the first time. Following the form of manuscripts that had been laboriously created by hand, the book has beautifully laid-out pages, wide margins, and readable print, like any well-produced book we see today. But a lot of preparation went into that perfection.

Gutenberg once referred to his early efforts to develop his invention as a period of *Afenteur und Kunst*—adventure and art. It was that and a good deal more; it was also a time of incessant industry and almost constant financial problems. What he set out to do demanded experience, craftsmanship, care, imagination, patience, determination—and ample underwriting. He had to design a suitable and practical type, one that could be easily read and understood by those who had previously known only handwritten characters. (Gutenberg's type was a faithful and beautiful rendering of the finest Gothic scripts of the time.) Each letter had to be cut on the head of a tiny steel punch and then stuck into a matrix into which molten lead was poured to be cast into an individual letter. In this last, very delicate operation, his early training as a goldsmith stood him in good stead. The complex job required highly skilled organization.

All in all, Gutenberg's font of type consisted of about 270 individual characters. The finished type was placed in wooden cases: the capital letters in the upper case, the smaller in the lower case. His Bible required about 2,500 pieces of such type for each of the 1,284 pages that constituted the final two volumes of the book. That amounted to around a third of a million such separate units for the entire job. Each of these had to be precisely made to align perfectly in a form that would be securely locked in a press for final printing. (To accommodate so many printed characters, the limited number of individual types had to be distributed back into their boxes about every twenty to forty pages and reassembled for the next batch of printing.)

While Gutenberg was assiduously working on his complex project, he was also working himself into debt and finally into bankruptcy. The Bible was brought to completion and went on sale in 1455 through the managerial enterprise of the highly accomplished associates who had bought him out. A member of this group described one of the books published only a few years later as having been fashioned "by an ingenious invention of printing and stamping without use of a pen." After having used a quill pen for so many years to record their thoughts, resorting to "artificial writing" must have seemed to many like a questionable breach of natural law. For decades to come, some printed books continued to assure incredulous readers that they had indeed been produced "without use of a pen."

Gutenberg's work was the climax of the endeavors of others as well as his own; it was he, however, who had succeeded in putting it all together. Shortly after that success, a bloody conflict took place between two rival archbishops in Mainz. Apparently, those who were expelled from the city as a result of the fracas included craftsmen who had learned the new art in the workshop of Gutenberg and his associates. When they left for other parts, they carried their special skills and knowledge with them. In the years that followed, the "secrets" of the new invention spread like wildfire across much of Europe.

Within a decade after the publication of the great Bible, itinerant German printers were at work in Italy. Within another decade, about seventeen European towns had working presses. By 1480, the number had increased to about 120, and by 1500, to about 255. Books produced in this period (that is, before 1501) are known as "incunabula," from the Latin word for "cradle," suggesting that they are from the infancy of this technology. Printing was becoming an important and constantly growing industry, and of course, publishing grew along with it. In practice, the two were not differentiated. Characteristically, one man not only decided what titles to publish but also saw to setting the type and printing the texts, and then tried to market the finished product. At the time, only a relatively modest portion of the population could read. Then, as now, some of those who could read simply did not buy books even when they were available for purchase.

2–1. Bible. *Mainz, Johann Gutenberg, ca. 1455. Rare Books and Manuscripts Division*
This was the first book printed by movable type in Europe. The Library's copy, purchased by James Lenox in 1847, was the first Gutenberg Bible *brought to the Western Hemisphere.*

The printer-producer-publisher had to reach beyond the limits of his own town or city to dispose of an edition, even though that customarily did not exceed a thousand copies. His problem in selling in an international market was somewhat lessened, however, by the universal currency of Latin, the language of the Church and most learned people throughout Europe.

Before going on to discuss some of the great books from the Library's collection of about a thousand incunabula, we should mention another technology that had an important role to play in the development and spread of printing. This was papermaking, and the crucial part it had to play in making printing possible cannot be underestimated.

Manuscripts had generally been written on vellum (calfskin) or parchment (goatskin), and since they were produced in limited numbers, the supply of animal skins generally was sufficient. When the possibility of producing books rapidly in multiple copies became a reality, then there was a need for a new writing surface. All the herds in Europe would not have been sufficient to meet the needs of the growing printing industry. What they needed was a relatively cheap and available surface, and paper provided them with it.

Paper had been invented in China as early as the first century A.D., but it was not produced in Europe until the tenth century, and it was not generally available until the fifteenth—just in time for Gutenberg. Paper history can be studied in depth at the Library thanks to the generosity of Leonard B. Schlosser, who presented his collection of some three thousand volumes on paper in 1986 to the the Wallach Division of Art, Prints and Photographs.

With paper on hand, the early printers of Europe could now meet the demand for their products. If one scans the list of titles in the Library's incunabula collection, it becomes quickly apparent that the greatest demand was for liturgical works. The Church and its clergy needed many copies of the tools of their trade, and so the presses of Germany, Italy, France, and the Netherlands churned out Bibles, missals, books of hours, and psalters for their use. Alongside this ecclesiastical torrent, there flowed as well a somewhat narrower stream of secular books for the educated layperson. These included editions of Greek and Roman authors, law books, medical books, and vernacular works, such as editions of Dante or travel literature.

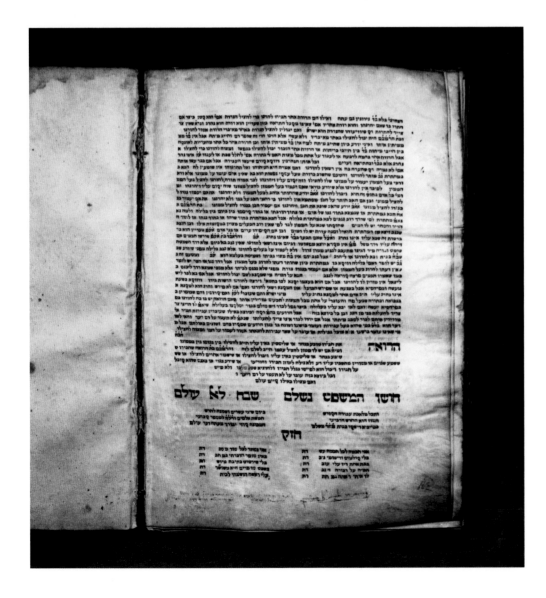

2–2. Arba'ah Turim [The Four Columns], *a code of Jewish law by Jacob ben Asher. Piove de Sacco (Italy), Meshullam Kozi, 1475. Jewish Division*
The two earliest Hebrew printed books to bear a date were both published in 1475; this is one of them. The two short columns at the bottom of the page are a rhymed colophon in praise of the printing press.

2–3. Hamisha Humshe Torah [Pentateuch]. *Bologna, Abraham B. Hayyim, 1482. First printed edition of the Hebrew Pentateuch, printed on vellum. Jewish Division*

The Torah or Pentateuch is read in the synagogue as part of the service on Sabbaths, festivals, the New Moon, and on Mondays and Thursdays.

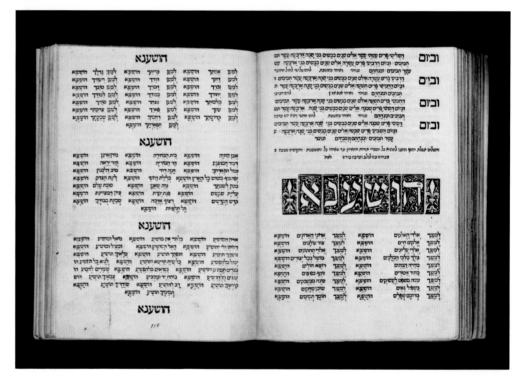

2–4. Mahzor [Festival Prayer Book] *2 volumes: Vol. I, Soncino, Joshua Solomon, 1485; Vol. II, Casal Maggiore (Italy), Joshua Solomon, 1486. Jewish Division*

This is the first printed text of the Hebrew festival prayer book. The second volume is opened to show the Hoshana (Hosanna, or "O, deliver") sequence recited at Sukkot (the Festival of Tabernacles).

Some of these works exceeded the strictly clerical product in their beauty, and some marked new directions in the appearance of books. The most important of these were produced by Nicolas Jenson in Venice in the 1470s. Jenson printed his books in a typeface that looked for its inspiration not to the Gothic script of the ecclesiastical manuscript tradition but to the "humanistic" or "Roman" script of the Italian Renaissance. In 1472, Jenson produced one of the most beautifully printed books of all time, his edition of Pliny the Younger's *Historia Naturalis*. The clarity and elegance of the type used in this book has been an inspiration to typographers right down to modern times. Even today, one can find books printed in typefaces based on those he used in this book. But his original was no inexpensive production. He printed a number of copies on vellum, reverting (as printers sometimes did for a luxurious effect) to the manuscript tradition. The smooth, off-white luster of the skin sets off the type in a remarkably beautiful fashion. As one can see from the copy of the book in the Library's Rare Books and Manuscripts Division, these vellum copies were then decorated with elaborately illuminated title pages and initial letters, drawn and painted by hand by highly skilled Venetian artists.

The illustrations of books in the incunabula period profited from the art of printmaking, which had emerged in the early fifteenth century. And though some printed books like Jenson's Pliny had their decoration added by hand after the printer had finished his task, other books were illustrated mechanically—text and illustration thus forming a technological unit. Among the most beautiful of these early illustrated books is Roberto Valturio's *De Re Militari,* printed in Verona in 1472. It is a book copiously illustrated with woodcuts clearly representing such contemporary developments as machine guns, portable bridges, and other examples of military and engineering hardware. They are wonderfully interesting and explicit diagrams that serve as a manual for scientists, engineers, mechanics, and others interested in up-to-date equipment for the armed forces of the day. With their accurately repeatable images of observed facts, such books opened an entirely new era in the advance of technology.

In 1499, there was published a rather curious work: Francesco de Colonna's *Hypnerotomachia Poliphili.* It was printed in Venice by Aldo Manuzio, far better remembered by his Latinized name, Aldus Manutius, who had set up his press at the sign of the Dolphin and Anchor about 1494. The title may be translated as "The Strife of Love in a Dream." This erotic epic was written by a not terribly religious Benedictine monk who, years later, when he was in his eighties, was convicted of seducing a young girl. The book is best remembered and treasured, however, not as a work of the literary imagination but as an artistic masterpiece. The unsigned woodcuts that illustrate it have been attributed to such Renaissance artists as Giovanni Bellini, Mantegna, Cima, and Carpaccio. Whoever executed them was indeed a master, for the woodcut technique here achieves a sophistication and elegance comparable to the better-known works of Dürer.

Like the Jenson Pliny, the *Hypnerotomachia* was printed in editions on vellum and on paper. The Library is fortunate to have one of each, and it is interesting to compare the different visual effect achieved by the different surfaces. The vellum has a luminosity that seems to absorb the contrasting black lines of the illustrations, while the paper seems to accentuate that contrast. Another difference between the Library's vellum and paper copies offers a footnote to the history of censorship. One of the illustrations, the so-called "Priapic" plate, shows the Roman god Priapus with an erect phallus, his customary attribute. In the paper copy, this has been scratched away; it remains in the vellum volume. Manutius had printed this book on commission, and it stands outside his usual range of production, which tended to concentrate on scholarly editions of classical authors in finely printed, small-scale formats, for he was one of the new breed of printer who was also a scholar.

When he set up his press in Venice, the city had become by far the largest center of bookmaking on the Continent. With its busy ships plying all the European waterways, Venice could provide a convenient, far-reaching agency for the distribution of all sorts of merchandise, including books. It also had a large Greek-speaking minority, refugees who had fled from the East after the fall of Constantinople to the Turks in 1453. Some of these were to provide Manutius with

2–5. Triod Tsvetnaya. Krakow, Fiol, 1491. Rare Books and Manuscripts Division

This missal of the Eastern Orthodox rite is the earliest-known example of printing in Cyrillic characters. It would be another seventy-five years before printing would be established in Russia.

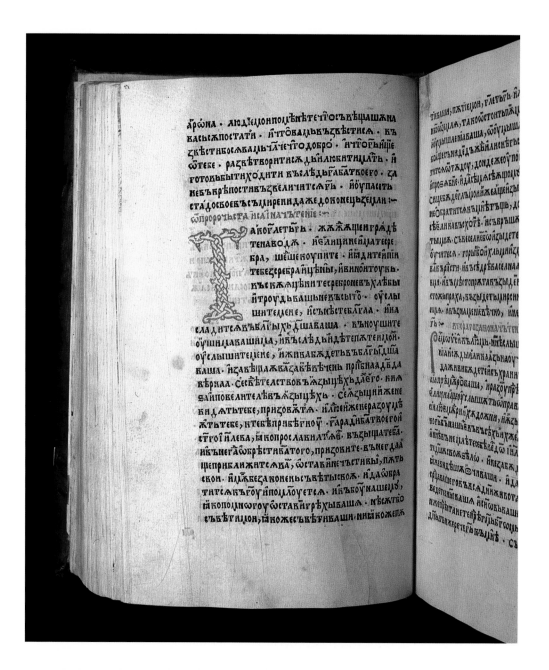

2–6. GAIUS PLINIUS SECUNDUS. *Historia Naturalis. Venice, Nicolas Jenson, 1472. Rare Books and Manuscripts Division*

Jenson's type has inspired typographers down to the present day. In this copy of one of his masterworks, the restrained, classical elegance of his letter-forms is complemented by initials in pen and watercolor by an anonymous artist known as the "Maestro dei Putti."

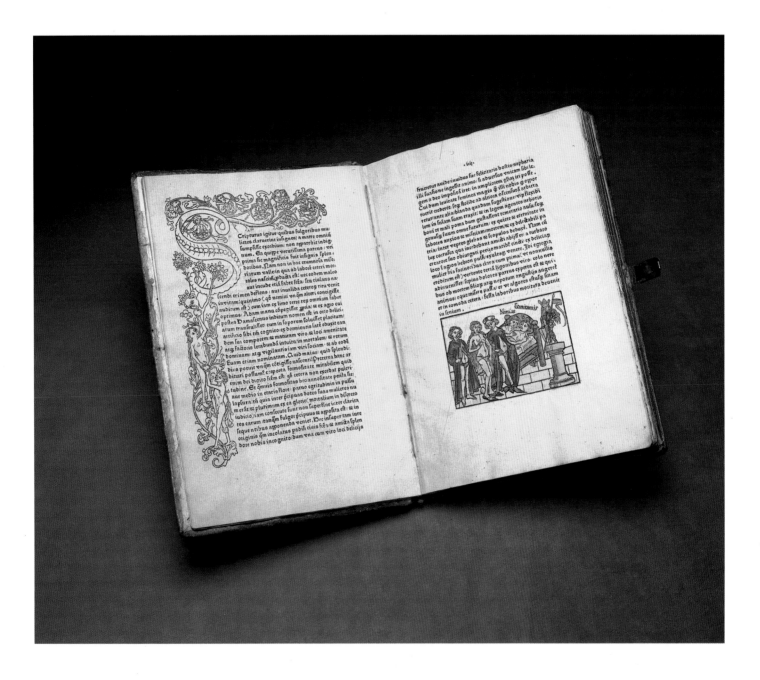

important assistance in his publishing endeavors. Unhappy scribes complained that the city was "stuffed with books" as they saw the presses eliminating the demand for their manuscripts.

Manutius had learned Greek at the university and served as tutor to Italian princes, who helped him financially when, without previous experience as a printer, he commenced his new career. He was a dedicated scholar who devoted the remainder of his life to publishing the classics in both Greek and Latin. It was the first time many of them had been printed. To further this end, he gathered in his home and his workshop émigré Greek-speaking associates, assistants, and fellow scholars. He was a competent businessman with editorial sagacity who could manage and coordinate men and machines and find his way to a remunerative market for what they produced—in short, an ideal publisher for that time or indeed any time. In 1501, he opened the way to new markets by initiating a series of books, starting with a Virgil *Opera* in a smaller, octavo format. These were the remote ancestors of today's convenient popular editions of little books, even the modern paperback. To condense the text for this format, he brought out a type based on contemporary cursive or chancellory scripts, with letters slanting to the

2–7. GIOVANNI BOCCACCIO. De Claris Mulieribus. *Ulm, Johann Zainer, 1473. Spencer Collection*

Boccaccio's stories of famous women enjoyed a certain popularity from the time they were written in the fourteenth century. This, the first Latin edition to be printed with illustrations, is remarkable both for its woodcuts and for the elaborate initial S shown here, which some have considered one of the most beautiful printer's ornaments ever designed.

2–8. ROBERTO
VALTURIO. *De Re Militari.*
Verona, Ioannes Veronensis,
1472. Spencer Collection
The eighty-two woodcuts that
illustrate this work, the first
book to be printed with techni-
cal illustrations, show the ma-
chinery and methods of
medieval warfare.

right, the ancestors of what we know as italic lettering or type. These convenient and attractive "pocket classics" found their way to all corners of Europe. Manutius was a model for what we think of as a true Renaissance man. His creative genius was many-sided; as a scholar, a publisher, printer, designer, and craftsman he left a firm imprint on his times.

With the death of Manutius in 1519, the heroic age of the printed book may be said to have come to an end. Printing had been established as a viable commercial and cultural force. The basic technology had been refined and was to remain virtually unchanged until the nineteenth century. Books, though still rather expensive, were produced in greater quantity and covered a broader range of subjects than had been possible or even conceivable in the manuscript period. The number of copies produced of a given book was much smaller than we are accustomed to today — often fewer than a thousand copies of a title were issued — but their impact on the life of the times belies their small number.

In 1517, Martin Luther nailed his historic Ninety-five Theses to the door of the church in Wittenberg, Germany. Within weeks, printed copies were being read

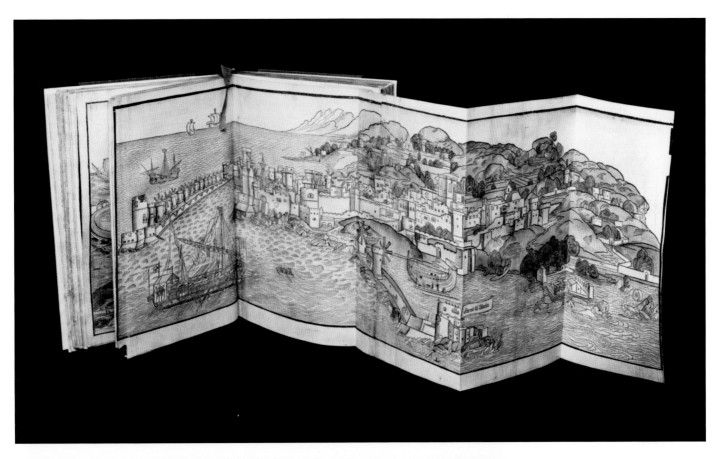

2–9. BERNHARD VON
BREYDENBACH.
Peregrinatio in Terram Sanctam.
Mainz, Erhard Reuwich, 1486.
Rare Books and Manuscripts
Division

Breydenbach made his pil-
grimage to Palestine in 1483–
1484, accompanied by the artist Erhard Reuwich. Upon their
return to Mainz, they produced
this combination of travelogue
and geographical textbook.

2–10. FRANCESCO DE
COLONNA. Hypnerotomachia
Poliphili. *Venice, Aldus Man-*
utius, 1499. Paper copy: Rare
Books and Manuscripts Divi-
sion; Vellum copy: Spencer
Collection

Colonna's erotic fantasy was
published in both paper and
vellum editions. In the Library's
copies, the controversial plate
showing a Priapus with an
erect phallus has been defaced
in the paper copy (above) and
remains intact in the vellum
one (below).

2–11. PUBLIUS VERGILIUS MARO. Opera. *Venice, Aldus Manutius, 1501. Rare Books and Manuscripts Division*

The Venetian publisher Aldus Manutius was known for the quality of his printing and the high scholarly standard of the texts he issued. Among his innovations was the production of important works in a smaller format (almost "pocket-size") than had heretofore been used for such works.

2–12. JACOBUS DE VARAGINE. The Golden Legend. *Westminster, William Caxton, ca. 1484. Rare Books and Manuscripts Division*

Caxton, who introduced printing to England, made this edition of a popular medieval compendium of Old and New Testament stories of interest to his local readership by including stories about English saints such as St. George and Thomas à Becket.

2–13. The Complutensian Polyglot. *Alcalà de Henares (Spain), Arnaldo Guillen de Bocar, 1514–1517. Rare Books and Manuscripts Division*

This massive six-volume work was commissioned by Cardinal Francisco de Cisneros de Ximenes. It is the earliest of the great polyglot Bibles, with texts in Hebrew, Greek, Latin, and Chaldean.

almost everywhere in Europe, and this was followed by scores of Luther's other religious tracts that were rapidly run through the press and sold to a host of eager readers. Five years later, this great reformer issued his translation into German of the New Testament, the so-called September Bible of 1522, which sold about five thousand copies in just over two months and was reprinted eighty times during Luther's own lifetime. As the historian A. G. Dickens has written, "Lutheranism was from the first the child of the printed book. . . . For the first time in history a great reading public judged the validity of revolutionary ideas through a mass medium which used the vernacular languages."

But it was not only Protestantism that took advantage of the useful tool that the printing press had become; the Church of Rome was also alert to its usefulness. Indeed, it was the belief of some Catholics that the Protestants should be attacked with their own weapons—philological research into original manuscript sources. In 1517, the same year Luther posted his Theses on the church door, one of the most ambitious publications of the sixteenth century came off the presses of Guillen de Bocar in Alcalá de Henares, Spain. This was the *Complutensian Polyglot,* a Bible printed in four languages. The text of the Old Testament was printed in Hebrew, Aramaic, Greek, and Latin. It was the first complete New Testament to be printed in Greek. The Hebrew version of the Old Testament was a turning point in the study of that language in Europe. Most subsequent translations of the Bible were based on this work. In addition to its scholarly value, it is a beautiful book; the Bible has always attracted the best printers, and this one is no exception.

2–14. Chertveroevangelie [The Four Gospels]. *Moscow, 1560s Slavonic Division*

The Library's collections include one of the West's most significant assemblages of Church Slavonic imprints, beginning with the earliest Cyrillic imprints of the late fifteenth century. Shown here is one of the rarest Muscovite Church Slavonic imprints that precede the first dated Cyrillic imprint, Ivan Fedorov's Apostol *(1564). Like many of the rarest items in the collection, it was purchased from Soviet sources during the 1930s.*

It was produced under the patronage of the powerful cardinal Francisco Ximénez de Cisneros, who had founded the university at Alcalá de Henares. To ensure accuracy in every detail, scholars from various parts of Europe were summoned to help in the undertaking, which took fifteen years to complete. Manuscripts from near and far had been gathered as reference materials—even some from the Vatican, the great treasury of such documents.

Some fifty years later, when the *Complutensian* had long been out of print, Christophe Plantin, working in Antwerp, filled the gap by producing another polyglot Bible. This one was printed in five languages, adding Syriac to those in the *Complutensian*. The Hebrew version was taken from that earlier book. For the rest, Plantin assembled a group of scholars and both manuscript and printed sources to document the book as thoroughly as possible. King Philip II of Spain promised to underwrite the project, and he summoned Benito Arias Montano out of retirement to supervise the editing. Montano was one of the most learned Orientalists of the time. Philip welshed on his promise, but the work was completed nevertheless.

As in the case of Manutius years earlier, Plantin's home and workshops attracted a flow of scholars, scientists, artists, and engravers. During his lifetime, he produced almost two thousand books, most of them scholarly, printed in a number of different languages and designed and produced with much distinction. With such works, he served as an active catalyst in the spread of learning throughout Europe.

While religious conflicts were being fought with books as well as guns, other, more intellectual battles were engendered by the printed book. In 1543, the Polish astronomer Nicolaus Copernicus published his *De Revolutionibus Orbium Coelestium* in which he laid the foundation of modern astronomy. Here Copernicus advanced his revolutionary ideas, firmly supported by mathematical calculations, that the earth is not stationary and the center of the universe but is rather only one of the myriad heavenly bodies that revolve around the sun. Copernicus's demonstration seemed both too heretical and too unlikely to gain wide acceptance; it took years before his position was considered tenable.

While the religious and scientific beliefs of Europeans were being challenged through the printed word, new voices in the arts were also being heard. As Protestantism changed the map of Europe and Copernicus's theories changed the map of the skies, so, too, the artistic landscape, particularly in architecture, was being reshaped. The only writing on architecture to survive from antiquity was *De Architectura*, a ten-volume treatise by the Roman architect Vitruvius (first century B.C.), which was dedicated to the emperor Augustus. Apparently, the work had only a minor impact on contemporary building, but when it appeared in print late

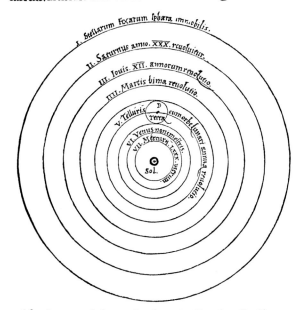

2–15. Nicolaus Copernicus. De Revolutionibus Orbium Coelestium. *Nuremberg, Ioannes Petreium, 1543. Rare Books and Manuscripts Division*
  Of major importance in the history of astronomy, Copernicus's work propounded the revolutionary theory of a heliocentric universe.

2–16. JOANNES DE KETHAM. *Fasciculo di medicina. Venice, Johannes et Gregoriis de Gregoriis de Forlivio, 1495. Spencer Collection*

Ketham's medical treatise is important in the history of printing for its content and its technique. It includes one of the first scenes of a dissection to appear in a printed book, and it is one of the earliest efforts at color printing.

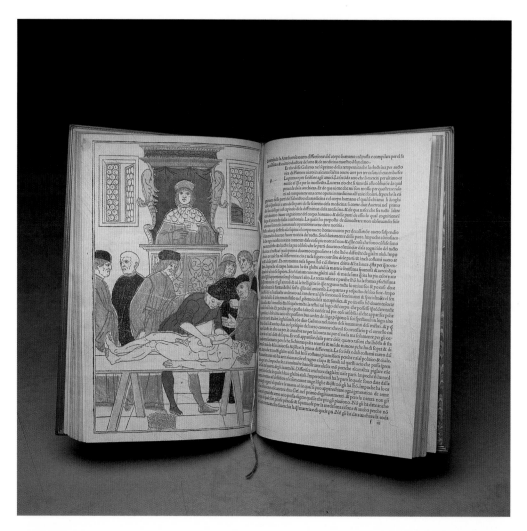

2–17. THOMAS GEMINUS. *Compendiosa Totius Anatomiae. London, Joannes Herford, 1545. Rare Books and Manuscripts Division and* ANDREAS VESALIUS. *De Humani Corporis Fabrica. 2d ed. Basel, Joannes Oporinus, 1555. Berg Collection*

Geminus's work was the first illustrated anatomical work published in England as well as the first book to employ copperplate engraving in its illustrations. The text and illustrations were pirated from the first edition of Vesalius's work, which, like the second edition, pictured here, was illustrated with woodcuts.

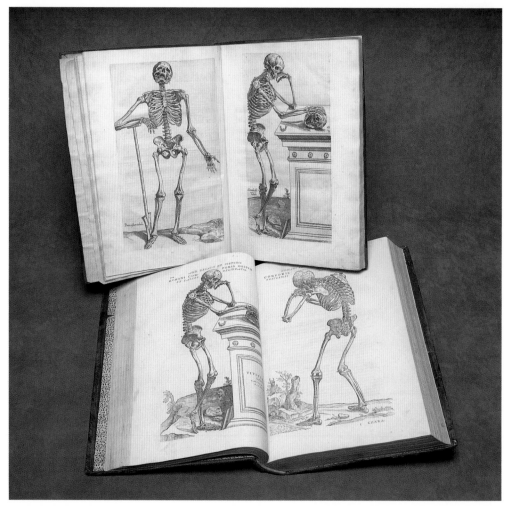

in the fifteenth century, it became virtually a bible for progressive architects
of the Italian Renaissance. Of all architects of that period who turned to Vitruvius
(and to the surviving remains of Roman architecture) for inspiration, the most
influential was Andrea Palladio, who in 1570 published his *Four Books of Architecture* in Venice and who referred to the ancient Roman as "my sole master and
guide." In its widespread and lasting acceptance throughout the Western world,
it may have been the most influential work on architecture ever printed. An indication of its continued importance can be gathered from a satirical comment by
the English artist William Hogarth two centuries after Palladio's first publication:
"Were a modern to build a palace in Lapland or the West Indies," he remarked,
"Palladio will be his guide, nor would he dare to stir a step without his book." Palladio taught the wide world to build in the Classical style; in reprints and adaptations his precepts spread like a brush fire from Venice to Poland, Norway, Hungary,
Russia, and above all, to England and her colonies in America and elsewhere.
Even today, Palladianism in one form or another serves as a hallmark of elegance
in many of our books, government buildings, and other public structures. It was
in the realization of "dear Impeccable Palladio's rule," as one eighteenth-century
English patron of the arts referred to it, that the Georgian architecture of that
period assumed its basic character.

   In the seventeenth century, we find a flowering of literary genius throughout
Europe. This was the age of Shakespeare and Milton, of Cervantes, of Racine and
Molière, and so on down a long list of other immortals. The Library has a half
dozen copies of the 1623 edition of Shakespeare's First Folio, which has been
called the "most famous and sought-after book in English literature." This edition
has singular importance in that it marked the first book to gather together the
works of the greatest dramatic poet the English-speaking world has produced.
Half of the plays had not been previously printed. Beyond that, an engraving
on the frontispiece reproduces what some believe to be the first known portrait

2–19. WILLIAM SHAKESPEARE. *Comedies, Histories and Tragedies. London, Isaac Iaggard & Ed. Blount, 1623. Rare Books and Manuscripts Division*

Known as the "First Folio" because of its format, this first collected edition of Shakespeare's works was published seven years after his death.

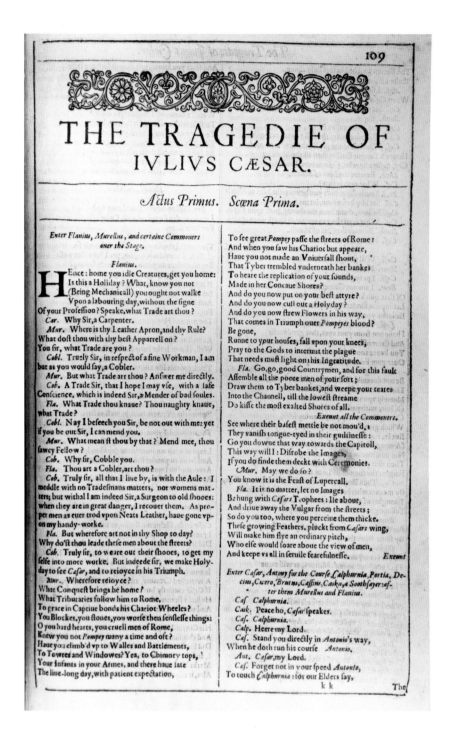

of "The Bard"—one that, in a "Note to the Reader" on the facing page, Ben Jonson, who knew Shakespeare well, declared to be a successful likeness of the man.

None of the highly esteemed folio editions was published in Shakespeare's lifetime. Some of his plays had appeared in smaller quarto books before his death—and sold at sixpence each. Many of these are considered greater rarities than the Folio, and the Library also has a number of these. Quite aside from the bibliophile's appreciation of these editions for themselves, with all their interesting and informative variations, and along with associated books, American scholars can write authoritatively about major aspects of Shakespeare and his world without having to go abroad to do their "homework."

Shakespeare's concerns with kingship and the authority of the state were reflected in contemporary political affairs, as Elizabeth I and James I consolidated their power and eliminated or trumped their rivals, both internally and externally.

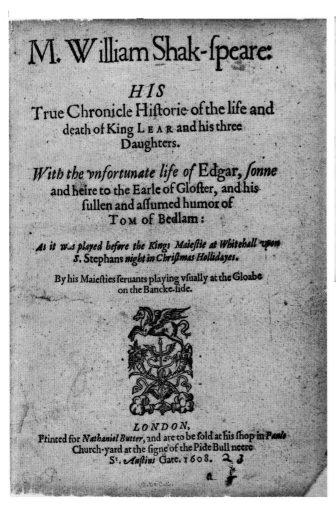

On the Continent, too, political power was being centralized, and in France the quintessential authoritarian nation-state was beginning to take shape. The man behind the throne was Cardinal Richelieu, the prime minister of France, for whom sanctity seems to have taken a rather distant second place in his list of priorities, the highest of which was service to the state, in the person of the king, Louis XIII.

Richelieu recognized the importance of printing as a device to further the power and prestige of France, and so, in 1640, he established the first government printing office, the Imprimerie Royale, or Typographia Regia, in Paris. It was his determined objective to add to the glory of his king by creating a royal press that would produce works of rare perfection. (Both the king and his minister had private presses of their own.) With his almost unlimited authority and resources, Richelieu had agents scour the best printing centers of Europe to recruit craftsmen skilled in all aspects of printing and to procure the finest equipment that would ensure the success of his very ambitious venture. Among their other missions, his scouts went to Holland where, he had been assured, there were inks to be found that "render the impression of the letter much more beautiful and distinct," but which could not then be had in France.

Within a matter of months, Richelieu reached his objective. The first book, a folio version of the *Imitation of Christ*, was completed by the end of the year. This devotional work was produced as a sumptuous tome, embellished with engraved copperplate vignettes, some after designs by the contemporary artist Nicolas Poussin. In the next decade, almost one hundred imposing titles were issued by the seven presses at the Imprimerie. It had become the only printing office in Europe

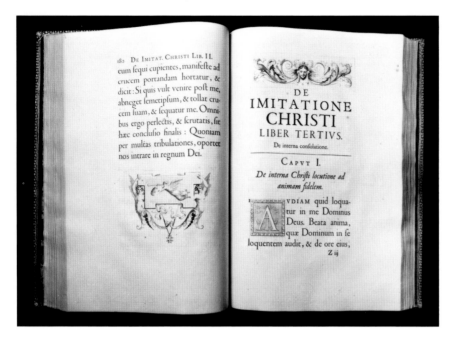

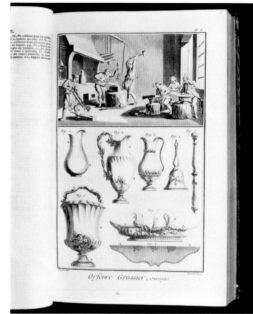

where the great tradition of fine bookmaking, typographic precision, technical skill, and aesthetic devotion were blended with such remarkable results.

About the middle of the next century, the presses of France were producing an abundant crop of new and radical publications that, in effect, proclaimed a revolution in ideas. The period became known as the Age of Reason or the Age of Enlightenment. Never before had man in the name of reason so thoroughly examined the nature of the human condition and the structure of his institutions. These were the days of Montesquieu, Buffon, Rousseau, Voltaire, and other inquiring critics.

The most successful publishing venture of the century was the monumental *Encyclopédie*, edited by the French philosopher Denis Diderot who, in collaboration with a constellation of eminent minds (including the authors just listed), after twenty-six years of productive labor, completed the work in thirty-three volumes with some 2,885 engraved illustrations in 1776–1777. This was accomplished in spite of the fact that the project was twice suppressed, and Diderot was repeatedly jailed because of the challenging and unorthodox views he announced so prominently in print.

The success of the *Encyclopédie* was immediate, for it embodied all the advanced thought of the century presented under a veneer of commonplace information. Indeed, in many ways it served as an introduction to the French Revolution, so soon to follow. Beyond that and probably of equal importance were its contributions to a knowledge of the arts and crafts, which had never before been given such knowing and precise explanations. For the first time, a highly literate man devoted lavish attention to the work of the everyday craftsmen whose inventions and practices played such an important role in the basic mechanics of society. By his personal observations and inquiries, Diderot understood the essentials of craftsmanship, and in text and illustrations, he explained them to the public. What had long been referred to as the "mysteries" of the crafts—and often jealously guarded as such—was converted into common knowledge for anyone who had access to its pages, including the man in the street.

Diderot's *Encyclopédie* was not only a manifestation of the spirit of the Enlightenment, which spread throughout Europe and the North American colonies in the eighteenth century, it was also a tribute to the rise of an energetic and enterprising middle class, whose interest in technology and industry was to transform the world economy in the nineteenth century. The printing and publishing industries were no less affected than any other sphere of human activity during what has come to be called the Industrial Revolution.

From Gutenberg's day until the nineteenth century, there had been no fundamental changes in the way books were printed and distributed. Then, as the industrial age gained momentum, a succession of innovations radically altered the nature of commercial printing. According to some, the newly developed power-driven rotary presses, machine-made paper, stereotype plates, and the speedy mechanical typesetting made possible by the invention of the Linotype and Monotype machines were as revolutionary (and salutary) as Gutenberg's invention of movable type four centuries earlier. Printing could now, at least, be a relatively inexpensive operation.

With the reduction in the cost of printing came a rise in the volume and variety of printed matter. The newspaper, which had been around in various guises since the sixteenth century, became commonplace. Literature with a frankly popular

2–23. Scientific Works. *Rare Books and Manuscripts Division*
The explosion of scientific activity that took place in Europe and North America in the seventeenth and eighteenth centuries was accompanied by a flood of important books such as the ones shown here by Johann Kepler, Isaac Newton, René Descartes, and Benjamin Franklin.

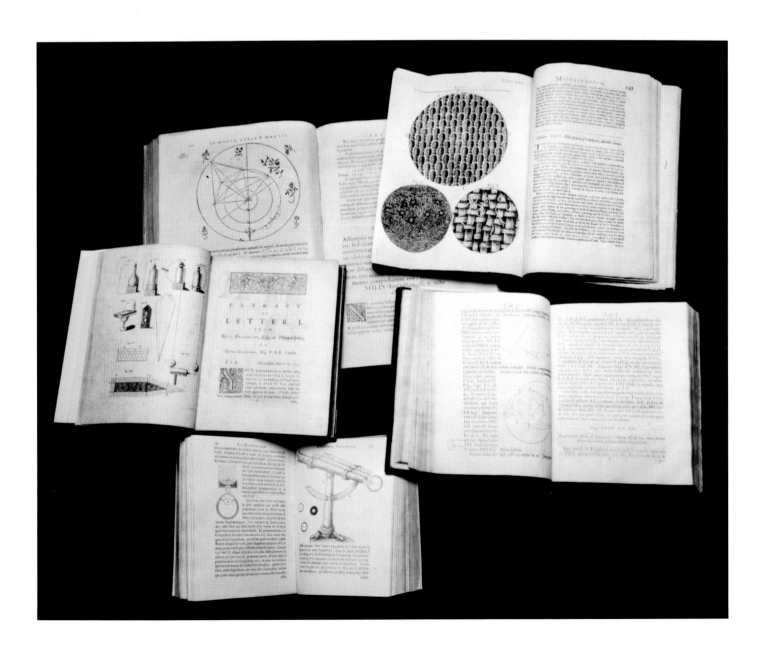

slant was produced in quantities sufficient to slake the thirst of the large, literate
middle-class and working-class audiences who sought diversion and entertainment
in their reading matter. The mid-nineteenth century also saw the rise of the modern
idea of the best-selling author whose celebrity was akin to that of more typical
public figures such as actresses or politicians.

Charles Dickens remains for us today the epitome of the popular author. His
works touched the hearts of hundreds of thousands of readers, who would sometimes buy his works in serial or part form. This sort of publication was one of
the new type fostered by the rise of literacy in combination with the capacity of
the new mechanical presses to produce large quantities of reading matter in a

rapid fashion. The Library's Arents Collection of Books in Parts (the companion to Arents's gift of his Tobacco Collection) offers a unique opportunity to explore this type of publication. Consisting of approximately fifteen hundred works, this is, in the words of one of its former curators, the only collection anywhere "assembled on the principle that the books therein appeared serially in separate numbers and are still in their natural state. Books in parts may be defined as works by an author or authors which are published piecemeal over a period of time, each unit having its special cover."

In this collection, Dickens's works have a prominent place, so that one may examine *Oliver Twist* (1837–1839) or *David Copperfield* (1849–1850) just as

2–25. CHARLES DICKENS. A Christmas Carol. *London, Bradbury and Evans, 1849. Shown with Dickens's desk. Berg Collection*

Dickens began public readings of A Christmas Carol *in 1853. Shown here is the prompt copy he used for sixteen years. The desk pictured here is from his house at Gad's Hill.*

they were experienced by the ordinary nineteenth-century reader who waited impatiently for each part to appear. Sometimes a part would end in mid-sentence so that a measure of anticipation was built up in the reader's mind for the next installment.

In addition to the works of Dickens and other literary figures, the Arents Collection of Books in Parts also features colorplate books, which were published serially not so much for popular consumption as for reasons of sound business practice. Although the printing of text and black-and-white line illustration had become quite cheap, the printing of elaborate colorplates was still an expensive proposition. Thus the capital required to produce a massive work with over three hundred illustrations, like John Gould's *Birds of Great Britain*, was beyond the capacity of most publishers. So the sale of each part helped to provide the wherewithal to produce subsequent parts.

The popular literature of the nineteenth century also includes a distinctive American strain, the dime novel, which can be studied in depth in the Rare Books and Manuscripts Division's Beadle Dime Novel collection. Erastus Beadle was the progenitor of this immensely popular type of publication, which in some cases achieved sales of 300,000 copies a year. He issued them in various formats, some items priced at less than a dime, some at more, and they were sold in the many millions. All in all, they made a substantial contribution of a special sort to American letters. Preachers and censorious parents denounced these paperbacks as "impossible trash," but children continued to read them. During the Civil War, soldiers devoured them. Abraham Lincoln read them. However elementary, they were full of patriotic fervor, pioneering adventures, and other wholesome themes.

There were many who foresaw in such offshoots of the new printing technology, with its radical changes from traditional procedures, the end of fine bookmaking. Most vocal among those early critics was the eminent English poet, artist, craftsman, and socialist William Morris, who believed that deserting long-tried principles that for so many years had served so well—in bookmaking as in everything else—was dehumanizing. To stem this menacing tide, in 1891 he literally took things in his own hands and established the famous Kelmscott Press as a "typographical adventure." He aspired to revive the integrity he saw in books that had been produced centuries earlier, and he succeeded remarkably well in such superb volumes as his editions of Dante and the Bible.

Morris could not turn the clock back, but in looking to the past for inspiration, he exerted a great influence on the future, setting new, high standards in design and workmanship. Actually, the menace was not as pervasive as Morris feared. There never has been a time, before or after the intrusion of these new devices, when exemplary books ceased to be produced or the demand for them slacked; since its beginnings, the Library has served as a custodian of the fine arts of bookmaking in all its aspects. The revivalist spirit that fired Morris was experienced in America and in other countries, with consequences that are still apparent today.

With Morris, it may be said, begins the tradition of "modern fine printing," which like "modern" art does not necessarily designate recently produced works. In quality and comprehensiveness, the Library's collections of books in this genre are without equal in this country. For over fifty years, the Rare Books and Manuscripts Division has been collecting finely printed books from all over the world to document the continuing devotion and attention that has been paid to the "book arts."

Hundreds of people in this century, in Europe and the United States, have set out to print books that are a joy just to hold and contemplate, as well as to read. Three of them stand out as particularly worthy successors to Gutenberg.

The first of these is Giovanni Mardersteig, whose career in some ways reflects the careers of the first fifteenth-century printers. Born Hans Mardersteig, in Weimar, Germany, in 1892, he set up his first press in 1922 in Montagnola di Lugano, Switzerland. In 1927, he moved that press, known as the Officina Bodoni, to Verona, where it remained until his death in 1977. It continues to be operated by his son, Martino. Mardersteig's typography has a chaste simplicity as its hallmark. His inspiration was drawn from the Italian printer and typographer Giambattista Bodoni, whose approach to the design of books was that of an austere Neoclassicist. In Bodoni's books there is no fussy decoration or fanciful typeface; there are letterforms based on Classical models and nothing more. This influence is evident in one of Mardersteig's masterpieces, his 1956 edition of Fra Luca Pac-cioli's *De Divina Proportione,* in which a suitably noble type sits in elegant and un-adorned splendor on the title page. It is no mere archaeological exercise, however, for the book is clearly a modern work, and that is perhaps the key to Mardersteig's genius: he used the past as a vehicle for creating something new. And this is the quintessential definition of Classicism: the past serves to provide the materials for the present, materials that may, within certain confines, be reworked to suit contemporary needs.

If Mardersteig may be said to be the greatest printer to have grown to maturity between World Wars I and II, it is not so easy to identify, as yet, the most important printers of the generations that followed World War II. The Library does, however, have its institutional preferences, and these may serve to indicate the standing of two of the practitioners of the craft. For we have acquired the archives of the

2–26. Dime Novels. *Rare Books and Manuscripts Division*
   Late-nineteenth-century popular American literature took many forms, among them the "dime novel" (so named because of its price). The novels took as their subjects tales of a sensational or adventurous nature.

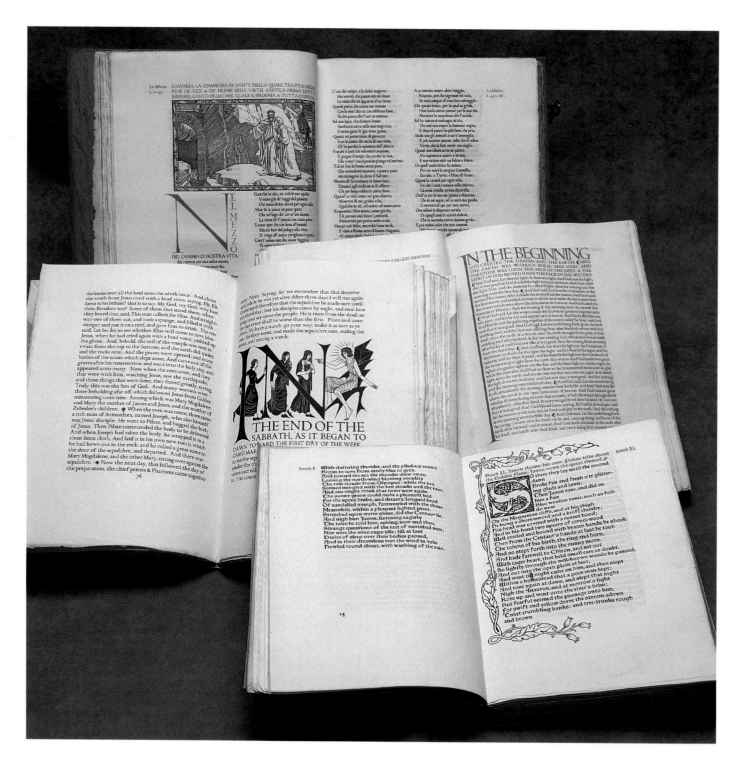

2–27. The Private Press. *Rare Books and Manuscripts Division*
In the late nineteenth and early twentieth centuries in England there was a great revival of interest in the art of printing. A number of significant private presses emerged, among them Kelmscot, Ashendene, Golden Cockerell, and Doves. Works by all of these presses are seen here.

Plain Wrapper Press, which was active in the 1970s, and of the Red Ozier Press, which continues to produce important books.

The Plain Wrapper Press was founded by Richard Gabriel Rummonds in 1966 in New York. Up until then, he had had a varied career as a set and industrial designer, commercial attaché at the U.S. embassy in Quito, Ecuador, and postulant at a Trappist monastery in Buenos Aires. He had also worked as a book designer for Alfred Knopf. His researches in the field of finely printed books brought him to the Rare Book Room of the Library, where the collection of modern fine printing and the helpfulness and encouragement of the staff inspired him to set up his own press.

In 1971, Rummonds moved the Plain Wrapper Press to Verona, Italy, the home of Mardersteig's Officina Bodoni. There, his interest in modern literature

FALCO CANDICANS.

2–28. JOHN GOULD. The Birds of Great Britain. *London, published by the author, 1862–1873. Arents Collections*
The greatest of nineteenth-century British bird illustrators, Gould produced a vast quantity of high-quality work employing the process of lithography.

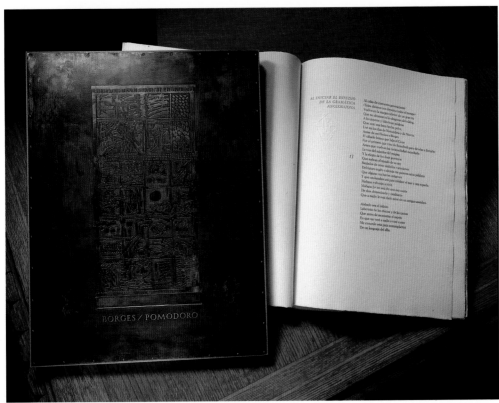

BORGES / POMODORO

2–29. JORGE LUIS BORGES. Seven Saxon Poems. *Verona, Plain Wrapper Press, 1974. Spencer Collection*
Gabriel Rummonds, an American printer, produced this deluxe edition of Borges's poems. It was illustrated by the Italian sculptor Arnaldo Pomodoro.

and art, combined with his mastery of the book arts, led him to produce a number of notable books, the greatest of which is his edition of Jorge Luis Borges's *Seven Saxon Poems*, which he published in 1974. It is a sumptuous book. The format is folio, which is to say the book is about sixteen inches tall. The typography, perhaps under the influence of Mardersteig, is simple and direct. There are intaglio illustrations (called "impressions") by the contemporary Italian sculptor Arnoldo Pomodoro. The whole is set within a binding of natural calfskin inlaid with three gilt bronze relief plaques by Pomodoro. As a finishing touch, the book is placed

2–30. FRA LUCA PACCIOLI. De Divina Proportione. Milan, Officina Bodoni, 1956. Rare Books and Manuscripts Division
Giovanni Mardersteig's masterpiece is this modern edition of a Renaissance text on proportion. In its restrained and severe look it is the epitome of the Officina Bodoni's typographical style.

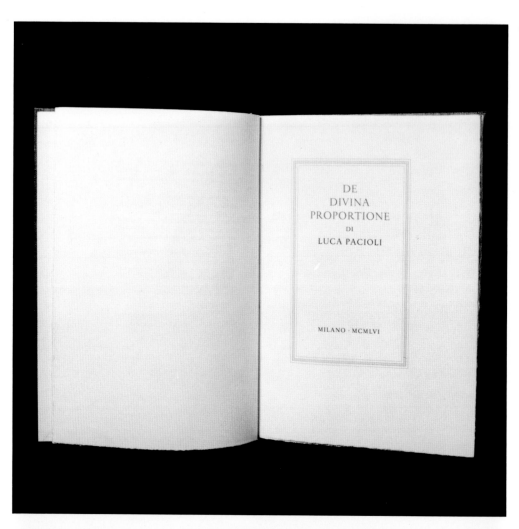

2–31. WILLIAM FAULKNER. Father Abraham. New York, Red Ozier Press, 1983. Arents Collections
The Red Ozier Press issued this edition of a heretofore unpublished Faulkner story as a gift to The New York Public Library. Its wood-engraved illustrations are by John de Pol.

in a case fitted on top with a bronze plate, also by Pomodoro. Contemplating his collaboration between printer, artist, and writer, the lover of finely made books receives assurance that the great tradition of bookmaking is not only alive in our century but thriving.

The Red Ozier Press was founded in New York City in 1976 by Steve Miller and Ken Botnick. Its particular interest is in publishing the works of contemporary authors in books that manifest a particularly American aesthetic of fine printing. The look of their books is not so severe as Mardersteig's or so lush as Rummonds's. In 1983, the Rare Books and Manuscripts Division commissioned the Red Ozier Press to publish the manuscript of a story, "Father Abraham," by William Faulkner. This work, from the Arents Tobacco Collection, is the first draft for the beginning of a novel that ultimately evolved into *The Hamlet*, which appeared in 1940. The Arents version had never before been published, and it was thought that Red Ozier would do the best job of bringing it out. And a great job they did! From its hand-lettered title page by Anita Karl, through its unfussy type, and on into its paste-paper-over-boards covers by Claire Maziarczyk, it is a stunning example of the best efforts that contemporary American craftspeople can achieve.

Although there has been talk in recent years of the "death of the book" and the "bookless library" by those infatuated with computer screens, the continuing efforts of printers like those at the Red Ozier Press may serve to convince us that the book has a while to go before it takes its last breath. The creativity of our young printers together with the enthusiastic collecting policy of private and institutional collectors like The New York Public Library suggest that its future is secure.

2–32. Veshch. *March–May, 1922. Berlin, 1922. Slavonic Division*
  This issue of the journal Veshch *was designed and edited by Lazar Markovitch El-Lizitsky, arguably one of the most influential designers of the post-World War I period. His co-editor was the influential journalist, memoirist, and political figure Ilya Ehrenburg.*

CHAPTER THREE

PRINTS AND ILLUSTRATED BOOKS

The New York Public Library has one of the country's great collections of prints and illustrated books, collections that owe their existence, as does the Library as a whole, to the generosity of a few private collectors and donors. In this case, it is not Astor, Lenox, or Tilden to whom we owe thanks but three gentlemen whose names appear on the pylons within, not over the great triumphal entryway to the Central Research Library: Samuel Putnam Avery, Isaac Newton Phelps Stokes, and William Augustus Spencer. Each in his particular way, together with the curators who have built upon these donors' gifts or endowments, helped to provide for the Library a distinctive place in the field of prints and illustrated books.

There had been small collections of prints in the Astor and Lenox libraries, but it was only with the gift by Avery in 1899 that a separate department devoted to prints was to be established in The New York Public Library. Avery, a native New Yorker, trained as a wood engraver and went on to become an art dealer and friend of artists. His interests and his financial success led him to the boards of The Metropolitan Museum of Art, the Grolier Club, and The New York Public Library.

While dealing in works of art, Avery had formed an unsurpassed collection of contemporary prints (some 17,775 works in all), together with a small group of drawings, representing the work of 978 artists. These he gave to The New York Public Library, thereby establishing the first public print collection in the city, preceding by seventeen years that of The Metropolitan Museum of Art. The strength of the Avery collection lies in French etchings and lithography of the second half of the nineteenth century, but it also includes some works by artists of other countries, especially Germany, the Netherlands, Belgium, and England. Superb examples of the works of Edouard Manet and Mary Cassatt enjoy the company of Turner's *Liber Studiorum* and an important set of Whistler's prints.

Avery's gift was joined, in 1930, by a major collection of rare American historical views presented to The New York Public Library by I. N. Phelps Stokes, in memory of his parents. Stokes, an architect, historian, and print collector, was a Library trustee with a passionate interest in the story of the development of America as told through visual evidence. His collection of over seven hundred items consists primarily of prints but also includes watercolors, drawings, and paintings that document this country's growth over four centuries, from its discovery to the end of the nineteenth century. The profound seriousness with which he undertook his collecting is reflected in his introduction to the book he co-authored with Daniel Haskell in 1933, *American Historical Prints*. He writes: "Can there be anyone so callous, so lacking in Romance as not to feel a thrill of emotion before such contemporary pictures?" He also suggests that such topographical views are "the silent bearers of many a half-read message, at once instructive and interesting." The prints he presented to the Library ranged from an early sixteenth-century Flemish view of Vespucci on the verge of arriving in the New World to a lithograph of the Statue of Liberty issued in 1886, the year of its unveiling.

With the gifts of Avery and Stokes the essential character of the Library's print collection was established. It was not to be primarily a collection of old masters on the model of the great European institutional collections, though, as we shall see, some fine old-master prints were acquired. It was to be a collection primarily of nineteenth- and twentieth-century works with a particular emphasis on the works of French and American artists and American historical views. This character was to be developed and reinforced by the longtime curator of the Print Room (as it was then known), Frank Weitenkampf, who served as head of the department from 1900 until his retirement in 1942. Weitenkampf, an autodidact, joined the Astor Library as a page in 1881. He became a friend of Avery and of many American artists whose work he added to the collections. Under Weitenkampf, the print collection built upon the Avery, Stokes, and other important early gifts and grew into one of the major departments of the Library and one of the most important departments of its kind in the nation.

Today, the Print Collection is a unit of the Miriam and Ira D. Wallach Division of Art, Prints and Photographs. It also serves as the reading room for the Spencer Collection of Illustrated Books and Fine Bindings. This collection is named for William Augustus Spencer, a New Yorker who lived in Paris around the turn of the century. Like his compatriot, Avery, he collected contemporary French art, but his particular interest was in book illustration and in the work of the great French bookbinders like Marius Michel and Georges Mercier, who were active at the time. The story goes that on a visit to New York in the first decade of this century Spencer was given a tour of the then-uncompleted Central Research Library. He was so impressed by what he saw that he resolved to make the Library the ultimate repository of his collection. In 1912, he left Europe for New York, on the maiden voyage of the *Titanic;* he died when it sank. His collection of some 232 books and the endowment that supports it came to the Library in 1920. It has evolved into one of the world's greatest collections of the art of the book. International in scope, it includes medieval manuscripts from Japan as well as from Europe, seventeenth-century Islamic bindings, as well as twentieth-century French ones, and books illustrated by Western artists from the fifteenth through the twentieth centuries. From the *Hypnerotomachia Poliphili* to recent works by Jasper Johns and Francesco Clemente, the Spencer Collection documents the development of the illustration of books with some of the best examples of work produced in the West in the last five hundred years, and in the Middle East and Far East over the last seven hundred years.

Together, the Print Collection and the Spencer Collection have, like the Library and the city they grace, grown up with the century. The Print Collection now contains about 175,000 items along with 15,000 illustrated and reference books. The Spencer Collection has about 10,000 books and manuscripts. The importance of these collections lies not merely in the sheer abundance and quality of the works they contain, they also serve to remind us of the various ways that artists have contrived to produce graphic images and, on occasion, to integrate those images with the printed word. These collections of prints and illustrated books are at once so broad and detailed as to provide plentiful evidence of the variety of contributions such graphic images have made to our cultural heritage.

Perhaps one of the most striking features of this heritage is how early the art of printmaking produced works of genius in the West. In this respect it is similar to its cousin, the printed book, which early on achieved a remarkable level of perfection. The first prints in the Western world were made in the late fourteenth century, preceded by several centuries by prints made in the Orient. These first efforts were woodcuts: images printed on paper (or vellum) from a block carved with the image in relief. They were simple images of saints or Jesus Christ and the Virgin Mary intended for popular devotional use. Some of these simple woodcuts appear in early printed books, others on separate sheets. Just as the printed book evolved into a technologically and aesthetically sophisticated object by the end of the fifteenth century, so, too, these images emerged as a distinctive art form, drawing to the genre some of the most accomplished and innovative artists of their time.

As with the printed book, the most successful early practitioners of printmaking came from northern Europe. And of these, the most significant was Albrecht Dürer, greatest of the early German painters and one of the major artists of the Renaissance and Reformation. The standards he set transformed the technique and concept of woodcuts throughout most of Europe. In some of his earliest works in this field, he produced prints that for the first time suggested the instinctive quality and freshness of drawing. Around 1498, when he was still in his twenties, Dürer designed one of his greatest masterpieces, *The Four Horsemen of the Apocalypse* (and he may have actually cut some of the blocks himself).

The Library's copy of the book in which the print appears is bound together with two other contemporary books also with illustrations by Dürer, *The "Large" Passion* and *The Life of the Virgin*. By the rarest of good fortune the three are still protected by their original cover of full blind-stamped sheepskin that seems as fresh today as when first applied almost five centuries ago.

Left
3–1. ALBRECHT DÜRER.
St. Jerome. *Woodcut, 1511.
Wallach Division of Art, Prints and Photographs*
In Dürer's hands the rather primitive and commonplace woodcut process became a distinctive and vital art medium.

Right
3–2. HARTMAN SCHEDEL.
Liber Chronicarum. *Nuremberg, Anton Koberger, 1493. Rare Books and Manuscripts Division*
Commonly known as "The Nuremberg Chronicle," this immensely popular work offered its readers a multitude of woodcut illustrations of good quality to accompany an essentially pedestrian text.

For several hundred years after its publication, this precious book belonged to the Franciscan nuns of the Convent of St. Bittrich in Munich. During the Napoleonic Wars, the Bavarian monasteries were suppressed, and in due time the volume reached the open book market. When, before an auction sale in 1876, it was rumored that the binding was made and applied at Dürer's own workshop, the book was regarded with exceptional interest and was spared from the extravagant rebinding that was fashionable practice in that generation. Thus it came to the Library from an auction sale early in this century as a great rarity, hardly touched by time.

In woodcut printing the blocks soon wear down with use or crack and chip under the pressure of the press. But, late in the fifteenth century artists and printers began experimenting with the use of engraved metal plates as a substitute for wooden blocks. Not only was the material that carried the original altered but also the method of printing: from the relief process to a method in which the image is incised or indented *into* a polished metal plate. In 1481, in Florence there was published an edition of Dante with tipped-in plates made from engravings in copper. The "copper-plate Dante," as it is sometimes called, was among the first books to be illustrated by the new process. The images, which have been attributed to Botticelli, are more finely detailed than contemporary woodcuts, and the plates themselves were able to produce a better-quality impression than could have been achieved with a woodblock.

Dürer in his *Engraved Passion* took this new technology a step farther along the road to fine art. He exploited its capacity for reproducing fine details exquisitely and faithfully. In this work, as in his suites of woodcuts, he liberated printmaking from the status of a second-class or reproductive art and set the stage and the standards for the achievements of those artists of his own period and later generations.

Among those artists of his time whom Dürer influenced was Hans Holbein, whose *Dance of Death* (1538) is one of the glories of early printmaking. In the Spencer Collection copy of this work we see Death represented as a skeleton or corpse leading his victims, high born and lowly, to their inevitable "last tango."

Another follower of Dürer's was a Dutch artist, Lucas van Leyden, who made an important technical advance in printmaking by combining etching with engraving. In this process, the artist coats the plate with a resistant element like wax, draws his design with a needle-sharp instrument on that element, and then bathes the plate in acid that "bites" into the metal where the incisions have been made. What van Leyden accomplished here was to save the artist (or his assistant) some of the effort involved in forcing his drawing into the surface of the metal plate.

While these technical advances were increasing the options available to printmakers in the sixteenth century, the use of illustration in printed books was becoming almost commonplace. The subject matter ranged from devotional images to scientific illustrations to flights of fancy. The quality and inventiveness of book illustrations in the sixteenth century ranged from the pedestrian to the brilliantly innovative. Among the latter variety is a work that stands out as one of the great illustrated books of all time, if one of the most difficult title-and-author combinations to pronounce: Melchior Pfinzing's *Theuerdank*. This work, printed in Nuremberg in 1517, was commissioned by the Holy Roman Emperor Maximilian I to celebrate his exploits, among them his marriage to Mary of Burgundy. It is among the earliest examples of the "edition de luxe," a work printed for a private patron and intended for distribution by him to his friends rather than for sale. The Library has two copies of this book, one a "plain" edition with uncolored woodcuts on paper and the other, hand-colored, printed on vellum. The latter is in the Rare Books and Manuscripts Division and the former in the Spencer Collection. The

3–3. MARTIN SCHÖNGAUER. St. Anthony. *Woodcut, ca. 1485. Wallach Division of Art, Prints and Photographs*
The possibilities that the woodcut offered were explored almost exclusively by German artists in the late fifteenth century. While technically they improved this "poor man's illumination," much of the subject matter remained concerned with religion.

3–4. LUCAS VAN LEYDEN. Christ Presented to the People. *Engraving, 1521. Wallach Division of Art, Prints and Photographs*
Influenced by Dürer and perhaps by his experiments with etching and engraving, Lucas van Leyden evolved his own distinctive style and signaled the emergence of a northern Mannerist tradition.

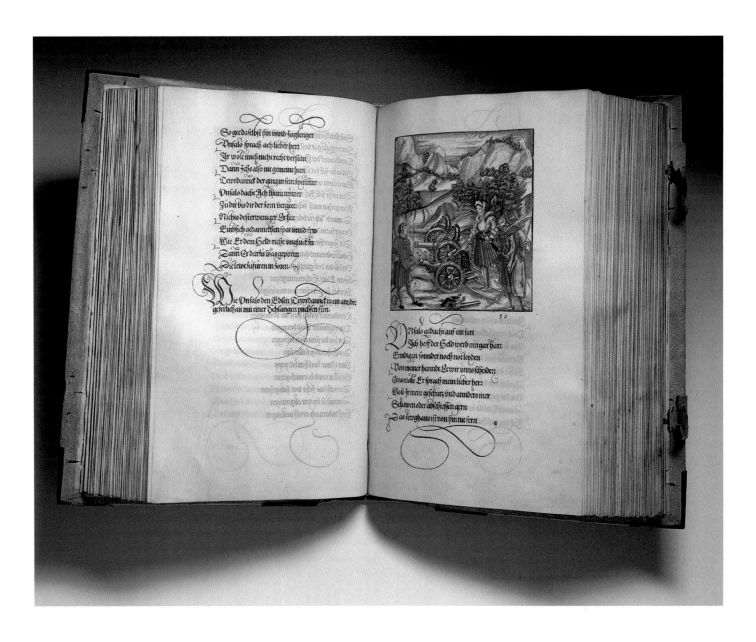

illustrations were the work of a group of six German artists, the most notable
of whom were Hans Schaufelein and Hans Burgkmair.

It was not until the beginning of the seventeenth century that some of the éclat
that characterizes early sixteenth-century printmaking and book illustration
was to be recovered. Among the artists who contributed to this revival were Peter
Paul Rubens and Pieter Brueghel the Elder. Aside from turning out an enormous
number of canvases with the help of a "factory" of helpers, Rubens also developed
a successful business by managing a large workshop of handpicked engravers
to reproduce his paintings and drawings. He supervised their work with scrupulous
care to impose his individual style on the final results. (Such were his demands
on his helpers that at least in one case even his most proficient workman was driven
to a nervous breakdown.) It was in good measure through such copies that his
influence spread throughout Europe.

So it also was in the case of Brueghel, who worked for engravers as a sideline.
It was through engraved copies of his memorable landscapes and genre scenes
of peasants at work and play that he became known and admired by thousands who
had never seen the originals. Even in this day of jet travel and proliferating public
museums, most of us are introduced to the great masterpieces of painting through
reproductions of one sort or another.

3–5. Theuerdank. *Nuremberg,
Johann Schönsperger, 1517.
Rare Books and Manuscripts
Division*

*This image is taken from one
of the forty copies of this book
printed on vellum for presentation by Maximilian I, the Holy
Roman Emperor, who commissioned it.*

Of all the seventeenth-century artists who worked on copperplates, Rembrandt was the greatest technician. He used any and every means to realize the special effects he envisioned. He is celebrated as the greatest of etchers — and he is also remembered, of course, as being one of the most searching and expressive of painters. He repeatedly reworked many of his plates in his continual quest for some improved rendering of light and shade, disregarding the limitations this may have imposed on the size of an edition and the higher income he might have gained from a single day's work. However, that practice proved to be the ultimate delight of connoisseurs who find special satisfaction in owning one or another of the different "states" of his etchings.

Louis XIV's power and personality set the tone for the eighteenth century, not merely for France, but for Europe. The French style in everything from architecture to clothing was copied throughout Europe, and French became the lingua franca of the educated and cultured classes. The best prints and illustrated books of this period, whether produced in France, Italy, or Germany, reflect a certain French quality of approach, a quality that combines technical mastery with a lightness and airiness of imagery. In the earlier part of this century, in which a wealth of beautiful books and prints was produced, a work of particular impressiveness is the edition of Molière's works that was printed with engraved illustrations after François Boucher in 1735. In these plates, illustrating scenes from the author's famous plays, we see revealed the actors and costumes of the contemporary French theater. The lightness of the mood is reflected in the lightness of the line, the economy of means appropriately brought to bear on the subject.

A work of rather heavier substance, Torquato Tasso's *Gerusalemme liberata* received a similarly feathery touch at the hands of Giovanni Battista Piazzetta when he illustrated it with etchings and engravings for an edition published by Giambatista Albrizzi in Venice in 1745. If Paris had any rival in the arts in the eighteenth century, it was Venice, where painters like Tiepolo, Belloto, Guardi, and Canaletto developed their own version of the rococo style. And considering the republic's size, there was also an immense output of prints and illustrated books, among which Piazzetta's Tasso stands out as the masterpiece. The inventive-

3–6. P I E T E R   B R U E G H E L   T H E   E L D E R . Summer. Engraving, ca. 1560. Wallach Division of Art, Prints and Photographs

One from a suite of four prints illustrating the seasons, this engraving reminds us of the increased use of profane subject matter in the art of the sixteenth century.

Iulius, Augustus, nec non et Iunius Aestas ·   AESTAS Adoles centis imago)   Frugiferas aruis fert Aestas torrida meßeis ·

3–7. REMBRANDT. St. Jerome Beside a Pollard Willow. *Etching with dry point, 1648. Wallach Division of Art, Prints and Photographs*

The most inventive and inspired of seventeenth-century prints were produced by Rembrandt who, like Dürer with the woodcut in the early sixteenth century, seemed to expand and explore the limits of the possible in engraving.

3–8. IL ROBETTA (CHRISTOFANO DI MICHELE MARTION). Allegory of Love. *Engraving, ca. 1510. Wallach Division of Art, Prints and Photographs*

A goldsmith by training, Il Robetta was influenced by Dürer and Schöngauer.

ness and spirit he brought to this Renaissance epic poem are breathtaking. The full-page illustrations of scenes from the poem are in themselves epic pictorial versions of the story. Around these elaborate images he weaved frames of a pronounced theatricality. And then in a magnificent kind of visual coda he supplied delightful vignettes to fill the spaces where each chapter of the poem comes to an end. There are no empty spaces in this book, and yet the overall effect is not one of overwhelming clutter and decoration, but rather of a fantastic balance on the part of an artist who knew just how far he could go, and then stopped.

The past was an ever-present force among artists of the eighteenth century, and nowhere is this fact more palpable than in the work of Giovanni Battista Piranesi, whose prints are represented in the superb Charrington set in the Library.

3–9. JEAN BAPTISTE MOLIÈRE. Oeuvres. Paris, 1735. Rare Books and Manuscripts Division
François Boucher provided the illustrations for this edition of Molière's plays. The combination of the playwright's light verbal touch and Boucher's feathery designs epitomizes the best of eighteenth-century French book design.

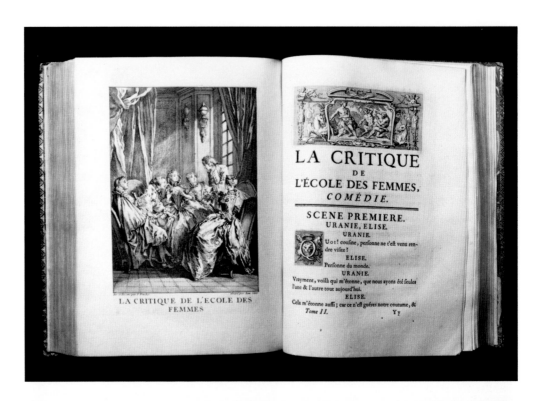

3–10. TORQUATO TASSO. La Gerusalemme liberata. Venice, Albrizzi, 1745. Spencer Collection
Giovanni Battista Piazzetta was commissioned by the great eighteenth-century Venetian publisher, Albrizzi, to illustrate this Renaissance epic of chivalry. In its scale and inventiveness it is, perhaps, the great masterpiece of book illustration of the eighteenth century.

Piranesi was a commercial manufacturer of architectural prints, but as an artist he etched the ancient ruins of Rome with an imagination and virtuoso technique that rendered hallucinatory and compelling a Rome that never was.

This striking visionary quality also appears in the work of one of the most powerful and resourceful printmakers (and painters) of the late eighteenth and early nineteenth century: the Spanish artist Francisco Jose de Goya y Lucientes. In 1799 he published eighty aquatints, which he called *Caprichos*, that were masterpieces of imaginative printmaking and the first works to extend his reputation outside of Spain. The Library's copy of this suite once graced the collection of the Pre-Raphaelite painter and poet Dante Gabriel Rossetti.

This was the first set of original and powerful works to be executed in aquatint. They remain the most popular of all Goya's works. Aquatint was a revival, or reinvention, of a technique that makes it possible to print tones as even as an ink wash, creating an effect closely resembling a watercolor.

If in his paintings and prints—especially the *Disasters of War* series—Goya looked outward and saw terror, the Englishman William Blake looked inward and saw visions that filled him full of awe. These he shared with the public in a series of works that illuminated both his own creations, such as his *Songs of Innocence* (1789) and *Songs of Experience* (1794), and works that shed a new light on the writings of others, such as *Night Thoughts* (1797) and *Milton* (1804). In the latter work, a copy of which is in the Rare Books and Manuscripts Division, Blake's facility as an engraver, combined with his dramatic and innovative sense of color, produced an extraordinary and unique illustrated book. Indeed, there has been nothing quite like Blake's *Milton* in the history of book illustration; the design and color appear to flow in and out of the text, waiting, it almost seems, to be read along with the words.

Less mesmerizing than Blake's visionary works but important for the history of nineteenth-century illustration are the wood engravings produced by the Englishman Thomas Bewick in the late eighteenth and early nineteenth centuries. For many long years, the art of woodcutting had been all but neglected. Then, about 1800 Bewick gave it an entirely new life by a relatively elementary but important change in the technique of cutting the wood. The standard method of working the block had always been to cut it along the grain of the wood, painstakingly gouging out the areas that were to constitute the white background of the image. Bewick's revolutionary practice was to use instead the end grain of smooth, hard boxwood, cutting the picture into the upright fibers with a metalworker's graver. The resulting printed image could be rendered with all the finest detail of a copper-plate engraving.

As we contemplate the Bewick collections in the Print Collection, we can see why the illustrations in Bewick's books with their rustic sentimentality, such as his *British Birds* or his pictures of farm creatures, immediately caught the public's fancy. It brought the woodblock back into books. Accompanied by attendant innovations in paper and presses, it made possible the printing of as many illustrations in the nineteenth century as had been produced in all the preceding centuries combined. Pictorial journalism could and did become a major enterprise, as witnessed by the founding of *Punch, Illustrated London News*, and *Harper's Weekly* in the years closely following Bewick's innovation.

Another late-eighteenth-century innovation in printmaking was the invention of lithography by the German Aloys Senefelder, who was not an artist but an experimenter who searched for an inexpensive method of printing words and musical notations. The technique involved is essentially a chemical process based on the simple principle of the antipathy of oil or grease for water: An image is drawn or brushed with greasy ink on a limestone surface. When the stone is moistened with a sponge, it will absorb the water except where the image has been drawn. When a greasy ink is, in turn, rolled over the entire surface, it will be accepted by the drawn areas and repelled by the moistened sections. The stone is ready for printing.

The lithograph method made it possible for the first time for artists to transfer their unique drawings directly to a printing surface without an intermediate copyist and to have them reproduced in multiples. Lithography can produce such faithful examples of an artist's work that it is not always easy to tell the reproduction from the original.

Few of the tragedies of wartime were pictured in the art of the time in Britain's peaceful isle. There was, however, an abundance of caricatures in which the follies of man at war were more or less humorously exposed, a fair number of which are represented in the Library's important collections of English caricatures. These include an extraordinary collection of almost all the satirical prints (and

3–11. GIOVANNI BATTISTA PIRANESI. A Prison. *Etching, 1750. Wallach Division of Art, Prints and Photographs*
This etching was published as part of the series issued under the title Carceri d'invenzione nuova. *Its nightmare vision gives more than a bit of a lie to the idea of eighteenth-century art as the exclusive domain of froth and bucolic idylls.*

FROM GRANDFATHER DOWNWARDS

many original drawings) produced by James Gillray, a master of the art. These were
the gift of the Tilden Trust.

In contrast to Goya's bloody encounters, one of Gillray's prints answers the
threat of Napoleon's planned invasion of England with taunting humor: A rag-
tag group of indifferently armed yokels defies the great emperor with jolly good
humor that brings to mind Britain's reaction to Hitler's contemplated invasion
of England in World War II.

If one were to name the important artists who turned to lithography as a medium
in the generations following Goya, Honoré Daumier would have to stand high
on any list. Today, Daumier is considered one of the outstanding artists of his
time. He is best remembered for the thousands of lithographs he produced, year
after year, for popular consumption. One of the most memorable of these may
well be his *Rue Transnonain, 15 April 1834,* a grisly report of the butchery of innocents in Paris by troops detailed to suppress a republican outburst during a civil
uprising. The violent events of those troubled times in France may well have been
all but forgotten had not Daumier recorded it in a lithograph of such unforgettable
poignancy. The shop window in Paris where the print was displayed attracted
such crowds that the police suppressed the edition as best they could while the
artist went to jail.

Before continuing our discussion of the glories of nineteenth-century prints,
which are the heart of Avery's collection, we should look to events across the
Atlantic where American printmaking was flourishing. Like printing itself, it
had come rather late to the North American continent, partly because the frontier
environment did not nurture the arts and partly because European products were

He set his face against Jerusalem to destroy the form of Albion

But Los hid Enitharmon from the sight of all these things.
Upon the Thames whose lulling harmony repos'd her soul:
Where Beulah lovely terminates in rocky Albion:
Terminating in Hyde Park. on Tyburns awful brook.

And the Mills of Satan were separated into a moony Space
Among the rocks of Albions Temples, and Satans Druid sons
Offer the Human Victims throughout all the Earth. and Albions
Dread Tomb immortal on his Rock, overshadowd the whole Earth:
Where Satan making to himself Laws from his own identity.
Compell'd others to serve him in moral gratitude & submission
Being call'd God: setting himself above all that is called God.
And all the Spectres of the Dead calling themselves Sons of God
In his Synagogues worship Satan under the Unutterable Name

And it was enquir'd: Why in a Great Solemn Assembly
The Innocent should be condemnd for the Guilty? Then an Eternal rose

Saying. If the Guilty should be condemnd he must be an Eternal Death
And one must die for another throughout all Eternity.
Satan is fall'n from his station & never can be redeemd
But must be new Created continually moment by moment
And therefore the Class of Satan shall be call'd the Elect, & those
Of Rintrah, the Reprobate. & those of Palamabron the Redeemd
For he is redeemd from Satans Law, the wrath falling on Rintrah.
And therefore Palamabron dared not to call a solemn Assembly
Till Satan had assumd Rintrahs wrath in the day of mourning
In a feminine delusion of false pride self-decievd.

So spake the Eternal and confirmd it with a thunderous oath.

But when Leutha (a Daughter of Beulah) beheld Satans condemna-
She down descended into the midst of the Great Solemn Assembly
Offering herself a Ransom for Satan, taking on her, his Sin

Mark well my words, they are of your eternal salvation:

And Leutha stood glowing with varying colours immortal, heart-pier-
And lovely: & her moth-like elegance shone over the Assembly

At length standing upon the golden floor of Palamabron
She spoke: I am the Author of this Sin! by my suggestion
My Parent power Satan has committed this transgression.
I loved Palamabron & I sought to approach his Tent,
But beautiful Elynittria with her silver arrows repelld me.
For

preferred over domestic, Colonial products. The American Revolution had, of course, provided the political break with Europe, but it was a long time before that breach led to a truly national style in the arts.

In the nineteenth century, the sense of a culture developing rather than of culture attained led some American artists to travel to Europe. There they sought a richer and more sympathetic environment for inspiration. Among these artists, Mary Cassatt and James McNeill Whistler stand out. Their works are well represented in the Avery collection, which contains a matchless group of Cassatt's color aquatints and an extraordinary set of Whistler's prints.

Mary Cassatt, a genteel and well-to-do spinster from Philadelphia, was the first important American woman artist and remains among the best. She moved to France where she became the only American artist to be associated with the

3–16. HONORÉ DAUMIER. Rue Transnonain, 15 April 1834. *Lithograph, 1834. Wallach Division of Art, Prints and Photographs*

This print records the butchery of innocents in Paris by troops detailed to suppress a republican insurrection.

3–17. MARY CASSATT. The Toilette. *Drypoint and aquatint, 1891. Wallach Division of Art, Prints and Photographs*

The first of America's great women artists, Mary Cassatt was associated with the French Impressionists.

central group of French Impressionists. Like Manet, Degas, and other painters of the time, she took to printmaking. Had she never painted a stroke, she would be remembered for the superb aquatints, etchings, and drypoints she produced. Here, more than in her paintings, she revealed the influence of Japanese art, especially prints, that could be seen in Paris in the last decades of the nineteenth century and that added an exotic and refreshing strain to the growing and ever-shifting current of modern art in Europe and America.

3–18. JAMES ABBOTT
MCNEILL WHISTLER.
Venice. *Etching, ca. 1885.*
*Wallach Division of Art, Prints
and Photographs*
  *The English Fine Arts So-
ciety commissioned Whistler to
etch a suite of twelve views of
Venice, of which this is one. In
his total mastery of the technique he has sometimes been
considered the greatest etcher
since Rembrandt.*

Cassatt's slightly younger fellow expatriate, James Abbott McNeill Whistler, also produced prints in addition to his suave and elegant oils. Not all his contemporaries appreciated his art. His canvas *Falling Rocket, Nocturne in Black and Gold,* among the paintings he is best remembered for today, infuriated the aging British critic and tastemaker John Ruskin. "I have seen, and heard, much of cockney impudence before now," Ruskin wrote, "but never expected to hear a coxcomb ask two hundred guineas for flinging a pot of paint in the public's face." Whistler sued for libel—largely for the sport of it. Thanks to his brilliant wit and merciless sarcasm, it was a very interesting case in court. Whistler won the suit but was awarded only one farthing for damages; the legal costs all but ruined him.

Very soon after that matter was concluded, he was commissioned by the Fine Arts Society to etch twelve views of Venice, and the success of these plates not only brought him a welcome income but confirmed his status as a rare artist. There were those who considered Whistler the greatest etcher since Rembrandt—and with his indomitable self-esteem, Whistler himself might well have agreed. Toward the end of his life, he created a large number of brilliant lithographs, with which he helped to reclaim the art from the hands of commercial lithographers. Both he and Mary Cassatt restricted their prints to limited editions, a device that was to become commonly used to distinguish between mere reproductions and original prints created and printed by the artist himself or under his close supervision.

It is in the period in which Whistler and Cassatt flourished that the greatest strengths of the Print Collection lie, owing to Avery's gift. Here we find not only familiar names like Bonnard and Manet, but also less familiar ones like Buhot, Bresdin, Méryon, and Klinger. Through his discerning eye and practically infallible taste Avery assembled a collection of prints of great range and quality, and they, in turn, reveal the world of the late-nineteenth-century European artist.

Avery had begun collecting Manet prints in 1884 (making his first purchases from the artist's widow), and he went on to build one of the most important collections of this artist's graphic work outside of France. He also acquired an occasional drawing, such as the watercolor for *Hat and Guitar* (1862), which was etched and used as the frontispiece for an edition of etchings. This simple image is extremely suggestive, calling to mind as it does Manet's fascination with Spain and with Spanish art, which influenced him so greatly.

The clarity and repose of Manet's vision was not the only road to art shared by artists in his time. Other printmakers, seized by a romantic attraction to the fanciful and the grotesque, created a highly personal and visionary art. Among these was Félix Buhot who was born, appropriately enough, on the rue de Fantasie in the Norman village of Valognes in 1847. In the 1870s and 1880s, he produced a series of views of Parisian street life full of foreboding and melancholy. He developed the practice of adding what he called *marges symphoniques* (symphonic margins) to his prints—around the image he would etch cartoons that commented on and amplified the central image of the print. Thus in his *Le Hibou, Pauca-Paucis* (1883) he sketched a devil, a figure climbing stairs, birds, and the full moon.

3–19. EDOUARD MANET.
Illustration from *Le Corbeau* by
Edgar A. Poe. *Lithograph,
1875. Wallach Division of Art,
Prints and Photographs*
   *Poe's poem was translated by
Stéphane Mallarmé who shared
with Baudelaire a respect for
the poet as mystifying to some
as the interest contemporary
French intellectuals show in the
work of Jerry Lewis.*

Buhot's view of a threatening and macabre urban environment is more than a step away from the images of bourgeois contentment that characterized so much of the art of the time. Its main concern is with imagination and sensation. And in this respect it supplies a link with the work of the late-nineteenth-century English artist Aubrey Beardsley whose imagery makes public a private and unique vision. In his black-and-white illustrations, at once stark and lush, for the late medieval romance, Malory's *Morte d'Arthur*, we see Beardsley not so much rendering visible the printed word as imaginatively recreating a story. His knights and ladies

3–20. FÉLIX BUHOT. Le Hibou, Pauca-Paucis. *Etching, 1883. Wallach Division of Art, Prints and Photographs*
In the margins of this print Buhot sketched a devil and other figures amplifying the dark mood and motif of the central image.

3–21. AUBREY
BEARDSLEY. Illustration for
Sir Thomas Malory's *Le Morte
d'Arthur. Wood engraving,
1893–1894. Arents Collection*
 The sinuous line and stark
contrast of Beardsley's illustrations for Malory's late-medieval
romance do not so much render
visible the printed word as they
imaginatively recreate the story.

are intended not so much to aid us in comprehending the story as they are meant to evoke a mood. Within their elaborate borders, they are set off from the text and lead a life of their own, seemingly independent of Malory's words.

This tension between word and image was to become one of the salient characteristics of the great illustrated books of the twentieth century. One of the most original and striking of these was the result of a collaboration between the painter Sonia Delaunay and the poet Blaise Cendrars. The text of this work, *La Prose du Transsibérien et de la petite Jehanne de France*, is a poem about a journey on the Trans-Siberian Railway from Moscow to Nikolskoye on the Sea of Japan. The work is striking for its inventive format as well as for its vividly colored illustrations. The four separate sheets that make up the book were meant to fold up like a map, and it is in this form that they are usually encountered. The copy in the Spencer Collection, however, remains in its original, unfolded form, perhaps the only one of the sixty-two copies of the book to survive in this state.

Delaunay's illustrations weave in and out of the text, arcing around it, filling a margin in one place, a space between lines of type in another. They manifest, along with the use of a variety of typefaces and of printing inks, an interest in thinking through the idea of just what an illustrated book is or has the potential to be. They also manifest the artist's theories about the relationships between color and form that culminated in the concept of "Simultaneity" developed by her and her husband, Robert. The book itself is one of the monuments of twentieth-century art and one of the major milestones in the history of the illustrated book.

Less innovative in design than the Delaunay/Cendrars collaboration were the books published by Ambrose Vollard in Paris in the 1930s. The importance of these luxurious volumes lies not in their design so much as in the artists who were commissioned to illustrate them. Most of the great names of the School of Paris were called upon to provide illustrations for the texts that Vollard selected. The illustrations accompany the words in the traditional way, with a full-page illustration facing the words or a vignette placed above the text block. The style of those illustrations was, however, decidedly *not* traditional. Artists like Picasso, Matisse, and Rouault brought their modern sensibilities to bear on the illustrated book, and the results reinforced the primacy of the French tradition in the annals of the history of book illustration. Among the Spencer Collection's holdings of Vollard books, the edition of Balzac's *Le chef d'oeuvre inconnu* (The Unknown Masterpiece) (1931) with etchings and wood engravings by Picasso stands out as another of the great illustrated books of the twentieth century. The grim underpinnings of Balzac's worldview are brilliantly represented in the dense and dark illustrations that accompany them.

Max Ernst, who was born in Germany, had played an important role in artistic circles in Paris in the 1920s and 1930s, emerging as the most important figure in the Dada and Surrealist movements. In 1941, he immigrated to the United States, joining the many European artists who had fled the war in Europe. In 1946, he married the American artist Dorothea Tanning. Ernst worked in a variety of mediums, turning his hand to sculpture, painting, and printmaking and bringing his own distinctive genius to each. He was also interested in illustrating books or, perhaps more precisely, creating them, as his collage novels such as *Une semaine de bonté* (1934) attest. This interest persisted late into his career, as did his capacity for inventiveness and freshness of vision. In 1964 he published his *Maximiliana* in collaboration with the Russian émigré typographer and graphic designer Iliazd (Ilya Zdanovitch).

This work brought together two of the main currents of twentieth-century art: Surrealism and Constructivism, for Iliazd had grown up with and contributed

BLAISE CENDRARS

La Prose du Transsibérien
et de la Petite Jehanne de France
Couleurs simultanées de M⁰⁰ DELAUNAY-TERK

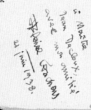

TIRAGE DE LUXE N° 47.
De 1 à 8 pour les exemplaires parchemin
De 9 à 36 pour les exemplaires japon
De 37 à 150 pour les exemplaires simili japon

ÉDITIONS
des
HOMMES NOUVEAUX
4, rue de Savoie, 4
PARIS
1913
Tous droits réservés

PROSE DU TRANSSIBÉRIEN
ET DE LA PETITE JEHANNE DE FRANCE

En ce temps-là j'étais en mon adolescence
J'avais à peine seize ans et je ne me souvenais déjà plus de mon enfance
J'étais à 16 000 lieues du lieu de ma naissance
J'étais à Moscou, dans la ville de mille et trois clochers et des sept gares
Et je n'avais pas assez des sept gares et des mille et trois tours
Car mon adolescence était alors si ardente et si folle
Que mon cœur, tour à tour, brûlait comme le temple d'Éphèse ou comme la Place Rouge de Moscou
    Quand le soleil se couche.
    Et mes yeux éclairaient des voies anciennes
    Et j'étais déjà si mauvais poète
    Que je ne savais pas aller jusqu'au bout.

Le Kremlin était comme un immense gâteau tartare
Croustillé d'or
Avec les grandes amandes des cathédrales toutes blanches
Et l'or mielleux des cloches...
Un vieux moine me lisait la légende de Novgorode
J'avais soif
Et je déchiffrais des caractères cunéiformes

    Puis, tout à coup, les pigeons du Saint-Esprit s'envolaient sur la place
    Et mes mains s'envolaient aussi, avec des bruissements d'albatros
    Et ceci, c'était les dernières réminiscences du dernier jour

        Du tout dernier voyage
        Et de la mer.

Pourtant, j'étais fort mauvais poète
Je ne savais pas aller jusqu'au bout
J'avais faim
Et tous les jours et toutes les femmes dans les cafés et tous les verres
J'aurais voulu les boire et les casser
Et toutes les vitrines et toutes les rues
Et toutes les maisons et toutes les vies
Et toutes les roues des fiacres qui tournaient en tourbillons sur les mauvais pavés
J'aurais voulu les plonger dans une fournaise de glaives
Et j'aurais voulu broyer tous les os
Et arracher toutes les langues
Et liquéfier tous ces grands corps étranges et nus sous les vêtements qui m'affolent...
Je pressentais la venue du grand Christ rouge de la révolution russe...
Et le soleil était une vilaine plaie
Qui s'ouvrait comme un brasier.

En ce temps-là j'étais en mon adolescence
J'avais à peine seize ans et je ne me souvenais déjà plus de ma naissance
J'étais à Moscou, où je voulais me nourrir de flammes
Et je n'avais pas assez des tours et des gares que constellaient mes yeux
En Sibérie tonnait le canon c'était la guerre
La faim le froid la peste le choléra
Et les eaux limoneuses de l'Amour charriaient des millions de charognes

Dans toutes les gares je voyais partir tous les derniers trains
Personne ne pouvait plus partir car on ne délivrait plus de billets
Et les soldats qui s'en allaient auraient bien voulu rester...
Un vieux moine me chantait la légende de Novgorode.

    Moi, le mauvais poète qui ne voulait aller nulle part, je pouvais aller partout
    Et aussi les marchands avaient encore assez d'argent
    Pour aller tenter faire fortune.
    Leur train partait tous les vendredis matin.
    On disait qu'il y avait beaucoup de morts.
    L'un emportait cent caisses de réveils et de coucous de la Forêt-Noire
    Un autre, des boîtes à chapeaux des cylindres et un assortiment de tire-bouchons de Sheffield
    Un autre, des cercueils de Malmoë remplis de boîtes de conserve et de sardines à l'huile.
    Puis il y avait beaucoup de femmes
    Des femmes des entre-jambes à louer qui pouvaient aussi servir
    Des cercueils
    Elles étaient toutes patentées
    On disait qu'il y avait beaucoup de morts là-bas
    Elles voyageaient à prix réduits
    Et avaient toutes un compte-courant à la banque.
    OR, UN VENDREDI MATIN CE FUT AUSSI MON TOUR
    ON ÉTAIT EN DÉCEMBRE
    ET JE PARTIS MOI AUSSI POUR ACCOMPAGNER LE VOYAGEUR EN BIJOUTERIE QUI SE RENDAIT À KHARBINE
    NOUS AVIONS DEUX COUPÉS DANS L'EXPRESS ET 34 COFFRES DE JOAILLERIE DE PFORZHEIM
    DE LA CAMELOTTE ALLEMANDE « MADE IN GERMANY »

IL M'AVAIT HABILLÉ DE NEUF ET EN MONTANT DANS LE TRAIN J'AVAIS PERDU UN BOUTON
— JE M'EN SOUVIENS, JE M'EN SOUVIENS, J'Y AI SOUVENT PENSÉ DEPUIS —
JE COUCHAIS SUR LES COFFRES ET J'ÉTAIS TOUT HEUREUX DE POUVOIR JOUER AVEC LE BROWNING NICKELÉ
QU'IL M'AVAIT AUSSI DONNÉ

J'étais très heureux insouciant
Je croyais jouer aux brigands
Nous avions volé le trésor de Golconde
Et nous allions grâce au transsibérien le cacher de l'autre côté du monde
Je devais le défendre contre les voleurs de l'Oural qui avaient attaqué les saltimbanques de Jules Verne
        Contre les khoungouzes les boxeurs de la Chine
        Et les enragés petits Mongols du Grand-Lama
        Alibaba et les quarante voleurs
        Et les fidèles du terrible Vieux de la montagne
        Et surtout, contre les plus modernes
        Les rats d'hôtel
        Et les spécialistes des express internationaux.

Et pourtant, et pourtant
J'étais triste comme un enfant
Les rythmes du train
La « moëlle chemin-de-fer » des psychiatres américains
Le bruit des portes des voix des essieux grinçant sur les rails congelés
Le ferlin d'or de mon avenir
Mon browning le piano et les jurons des joueurs de cartes dans le compartiment d'à côté

Ne fronce plus ces sourcils-ci,
Casta, ni cette bouche-ci,
Laisse-moi puiser tous tes baumes,
Piana, sucrés, salés, poivrés,
Et laisse-moi boire, poivrés,
Salés, sucrés, tes sacrés baumes.

33

Opposite
3–22. BLAISE CENDRARS.
La Prose du Transsibérien et de
la petite Jehanne de France.
*Paris, Editions des Hommes
Nouveaux, 1913. Spencer
Collection*
    Sonia Delaunay collaborated
with the author in the creation
of pochoir—stencil process—illustrations for his poem. One of
the monuments of book illustration in the twentieth century,
this work heralds the imaginative collaborations that pervade
this genre in our time.

This page
3–23. PIERRE BONNARD.
Illustration for Paul Verlaine's
*Parallèlment. Lithograph,
1900. Spencer Collection*
    The 109 lithographs that
Bonnard created to accompany
Verlaine's text set the stage for
the twentieth-century livre d'ar-
tiste. *For the rest of the century
esteemed painters would be
commissioned to provide illustrations for luxury books
meant to be contemplated rather
than read.*

3–24. PABLO PICASSO. Le
repas frugal. *Etching, 1904.*
Wallach Division of Art, Prints
and Photographs
   In this early work, which
antedates his experiments with
Cubism, Picasso reveals his
mastery of design and technique
with a relatively conventional
image.

to the great flowering of the arts that had taken place in Russia just before and
after the Revolution of 1917. The book is almost a dialogue between the artist and
his designer, as the relationship of text and illustration shifts from page to page.
At one point, the words cascade down the page, one letter above another, echoing
the verticality of the image they accompany. At another point, they are shunted
off to the edge of the page, which is dominated by an image of doodling that par-
odies learned textual commentaries. The thirty folded folios all suggest the
seemingly limitless possibilities of interplay between text and image on the printed
page. The presence of this monumental book in the Library's Spencer Collection
is due to the generosity of Dorothea Tanning who, in 1983, gave to the Library more
than one hundred fifty etchings, aquatints, and lithographs made by her husband
along with a copy of *Maximiliana.*
   It seems that there are as many variations on that theme as there are writers
and artists who choose to collaborate. Indeed, so long as there are creative and
adventuresome artists and writers, magnificent illustrated books will continue
to be produced, each exploring and testing, in its own fashion, the limits of the

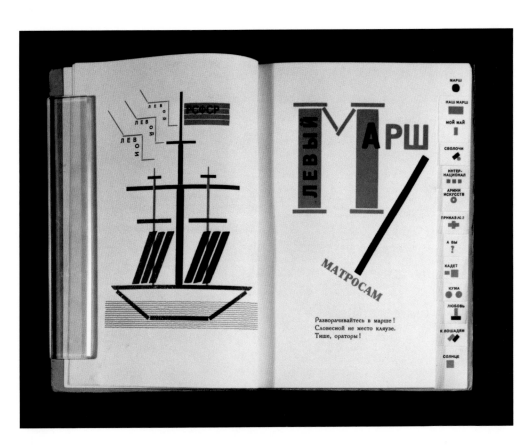

3–25. VLADIMIR
MAYAKOVSKY. Dlya Golosa
[For the Voice]. *Berlin, 1923.*
Spencer Collection
    *El Lissitsky designed this
book, a startling evocation of
the inventiveness and energy of
the book arts in the Soviet
Union in the years immediately
after the 1917 Revolution.*

3–26. MAX ERNST.
Maximiliana. *Paris, Le Degré
Quarante et Un, 1964. Spencer
Collection*
    *The great Surrealist artist
Max Ernst carried his inventiveness and freshness of vision into
his last decades. In Max-
imiliana he collaborated with
the Russian émigré typographer
and graphic designer Iliazd
(Ilya Zdanovitch).*

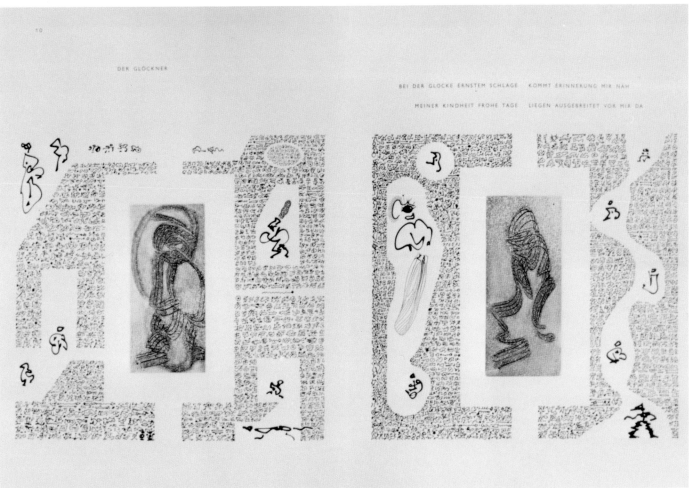

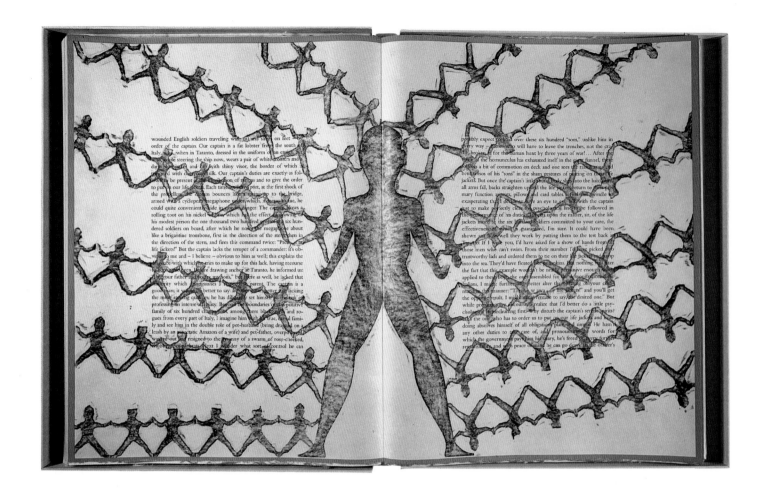

3–27. FRANCESCO
CLEMENTE. Illustration for
The Departure of the Argonaut.
*Lithograph, 1986. Spencer
Collection*

*Savinio's text, first published
in 1917, is an imaginative recreation of his experiences as
an Italian soldier in the First
World War. Clemente has built
over and around it a series of
vivid images whose power recalls the work of Blake and
Delaunay.*

If you are far away from home

A keepsake will remind you of
those who love you

possible. The resilience of the tradition of book illustration is best represented in recent work by Francesco Clemente's lithographs for the 1986 edition of Alberto Savinio's *The Departure of the Argonaut*, first published in 1917. The text is an imaginative recreation of Savinio's experiences as an Italian soldier in the First World War. In approaching this text, Clemente has, it seems, taken his cue from Blake and Delaunay. There is no fixed relationship between the illustrations and the text. The images run over, around, and alongside the work. The startling shifts of color from page to page reinforce in the viewer's mind the sense of voyage and the experience of discovery. The figural allusions to classic forms, to nature, and to navigation recreate for us, with an impressive economy of means, a voyage through the Mediterranean that is at once timeless and contemporary.

Clemente's and Savinio's book brings us to the end of our survey of the collections of prints and illustrated books at the Library. The image of a voyage that it offers is a useful one with which to conclude this chapter. Like any traveler on a whirlwind tour, there is much that we have missed. But that offers us a reason to return, perhaps without the long-winded tour guide, to make our own discoveries and to find our own treasures. The exhibitions that the Print Collection regularly mounts in the Central Research Library should make this return voyage smooth and rewarding. Like any favored place, this collection will never run out of delightful experiences for the returning traveler, whether he should come back once or a hundred times.

3–28. DONALD SULTAN. Illustration for David Mamet's *Warm and Cold. Lithograph, 1985. Spencer Collection*
The author and artist both became fathers at about the same time. Inspired by this co-incidence, they collaborated on this book, which explores the sometimes ambivalent emotions of parenthood.

CHAPTER FOUR

PHOTOGRAPHY

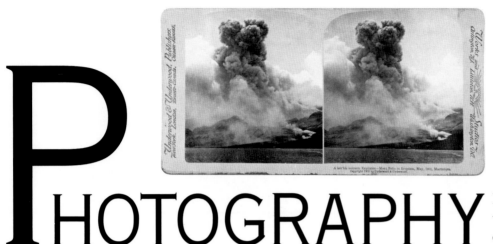

For those who contemplate the development of the varied collections of The New York Public Library, it sometimes seems that significant holdings of materials have sprung up while no one was looking. One is reminded of a line from Arthur Hugh Clough's poem "Say not the struggle naught availeth," which speaks of a great torrent, fed by rivulets, and gathering force until: "Comes silent, flooding in, the main." This silent growth of the collections is particularly noteworthy in discussing the Library's millions of photographs, which, scattered throughout its many divisions, comprise one of the major collections in the world. And yet, it was only in 1980 that a separate curatorial department for photography was established, as a unit of the Miriam and Ira D. Wallach Division of Art, Prints and Photographs. Over the years, each division of the Library accumulated collections of photographs, sometimes by themselves and sometimes as supplements to gifts of books. The collections at the Performing Arts Research Center, at the Schomburg Center for Research in Black Culture, and in the Central Research Library had evolved into a world-class assemblage documenting the history and development of photography almost without any intention of doing so.

Each of the three "parental" libraries that merged their resources in 1895 to form The New York Public Library included collections of photographs in their holdings. Shortly after the earliest successful demonstrations of the camera, the Astor Library acquired significant products of the new invention. Both the Lenox Library and the private library of Samuel J. Tilden also brought to the merger files of photographs of exceptional interest that remain among the Library's prized holdings in this field. Along with this material, as a matter of course, there came the literature that explained the processes and equipment by which means such remarkable results were made possible.

"Remarkable" is an apt word here, for in many instances the quality of the images produced in these early photographs has yet to be improved upon. Aside from such high standards of performance, the second half of the nineteenth century and the years immediately following witnessed the rapid development of photography from a sensational novelty to a commonplace necessity of daily experience.

The earliest observations that forecast the future of the camera go back to ancient times. More than three centuries before the birth of Christ, Aristotle had noted that, when daylight was admitted into a dark chamber through a tiny aperture, an image of the outside world could be projected against the opposite walls of the enclosure. This is the simple principle of a child's pinhole camera. The projected image appears upside down, but otherwise it is magically realistic when the picture plane is placed in proper focus. (In the Middle Ages, an Arab scientist used such a device for observing eclipses of the sun, which he knew would be harmful if gazed at directly with the naked eye.)

An elementary device that could cause light waves to converge or change rays of light to form a sharp image — the lens — was also well known to the ancients. Before the invention of glass of suitable quality, magnifiers were often made of dark rock crystal to serve as short-focus lenses used for cutting seals and gems in such minute designs as were scarcely legible by the naked eye. They were so precise in execution that when enlarged to the scale of murals, as has been done in photographs of our own day, they show little or no distortion of details. In his *Natural History*, written in the first century A.D., Pliny the Elder recommended using rock crystal for focusing the sun's rays to a pinpoint for cauterizing wounds. Even earlier, the Egyptians had given their statues and coffins covered eyes with rock-crystal corneas that could have been quite easily used as lenses.

It was not until the sixteenth century, however, that a proposal was made to control and sharpen the images projected by a small source of light into a darkened interior with the aid of a lens. This discovery marked the origin of the camera obscura (the Italian term for a darkened room). This contrivance, it was reported, made it possible to capture a "whole view as it really is with its distances, its colors, and shadows and motion, the clouds, the water twinkling, the birds flying." With such a faithful image to guide him, the artist had an unprecedented tool for ensuring accuracy in rendering whatever subject he chose, and in a portable form it soon became a widely used device. It was discarded only in the nineteenth century, when photographs became available to serve the same purpose more conveniently and effectively.

Years before there were any practical achievements in that direction, it was predicted that a day would come when it would be possible to permanently fix an image as it appeared at any chosen moment in a camera obscura. The possibility persisted in the minds of inventive spirits who labored to make it come true, and in time some of these achieved a measure of success in their experiments.

The real breakthrough came in 1839 when the Frenchman Louis Jacques Daguerre and the Englishman William Henry Fox Talbot publicly announced they had reached the ultimate goal. Each had solved the problem in a different way, but both were able successfully to preserve on a durable surface the fugitive view on which they had focused their cameras.

When the compulsive diarist Philip Hone saw his first pictures by Daguerre in 1839, he could hardly contain his enthusiasm:

> Every object, however minute, is a perfect transcript of the thing itself; the hair of the human head, the gravel of the roadside, the texture of a silk curtain, or the shadow of the smaller leaf reflected on the wall, are all imprinted as carefully as nature or art has created them in the objects transferred; and those things which are invisible to the naked eye are rendered apparent by the help of a magnifying glass. . . . How greatly ashamed of their ignorance the by-gone generations of mankind ought to be!

It was electrifying news, all but incredible. Even when Daguerre was on the brink of proclaiming his discovery, an article in a German publication had scoffed at such a possibility. "If this thing were at all possible," wrote the author, "then something similar would have been done a long time ago in antiquity by men like Archimedes or Moses. But if these wise men knew nothing of mirror pictures made permanent, then one can straightaway call the Frenchman Daguerre, who boasts of such an unheard of thing, the fool of fools." Even Mme Daguerre is said to have questioned her husband's sanity for attempting to capture "evansecent reflections" with a man-made machine.

The rest is history. Inundated as we now are by photographs and photographic reproductions, it is impossible for us to recapture the public frenzy, at every

level of society, that greeted the advent of daguerreotypes. One contemporary
reporter wrote that "their exquisite perfection almost transcends the bounds of
sober belief." Edgar Allan Poe observed that the daguerreotype was "infinitely
more accurate in its presentation than any painting by human hands." In this
he was quite right. That is, so long as the artist sought consummate realism in
his work, he would now be outdone by the camera's lense, if for the time being
only in black and white. The celebrated English artist Charles Landseer warned
his colleagues that science had produced what might be termed a foe-to-graphic
art—a device that would seriously diminish the importance of artistic talent and
possibly even eliminate any need of it.

On seeing his first daguerreotype, a French contemporary flatly stated: "From
today painting is dead." No such dire consequences followed, of course, but
it became increasingly apparent that the art of painting would change its traditional
course.

In 1839, shortly after Daguerre had announced his discovery, the artist and
inventor Samuel F. B. Morse visited Paris to promote interest in his electric telegraph—to no avail. As he wrote home, while he was there he heard of "Daguerre's
wonderful results in freeing the image of the camera obscura." He visited the
Frenchman in his studio and wrote that "no painting or engraving ever approached"
the daguerreotypes he saw there. He added that this was "Rembrandt perfected"
and further predicted that Daguerre had opened a field of research beyond the
range of the microscope, a new kingdom for the naturalist to explore.

Upon his return to New York, Morse successfully undertook to make daguerreotypes on his own with the brief collaboration of Dr. John William Draper, professor of chemistry at New York University (Draper was the first to photograph the

moon). Interested American students came to Morse to learn what they could of the process. Some of them went on to practice on their own. Among them was Albert S. Southworth who proceeded to set up a very successful shop in Boston in partnership with Jonah Johnson Hawes. They attracted such sitters as Edgar Allan Poe, Henry Wadsworth Longfellow, John Quincy Adams, Daniel Webster, and, hardly less celebrated at the time, the Irish dancer and adventuress Lola Montez, who posed languidly with a cigarette dangling between her fingers. These were intensely sensitive and penetrating portraits as well as technically faultless reproductions.

Southworth could not suppress his exultation over the success of his operation. "I cannot in a letter describe all the wonders of this Apparatus," he wrote to his sister. "Suffice it to say, that I can now make a *perfect* picture, in one hour's time, that would take a Painter weeks to draw." The next year he again wrote her, "Our miniatures are by far the best of America, probably in the world. We sent specimens to England last October and have just heard from them. None as good there."

At the Great Exhibition held at London in 1851 American daguerreotypes won three gold medals and extravagant praise from critics. Horace Greeley observed that this exceptional quality was due to the smoke-free air of most American cities. One European visitor likened the galleries in the major cities to palaces, opulently furbished as they were to beguile customers. Whatever the inducements, by 1853 it was estimated that there were at least two thousand operators in New York alone, producing some three million daguerreotypes annually.

Probably the most important of the daguerreotypes in the Library's collections is a striking portrait of a Native American taken about 1848. It shows Ely Spencer Parker, a Seneca, born on the Tonawanda Reservation in western New York in 1828. He is shown in native dress, which belies his later, varied career as a lawyer, engineer, and general in the Union Army. He also became Grand Sachem of the Iroquois Confederacy. In this touching portrait, we see a faint echo of the pride and dignity of the Native American before his assimilation into the white man's world.

American daguerreotypers also took to the back roads in horse-drawn vans to look for customers in rural and frontier areas where they vied with itinerant limners who were painting likenesses of country folk to make a scant living. One daguerreotyper made a fourteen-hundred-mile journey down the Mississippi by flatboat equipped with a sitting room and a chemical room. He took more than one thousand portraits but still found time to fish and hunt along the riverbanks between appointments.

Making a daguerreotype was an exacting process. A silver-copper plate, burnished until it was as bright as a mirror, was treated with iodine vapor to render it sensitive to light. The exposed plate was developed over heated mercury, fixed in hyposulphite of soda (the same "hypo" still used in darkrooms), rinsed in distilled water, dried, and mounted under glass to protect the perishable film of mercury, which "held" the image.

Ingenious, attractive, inexpensive, and popular as they were, daguerreotypes had severe limitations. The image was necessarily small and reversed and could only be registered in bright daylight. The pictures could be seen only when the plate was held at a proper angle and, importantly, could not be reproduced. By about 1860, they went out of fashion, never to be revived. They were replaced by true photographs, which were free of all these limitations and had already won a widespread popularity since they were first produced by Talbot.

These "photogenic drawings," as Talbot referred to them (he also called them calotypes or Talbotypes), did not have the glittering brilliance of daguerreotypes, but they were produced by the negative-positive process, which charted the course of future developments in photography. Of further, vital importance, the process made possible the endless recreation of exact copies from a single negative—as the engraver had found it possible to duplicate his designs from woodblocks and copperplates. A vague notion of such a process had come to Talbot some years before during a sojourn in Italy. He loved the inimitable landscapes of that country and yearned to record his impressions of them. He had no talent for sketching, but at one point he recalled an old camera obscura he had used some years earlier to further his attempts to draw adequately. "It was during these thoughts," he wrote, "that the idea occurred to me . . . how charming it would be if it were possible to cause these natural images to imprint themselves durably, and remain fixed upon the paper!"

On January 31, 1839, Talbot reported to the Royal Society that he had, in fact, invented a process "by Which Natural Objects May Be Made to Delineate Themselves without the Aid of the Artist's Pencil." A few weeks later he submitted another paper in which he explained that he had managed to fix his image simply by using a solution of common salt. A few years after he announced his discovery, Talbot published a book in six parts (from 1844 to 1846) entitled *The Pencil of Nature*, which he illustrated by pasting in a group of his own photographs. It was not only the first publication to use photographic reproductions but the first demonstration of the mass production of photographic positives from single negatives. Only a few hundred copies of this seminal publication were issued and only a small number of these have survived—one of them in the Library's Rare Books and Manuscripts Division.

Beaumont Newhall has described this book as having for the history of photography the importance that the Gutenberg Bible has for the history of printing. The author himself, however, was somewhat self-effacing. In his "Introductory Remarks," he describes the book as a "little work" and apologizes for the quality of the images with the comment that "what they want as yet of delicacy and finish of execution arises chiefly from our want of sufficient knowledge of [Nature's] laws."

The images in *The Pencil of Nature* form a kind of catalogue of photographic subject matter. Talbot trained his eye on architecture, sculpture, decorative arts, two shelves of books, a page of text from an old book, and so forth. He suggested the varied uses to which photography could be put both practically and aesthetically.

In ensuing years, down to the present day, frequent changes have been made in the chemicals, papers, and other factors in the process of making a photograph. Some were introduced by Talbot himself, others by men who kept their innovations secret or did not bother to publicize the results. Occasionally, the same discovery was made by several men at the same time, as so often happens in the history of inventions; all of which tends to confuse any accurate or complete record of just who did what and when. However, the Library's collection of books and other documents relating to photography—past, present, and prospective—can provide a fair answer to any reasonable question that may arise. (It is not altogether beside the point to observe that preliminary research on the Polaroid camera was conducted in the Library's Science and Technology Research Center.)

One significant invention, the introduction of the wet-collodion process in 1850, had a revolutionary impact on photography. This method facilitated the preparation of plates and resulted in a delicacy and refinement of detail unmatched by previous negatives. It also saved time and money. The speedier action it ensured led to a different character in the resulting images than had been possible before. With new and improved equipment, photographers ventured into different and

distant fields in quest of the exotic and the unusual, and also, close at home, found a new look in the commonplace.

One novel and immensely popular outcome of this awakened interest in camera work came around the middle of the century with the development of the stereo- scope. This instrument, with its two photographs of the same subject taken from slightly different angles and viewed through two eyepieces—just as our separate eyes view the world about us—presents a convincing illusion of three-dimensional space. Public excitement over this new diversion was explosive. Not long after one promoter coined the slogan "no home without a stereoscope," that, in fact, seemed to be the case. Stereoscopic viewers were early versions of television sets. Oliver Wendell Holmes professed that this inexpensive gadget had allowed him to be "a spectator to the best views the world had to offer." He urged his readers to join him in viewing "the wonders of the Nile, the ruins of Baalbek, Ann Hathaway's cottage, the rawest Western settlement and the Shanties of Pike's Peak." He admitted that he had himself viewed a hundred thousand such slides. To make it easier, he invented a simple hand-held framer with a sliding rack for ad- justing the focus. Everything and anything was photographed to satisfy the demand for more and different subjects. Large collections of these stereographs, such as the Library's Robert Dennis collection, frequently contain pictorial information of substantial interest to the historian, evidence that can be found nowhere else.

The Dennis collection now totals about 72,000 stereoscopic views, making it one of the largest collections of its type in the world and one of the treasures of the Miriam and Ira D. Wallach Division of Art, Prints and Photographs. In 1941, 35,000 of these were purchased from Robert Dennis for the Library's American History Division (now the renamed U.S. History, Local History and Genealogy Di- vision) with the enthusiastic support of the division's chief, who described them "as truly American as local imprints." Forty years later, Dennis gave the Library an additional 32,000 stereos that he had acquired since 1941. They arrived at Fifth Avenue and Forty-second Street on the day he died, at the age of eighty.

Almost three-quarters of the collection deals with geographical subjects, em- phasizing the fact that nothing on earth seemed to be off the track beaten by roving cameramen, from the rain forests of Central America to the frozen seas of the Arctic, from remains of ancient civilizations in the Near and Far East to the un- touched wilderness of the American West. Illustrated reports of these various parts of the world, many of them sights never before seen by Western eyes, excited

4–3. ANNA ATKINS. British
Algae: Cyanotype Impressions,
1850–1851. Spencer Collection
   *In her experiments with the
cyanotype process, Anna Atkins
made a significant contribution
to the development of
photography.*

4–4. FRANCIS FRITH.
Egypt and Palestine
Photographed and Described.
*London and New York, James
S. Virtue, 1858–1859. Wallach
Division of Art, Prints and
Photographs*
 Frith traveled through the
Middle East in a covered
wagon, taking photographs that
he would later use in a variety
of publications, including an
edition of the Bible.

4–5. MAXIME DU CAMP.
Egypte, Nubie, Palestine et
Syrie. *Paris, Gide et J. Baudry,
1852. Wallach Division of Art,
Prints and Photographs*
 Traveling in the Middle East
with his friend Gustave
Flaubert, Du Camp used the
still relatively new process of
photography to good advantage.
On his return, he published his
collection of 122 views of historical monuments.

4–6. A Terrible Volcanic Explosion—Mont Pelée (Martinique) in Eruption, May 1902. Stereographic view, 1902. Wallach Division of Art, Prints and Photographs

Stereo views were produced by the millions between the 1850s and 1930s, and geographical subjects were a primary interest of those who made and bought "stereos."

public interest, and publishers looked to them for a growing and profitable market, underwriting expeditions to gather new views.

In 1850, the French writer and photographer Maxime Du Camp set off on a tour of the Middle East with his close friend Gustave Flaubert, who was yet to publish his first work. Flaubert was entranced by what he saw, and Du Camp took some brilliant photographs under almost impossible conditions. In 1852, the resulting book was published with the title *Egypte, Nubie, Palestine et Syrie* and illustrated with 125 of Du Camp's photos. It was probably the first of such illustrated books to be published, but it was quickly followed by a host of others. (A copy of Du Camp's book was one of the early acquisitions of the Astor Library.)

In the 1850s, Francis Frith, who was a publisher as well as a skilled photographer, made three trips to the Holy Land and ended by publishing seven books. Among them was his *Egypt and Palestine Photographed and Described* (1858–1859). As in Du Camp's case, Frith underwent almost maddening difficulties in his fieldwork. All the sensitizing, developing, and washing required to produce his negatives had to be carried out within a tent where the temperature often reached 130 degrees. At times, his collodion boiled and the fumes from evaporating ether were all but suffocating. Outside the tent, sudden desert sandstorms damaged his plates; insects and animals conspired to ruin plates and spoil chemicals. But Frith's dedication to his task was unconquerable, and his finished prints were superb.

Two of Frith's French contemporaries, Louis Auguste Bisson and his brother Auguste Rosalie, went to the opposite extremes on a trip to Switzerland they made in the company of Emperor Napoleon III and his beautiful empress Eugénie. In sub-zero weather, the photographers made several ascents of the formidable peaks of Mont Blanc. (Royalty remained discreetly behind to await developments.) At these windswept, frigid heights, their collodion barely flowed, and the developed plates had to be washed with melted snow. Yet the finished photographs, some as large as 12 × 17 inches, were among the finest views of such snow-and-ice mountain scenery that have ever been made.

4–7. LOUIS AUGUSTE AND
AUGUSTE ROSALIE
BISSON. Ascending Mont
Blanc, *ca. 1862. Wallach Division of Art, Prints and
Photographs*
   The Bisson brothers were
among the founding members of
the Société Française Photographique. Between 1855 and
1868, they made a number of
expeditions to the Alps.

4–8. TIMOTHY H.
O'SULLIVAN. A Harvest of
Death, Gettysburg, Pennsyl-
vania, *July 1863. Rare Books
and Manuscripts Division*

*This photograph, by a former
member of Mathew Brady's studio, was published in Alexander
Gardner's* Photographic Sketch-
book of the War *(Washington,
D.C., 1865–1866), a work
whose purpose was to show "the
dreadful details" of the Civil
War.*

In the United States, these were the critical years when the nation was inexorably
moving toward a civil war that threatened to dismember it altogether. Oliver Wendell Holmes had predicted that the stereoscope would be used to report "the next
European war," but the next major war was enacted on American soil, and it
was exhaustively reported by photographers.

Among photographers on both sides of the conflict, the most memorable was
Mathew B. Brady, a one-time pupil of Morse (and earlier a student of the American
painter William Page). Brady organized the first news-picture agency, and he
dispatched teams of photographers to every front line and encampment. There
resulted such scenes of carnage as will probably forever haunt the nation's memory
of that tragic conflict and try its conscience. One recorder of such macabre scenes
hoped that their awful reality would help put an end to such ghastly warfare; it
is a hope revived as each generation looks to some new and ultimate deterrent.

It was only after the Civil War that the nation as a whole became truly aware
of its continental dimensions and turned to the camera for eyewitness evidence of
what might be seen in the Great West. Even before the war was concluded, pioneer
cameramen had ventured into those little-known regions and brought back dramatic
disclosures. Prominent among them were two independent photographers, Charles
L. Weed and C. E. Watkins, both California based. Weed was apparently the
first to photograph Yosemite, in 1859, two years before Watkins. In the 1860s,
both men would produce giant portfolios of photographs of that magnificent valley,
such views as hardly seemed credible when they were shown in the sedate confines
of Eastern parlors.

During the decade after the South's surrender at Appomattox, the discovery of America seemed to be taking place all over again as the unfamiliar treasure-house of the West was explored by an army of investigators. The government sent out a succession of expeditions conducted by Clarence King, Major John Wesley Powell, Lieutenant George Wheeler, and others—men who were keenly alive to the epic character of their assignments. Even the official reports of these parties bristle with excitement and wonder over what was seen and learned of the spectacular nature of America's Western wilderness. And everywhere these parties (and individuals) went they were accompanied by artists and photographers to provide graphic evidence of what they saw on their surveys. That the photographers could overcome the hardships, difficulties, and downright dangers they faced in order to reflect these wonders on film was cause for wonder in itself.

Some of those who took part in these adventures were strongly affected by less creditable aspects of their experience. All too obviously, they saw that in these westward marches of civilization, the Native Americans were being forced to modify and abandon a traditional way of life they justifiably considered their birthright. The photographer Edward S. Curtis labored for twenty-five years to report those vanishing cultures before it was too late. He produced twenty illustrated volumes of well-documented photographic reproductions of what he had seen (largely with financial aid from J. P. Morgan and his estate). The Library's examples

4–9. CHARLES LEANDER WEED. Cascade—Little Yo-Semite Valley, ca. 1864–1865. *Wallach Division of Art, Prints and Photographs*
Weed was the first photographer to capture the natural wonders of the Yosemite Valley. His views were not meant to be simple documentary images; they were intended to be works of art.

of Curtis's works with their price labels still attached to the mounts may have been his first attempt to raise funds for his project.

The unique importance of a good photograph as a reliable source of documentation in every field of endeavor, from journalism to technology, became evident almost from the start. Its inherent literalness was its prime attribute. But whether such precise and detailed reproduction was an index of artistic merit, as many highly regarded early critics contended, or rather simply a form of technical wizardry, posed a question that is still sometimes raised.

In *The Pencil of Nature* Talbot included among his illustrations representations of glassware and of the open door of a rural cottage, along with other disparate subjects. "We have sufficient authority in the Dutch school of art," he wrote, "for taking as subjects of representation scenes of daily life and familiar occurrence." By this he intimated that he had fair reason for categorizing these homely products of his camera with the works of the Dutch "Little Masters" of the seventeenth century, who had found in the scenes and objects of everyday bourgeois life subjects fit for "art."

4–12. J. X. RAOULT.
Neskol'ko narodnykh tipov
Rossii. Pervoe izdanie . . .
[Some Russian Types . . .]
Odessa, 1870s or 1880s.
Slavonic Division

Much of the rare photo-
graphic material in The New
York Public Library's Slavonic
Division was at one time owned
by the Russian imperial family,
many of which were purchased
in 1931 from the library of
Grand Duke Vladimir Alex-
androvich, uncle of Tsar Nicholas II. Representative of the
many photographic and icono-
graphic volumes in the Library's
collection is this work of 224
photographs taken during the
1870s and 1880s, originally in
the library of Tsar Alexander
III. This photograph depicts a
troop of the Kuban Cossack
calvary.

4–13. Album of a costume ball
at the Winter Palace, February
1903. *St. Petersburg, 1904. 3*
vols. Slavonic Division

One of the strengths of the
Library lies in its holdings of
materials relating to the Russian imperial family and the
administrative and military
structure of the Russian Empire.
Depicted here in medieval Muscovite costume is Tsar Nicholas
II, as he presided over one of
the grandest costume balls of
the ancien régime, that which
took place at the Winter Palace
(now the Hermitage Museum) in
February 1903.

4–14. TIMOTHY H. O'SULLIVAN. Looking Across the Colorado River to the Mouth of Paria Creek, *ca. 1871. Wallach Division of Art, Prints and Photographs*

Lt. General George Wheeler's expedition to the Southwest enjoyed for a time the services of T. H. O'Sullivan as official photographer. O'Sullivan's landscapes vividly capture the heroic scale and natural beauty of the area.

4–15. EDWARD S. CURTIS. The North American Indians. *Seattle, 1900–1928. Rare Books and Manuscripts Division*

Curtis's record of the American Indian was published in twenty volumes, with the financial support of J. P. Morgan. Their ethnographic intent and usefulness is matched by their beauty, an indication of Curtis's reverence for the cultures he was documenting.

Not long after that statement was published, Sir William J. Newton, an eminent English miniaturist, delivered a startling paper of quite different import before the newly formed Photographic Society of Great Britain:

> I do not conceive it to be necessary or desirable for an artist to represent, or aim at, the attainment of every minute detail, but to endeavor at produc- ing a broad general effect. . . . I do not consider that the whole of a subject should be in what is called "in focus"; on the contrary I have found in many instances that the subject is better attained by the whole subject being a little out of focus.

On the surface, that sounded like an unprecedented disavowal of the camera's basic function of providing incomparably exact reproductions. Actually, Newton's advice was aimed at photographers whose works were intended as studies for paintings or drawings, as mechanically contrived "sketch pads" such as even the most esteemed artists of the time were learning to use in preparing their fin- ished works. It is a practice that has continued ever since.

As the insistance on sharp-focus camera work relaxed, the results suggested further experiments that brought about new concepts of photography as an indepen- dent art form. Before the end of the nineteenth century, various rebel groups in different countries rallied to support their claims of special distinction in this new direction. In the periodic exhibitions of contemporary photography, separate areas were reserved for "art photography." Soon, a substantial number of photographers "seceded" from the more traditional organizations and held their own shows.

The decisive figure in this international movement was Alfred Stieglitz, the American-born son of a German immigrant. It was he more than any other person who brought about a general recognition of photography as a form of fine art. A highly accomplished photographer himself, it was he who most convincingly insisted that photography was more than a handmaiden of art — or a means of accurately recording an event, a scene, or a person. He helped enormously to advance the notion that photography could be, in fact, a medium of personal expression with its own aesthetic — the first entirely new medium to have evolved in many centuries. His famous gallery "291" at 291 Fifth Avenue in New York became an international center for the "photo-secessionists"; the publications he directed, notably the handsome periodical *Camera Work* (1902–1917), became their organ. Among his other accomplishments, he was in good part responsible for initiating Americans into the world of modern art as it was practiced in Europe and then in America, a growing awareness of which influenced photographic aesthetics. (The flight from realism that attended that advanced style occasioned Frank Lloyd Wright to quip that if one saw a cow in a painting that looked like a real cow, it would be better to buy a cow because the painting was probably worthless.)

In any case, since the days of Daguerre and Talbot photography has played a constantly increasing role in human concerns. Although it is not always recognized, virtually every aspect of our daily experience is in one way or another affected by what the camera tells us. The camera has, in fact, become a major tool in shaping the course of civilization. Without the piercing insights provided by modern photography, our current knowledge of the nature of light, like that of the atom, would not have been possible; today's advances in science and technology would have been inconceivable.

With such prodigies already realized, it can be said that the contribution of photography to our cultural heritage is hardly less than that made by the invention of the printing press more than five hundred years ago. In modern times, photographs have, in their own way, become as important as words to our understanding of ourselves and the world we live in.

CHAPTER FIVE

CHILDREN'S LITERATURE

In his autobiography, *Without Stopping*, the American writer and composer Paul Bowles remembers wandering around New York by himself at the age of seven or eight, in about 1918. His itinerary included a visit to the Central Research Library, where the Central Children's Room was then located.

> About once a month I stopped by the Public Library to see Miss Moore. She always had time to talk for a few minutes, and she generally gave me a book to add to my growing collection. Often she had the authors dedicate them to me beforehand. Hugh Lofting wrote a whole page in the front of *The Story of Dr. Dolittle* and embellished it with drawings, as did Henrik Willem van Loon in *A Short History of Discovery,* who drew me a portrait of himself smoking a pipe. She had Carl Sandburg inscribe his *Rootabaga Stories* for me.

The "Miss Moore" of this illuminating anecdote was Anne Carroll Moore, who in 1906 had been appointed The New York Public Library's superintendent of services for children and who, in 1911, had presided over the opening of the Central Children's Room in the newly opened Central Research Library. Miss Moore set the tone and established the tradition of the Library's facilities for children, and under her leadership the collecting of children's literature began.

In a book such as this, we must concentrate on the objects in the Library's collection, since they are most easily captured in word and image, but we must note that children's programs are among the truly great treasures of The New York Public Library. Through the work of dedicated librarians, countless children, from all the economic and racial groups that make up this city, have been introduced not only to the pleasures of books and the delights of the imagination but also to sincere and inspiring public servants. Paul Bowles, for example, may well have grown up to be a writer without having met Miss Moore, but we suspect the welcome he received when he visited the Central Children's Room and the books he so happily took away must have suggested to him that the world of literature was a pleasant one to inhabit.

Miss Moore was not only interested in welcoming children and providing them with books, she was also interested in the adults who wrote and illustrated those books and in the history of children's literature. Since her day, the Central

Children's Room has been an international center of information in this field. Publishers, editors, and illustrators, as well as librarians and authors, have come here from all over to understand better this special territory in the world of books and to further their own professional undertakings. With all this, the Library has played no small part in raising the standards by which the quality and importance of books for the young may fairly be judged.

The Central Children's Room was established as part of The Research Libraries (in 1906 called the "Reference Department"). In 1949, it became part of the Branch Library system, and it is now housed in the Donnell Library Center on Fifty-third Street, opposite The Museum of Modern Art. Its collections have grown to over 100,000 books, drawings, paintings, toys, and ephemera, including an important collection of Valentine Day cards. It ranks as one of the major collections for researchers in the field of children's literature in the world. But it is also an active children's library. Recent books are lent to children and their parents; story hours are held; and the Feast of St. Nicholas, especially dear to Miss Moore, is still observed each year.

In addition to the great collection on Fifty-third Street, other collections of children's literature are found in units of The Research Libraries. Recently, the Schomburg Center for Research in Black Culture has developed a children's collection relating to the black experience that now numbers more than fifteen hundred titles. In the General Research Division, the Central Research Library holds the Schatzki collection of some three hundred eighteenth- and nineteenth-century European children's books and some four hundred volumes published by the Darton family in nineteenth-century England. The Slavonic Division holds an important assemblage of Russian children's books. There are important individual items of children's literature in just about all of The Research Libraries' units. They present a picture of a literary genre of interest not only to children themselves but also to adults who care about the history of books and who feel, perhaps, a twinge of nostalgia for that day, long ago, when they first came to love them.

Viewed across the years, children's books provide a field of rich interest for the social historian, for they clearly reflect what parents and educators have thought youngsters should read and know to guide them into their adult years. In the earliest books directed at a juvenile audience, moral strictures were stressed, almost unmercifully, in order to teach children how to think and behave as grown-ups before they were prepared to understand or undertake what might be expected from them as mature men or women. It was in much this same spirit that for centuries young folk were dressed in costumes that were cut to the pattern of adults' clothing—or, one might say, imprisoned in garments that inhibited their healthy childish antics. So they are shown in family portraits of past centuries—stiffly posed, miniature replicas of their parents.

What can we suppose a youngster's reaction to have been upon encountering a book (published in London in 1763 and now in the Library's collections) entitled, *The Newtonian System of Philosophy, Adapted to the Capacities of Young Gentlemen and Ladies, and Familiarized and Made Entertaining by Objects with Which They Are Intimately Acquainted?* As one writer has observed, perhaps this is the stuff of which the British Empire was built, but as entertaining fare, its success was at best dubious. And could American tots a century earlier have found pleasure in the New England clergyman John Cotton's message in the first children's book printed in this country, with the awesome title, *Spiritual Milk for Boston Babes in Either England Drawn out of the Breast of both Testaments for their Souls Nourishment* (1656)? However, the Rare Book Room houses and cherishes the only known copy of this edition as a fascinating historic rarity—and a harbinger of a multitude of primers to follow.

In 1539, Martin Luther had in the same spirit published a book designed specifically for children. *Catechismus pro Pueris et Iuventute*, as it was titled, was

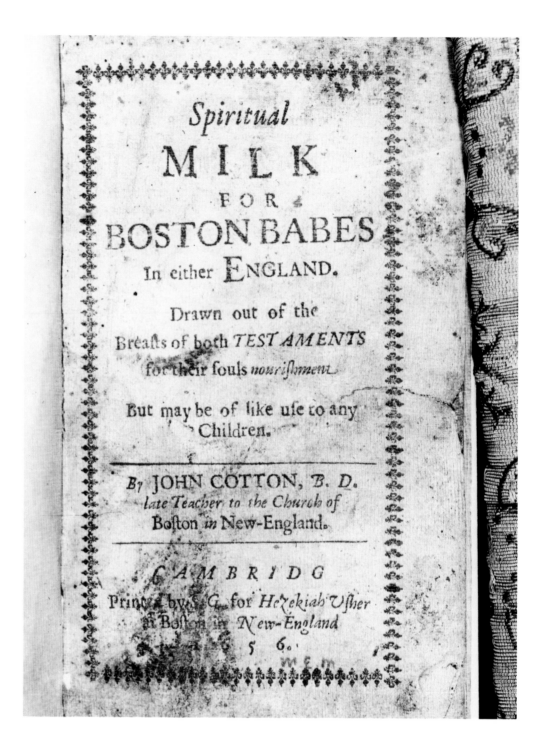

intended to teach the Lutheran catechism to the young people of Europe.

   In more recent times, children have had a large voice, and a larger choice, in what they will read. Often enough, they have an instinctive capacity for appreciating what books will best serve them. As much as their elders, they have put their stamp on the classics that will appeal to generation after generation of young readers in edition after edition. Neither his English nor American publisher was initially much impressed by Kenneth Grahame's engaging pastoral, *The Wind in the Willows* (1908), nor by any means were all reviewers. However, it has enjoyed a success with children for eight decades and shows no sign of losing its appeal.

   The origins of what came to be regarded as children's books can be traced to very ancient times. Long before there were written records of such performances, adults as well as children gathered about the fireside in courts and cottages to listen to recitations of myths and legends, epics and sagas that had been passed down from one generation to the next for countless centuries. A good part of this traditional oral recounting, with its tales of natural wonders, heroic adventure, and mysterious, beguiling episodes, was imperishable and, in one form or another, ultimately found its way into the books that children read today. And new books continue to appear whose stories have their roots in the folktales of Africa, Asia, Europe, the Caribbean, and America as verbally transmitted from times long past.

Children have a way of finding in some books written primarily for their elders elements that excite their imagination, and they appropriate such books, with or without adaptations, for themselves. So it has been, for example, with John Bunyan's allegory, *Pilgrim's Progress* (1678), Daniel Defoe's *Robinson Crusoe* (1719), and Jonathan Swift's *Gulliver's Travels* (1726). All three were written with an adult audience in mind; all three have passages whose serious messages young children could not be expected to comprehend fully; and all three stories have won permanent niches in libraries, enjoyed by youngsters on their own terms. This is by no means limited to books written in English. Pushkin, Chekhov, and authors of other lands have also had their serious writings mined by children in search of stories that would interest them. The underlying truths they may imply about humankind will not be lost on children who are captivated by the dramatic context in which they are presented. (Jean Jacques Rousseau allowed Emile to read *Crusoe* as part of his studiously monitored education.)

Charles Perrault was a distinguished seventeenth-century author and a member of the French Academy. However, for children and their parents, wherever they may be, he will always be best remembered for the stories he published in 1697

5–2. Catechismus pro Pueris et Iuventute. *Wittenberg, Peter Seitz, 1539. Spencer Collection*
  This Catechism *is among the earliest children's books to propagate the Protestant viewpoint of the Reformation. It consists of catechetical sermons and selections from Luther's writings.*

LE MAISTRE CHAT,
O U
LE CHAT BOTTE'.
C O N T E.

 N Meusnier ne
laissa pour tout
biens à trois en-
fans qu'il avoit, que son

PETIT CHAPERON
R O U G E.
C O N T E.

 L estoit une fois
une petite fille de
Village, la plus
jolie qu'on eut sçû voir;

under the title *Histoires ou contes du temps passé, avec des moralités* with the legend
on the frontispiece, *Contes de ma mère l'oye (Mother Goose's Tales)*. For all Perrault's
academic distinctions, this is the only one of his works that is still widely read.
He may have been tempted into the project by the taste for fairy tales and Oriental
stories that was current in the French court at the end of the seventeenth century,
a vogue that was noted by Mme de Sévigné in her entertaining letters.

Perrault's *Mother Goose* was a compilation of numerous popular tales drawn
from various and sometimes remote sources in different lands. The book was
soon translated into English, the first fairy tales to be published in the language,
and included such unforgettable stories as "The Sleeping Beauty," "Red Riding
Hood," "Blue Beard," "Puss-in-Boots," and "Cinderella," among other imperishable tales that every generation of children has cherished. It is quite possible
that those who were not exposed to such tales when they were little will never fully
understand others who have been. Our daily speech frequently includes words
and terms that, whether or not we are always aware of it, are allusions to characters
and situations that appear in ancient and not-so-ancient fables.

A prophetic development took place in London in 1744 when one John Newbery
opened a book shop in St. Paul's churchyard devoted largely to juvenile literature—
the first of its kind. Newbery was a publisher as well as a bookseller, and one
of his various productions was *Goody Two Shoes,* the well-known nursery tale that
some have attributed to the poet, playwright, and novelist Oliver Goldsmith,
whose talented pen Newbery sometimes turned to in exchange for financial help.
(Goldsmith mentioned Newbery in his novel *The Vicar of Wakefield* in 1766.)
Newbery, a shrewd tradesman, helped promote the book by claiming the story
was printed from an original manuscript found in the Vatican! Goldsmith may
also have brought together the nursery rhymes of *Mother Goose's Melody,* whose
origins are lost but whose essence has remained a source of many modern
adaptations.

The first "books" used by children were, in America as in England, hornbooks. These consisted of a printed alphabet sheet with a few one-syllable words and the Lord's Prayer, mounted on a wooden frame, with a sheet of horn to protect the surface. (The prolific Puritan diarist Samuel Sewall left us a touching picture of one of his little New England neighbors, almost three years of age, toddling off to his first day at school with his teenaged cousin who carried his hornbook for him.)

The founding fathers of New England were much concerned with the proper education of youngsters. Late in the seventeenth century, the first *New England Primer*, specially printed for the very young, was published in Boston. It was compiled by Benjamin Harris, an English bookseller who lived in Boston from 1686 to 1695. But such is the damage very young people can so quickly wreak on books they handle that the only copy of the earliest-known surviving example is the Library's copy of the 1727 edition. This little document has been termed, somewhat extravagantly but impressively, "the most famous children's book ever published." This tiny book is the centerpiece of a collection of primers printed in the eighteenth and nineteenth centuries and housed in the Rare Books and

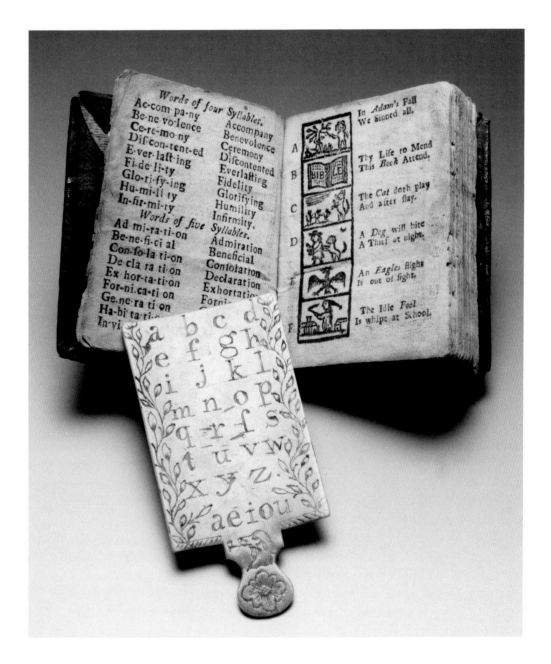

5–4. The New England Primer. Boston, Kneeland and Green, 1727, and Hornbook, English, 18th century. Rare Books and Manuscripts Division

The standard textbook for beginning readers in eighteenth-century North America was The New England Primer. *Contemporary with it in both England and America was the use of a hornbook, which was a single sheet with letters and numbers printed on it, inserted in a palette with a piece of horn to protect it.*

Manuscripts Division. These made little or no pretense at providing entertainment, of course, but rather concentrated on the need to develop a literate, informed, and God-fearing community in the spirit of Martin Luther. Puritan primers always combined religious with secular instructions. In the *New England Primer*, the alphabet starts:

> In Adams fall
> We sinned all

and ends:

> Zaccheus he
> Did climb the tree
> His Lord to see

These are verses that must have been well rehearsed by untold numbers of early American children.

The foremost of the early Yankee educators was Noah Webster. Copies of many of his schoolbooks on the shelves of the Rare Books and Manuscripts Division are from his personal library, along with his voluminous correspondence. In 1787, when he was still in his twenties, Webster published *A Grammatical Institute of the English Language*, the first part of which is best known as the "blue-backed speller." It was to have a long and important history and remains high on the list of all-time best-sellers in this country. It played a major role in standardizing American spelling and, to a degree, pronunciation as well. When it first appeared, before the American Revolution was formally concluded, it sounded, in effect, a declaration of independence from British precedents in such matters. The national honor, Webster insisted, demanded "a system of our own, in language as well as in government." Much of Webster's later life was devoted to compiling new dictionaries, which capped his fame and left his name a household word wherever the English language is spoken.

The first art designed to attract the attention and interest of children as they explore the strange planet they are born into is the illustrations in their nursery books; they will never be more impressionable than when they confront these images. That the pictures may not conform to observed reality is of small moment; to the untraveled mind, all unseen lands and things reportedly therein can be equally plausible. In the fourteenth century, John de Mandeville's very tall tales of a world beyond the horizon seemed awesome but, to receptive minds, not incredible reporting. As the woodcuts they engendered amply demonstrate, they fired the imagination as they were intended to do.

In our time, a children's book without inviting pictures to complement the text is all but unthinkable. But young people of earlier centuries had no such inducements. At best, the books that they were offered had little or nothing by way of illustration except for small, crude woodcuts supplied by anonymous craftsmen. What may have been the first of these was issued in 1658 by the Moravian educator Johann Amos Comenius. The Latin title, *Orbis Sensualium Pictus*, is hardly inviting, and the woodcuts do little to encourage further exploration of the text, quaint as they may seem to us and interesting as they undoubtedly are to bibliophiles. It remained this way for more than a century.

Around the end of the eighteenth century, there emerged a body of illustrated literature that was genuinely intended to amuse and delight as well as instruct children. Into the bleak world of catechisms, moralizing rhymes, and crudely illustrated primers came William Roscoe's *The Butterfly's Ball*, and its opening stanza announced that a new kind of children's literature was born:

Come take up your hats, and away let us haste,
To the Butterfly's Ball and the Grasshopper's Feast.

Roscoe, a member of the British Parliament, is thought to have written this little book for the entertainment of his ten children. It was published in 1807 in London with fanciful illustrations by the Irish artist William Mulready. As the first book written in English expressly to entertain rather than browbeat children, it is a major milestone in the history of this genre. The Library's Spencer Collection of Illustrated Books contains a copy of the first edition of this work together with a number of Mulready's original pencil drawings for the illustrations.

Learning, too, began to be approached in a playful fashion. In 1985, the Arents Collections acquired a unique children's item produced in England around 1810;

5–5. WILLIAM MULREADY. *Original pencil drawings for William Roscoe's* The Butterfly's Ball. *England, ca. 1807. Spencer Collection*

Roscoe's The Butterfly's Ball *is thought to be the first book written in English purely to entertain rather than instruct children. The Irish artist William Mulready provided a series of suitably fanciful images with which to illustrate it.*

5–6. The Doll's Casket.
*England, ca. 1810. Arents
Collections*
    *This tiny toy chest (3 × 5
× 3 inches) contains materials
for instructional play, including
letters, numbers, pictures of animals and household objects,
and a map.*

it is called "The Doll's Casket," but it is not at all macabre. "Casket" is used here as a synonym for "box" or "chest," and it is a kind of miniature toy chest with small maps for teaching geography and tiny books with pictures of birds, fish, and familiar objects, such as a tobacco pipe, all of which were to be used to make a child's learning experience a game and a pleasure rather than an affliction.

As the century progressed, cravings for a literature children could possess in their own right were being satisfied with a growing abundance of what are recognized as early masterpieces in the genre. With the nineteenth century came Grimm's *Household Stories*. Wilhelm Grimm, like his brother Jakob, was an eminent scholar. Together they industriously scoured the German countryside, recording the old tales that were remembered by the common folk. As these stories were translated into English and other languages, Grimm's fairy tales became virtually universal, familiar to both young and old. (The poet W. H. Auden ranked the book next to the Bible in importance.) The stories were quickly translated into English and found a worthy illustrator in the popular artist George Cruikshank. At the end of the century, another British artist, Arthur Rackham, was commissioned to illustrate the tales anew, and this he did with an inimitable style that won him lasting fame. With pen and ink, as well as watercolor, Rackham created a vivid imagery that gave life and spirit to the creatures of his fancy.

Much the same thing happened a few years later when the Danish author Hans Christian Andersen's *Wonderful Stories for Children* was published; it was translated into other languages and soon won a high place in the enduring heritage of children everywhere. One very discerning critic has observed that when we finish reading Andersen's tales, with their magical combination of fantasy and folklore, we are not entirely the same as we were when we began them. Anyone who has not read them has been pitifully deprived of one of the great joys of childhood. It has been said that whenever Andersen finished writing a new story he would tell it to a group of children. For their further delight, and his own, he would also scissor out paper likenesses of kings, queens, mountebanks, and other subjects

5–7. St. Nicholas, *from the illustration by Boyd for Clement Clark Moore's* A Visit from St. Nicholas. *New York, Spalding and Shepard, 1849. Rare Books and Manuscripts Division*

This illustration of St. Nicholas comes from one of the two known copies of the first separate printing of Moore's poem.

5–8. GEORGE
CRUIKSHANK. Hop O' My
Thumb. *London, D. Bogue,
1853, together with the auto-
graph manuscript of the tale.
Arents Collections*

*Cruikshank used his literary
and visual imagination to re-
cast this fairy tale into a tem-
perance tract.*

that suited his fancy and paste them down in agreeable designs. The Central Children's Room owns two of these marvelous cutouts.

Edward Lear's *Book of Nonsense* was published in parts in 1846, and it is housed
with the Arents Collections in that form. This unprecedented combination of
extravagantly whimsical verse and equally improbable drawings shattered for once
and for all the convention that a children's book must be charged with moral under-
tones or heavily overlaid with sentimentality to provide suitable reading during
the formative years. It could be pure wit and fun and be nonetheless wholesome
for that. Lear wrote the book and drew the illustrations to amuse the grandchildren
of his patron, the earl of Derby, but his facetious jingles, which have come to
be called limericks, have won imitators of every age and all degrees of respect-

ability. Lear's "nonsense" often lightly veils a critical observation of the world he viewed about him, as he did in his ridicule of English pronunciation of French:

> There was an old man of Boolong,
> Who frightened the birds with his song.
>> It wasn't the words
>> That frightened the birds,
> But the horrible *dooble ong tong*.

(Quoting Lear is a benign infection for which there is no known antidote, and little need of one.) The preeminent critic of the time, John Ruskin, hailed the *Book of Nonsense* as "the most beneficent and innocent of all books yet produced."

Like many other memorable illustrators of children's books, Lear was a competent artist whose paintings, especially his landscapes and nature studies, were well regarded by critics. One noted ornithologist of the day claimed that, at best, Lear's portraits of birds equaled in anatomical accuracy and grace of design any figure painted by Audubon. But it is his "nonsensical" distorted drawings that secure his fame.

The name of Sir John Tenniel, a popular nineteenth-century cartoonist for *Punch* magazine (he drew more than twenty-five hundred cartoons), will always be associated with the illustrations he provided for Lewis Carroll's *Alice's Adventures in Wonderland* (1866) and *Through the Looking Glass* (1872). More than a hundred different artists have turned their hands to illustrating these books, but none have surpassed Tenniel's creations in their popular appeal. With its art and nonsense, *Alice* echoed the spirit of Lear's books and strengthened the revolutionary trend they had established.

Lewis Carroll was the pen name of Charles Lutwidge Dodgson, by profession a mathematics tutor at Christ Church College, Oxford, and a close contemporary of Lear's. His digs overlooked the gardens of the dean of Christ Church Cathedral, Henry George Liddell, of whose three young daughters Carroll became an attentive and frequent companion. Alice Liddell was his great favorite. On one of the foursome's boating excursions on an idyllic afternoon, Carroll told them a made-up story that Alice found so delightful she pleaded with him to write it down. He

ASKALOTTE

Children, Behold Miss ASKALOTTE,
A most Attractive little Tot;
She was not Rude, nor yet Unkind,
I Never Knew her Not to Mind;
Yet she was always Asking Questions,
And Making most Ill-Timed Suggestions.

(This Goop is called ASKALOTTE because she asks such a lot of needless questions)
(55)

5–9. GELETT BURGESS. Goop Tales. *New York, F. A. Stokes Co., 1904. General Research Division*
In the modern version of the admonitory or instructive children's book, the approach, as is shown here, is to encourage good behavior in a jocular fashion.

"Oh, you're sure to do that," said the Cat, "if you only walk long enough."

Alice felt that this could not be denied, so she tried another question. "What sort of people live about here?"

"In *that* direction," the Cat said, waving its right paw round, "lives a Hatter: and in *that* direction," waving the other paw, "lives a March Hare. Visit either you like: they're both mad."

"But I don't want to go among mad people," Alice remarked.

"Oh, you can't help that," said the Cat: "we're all mad here. I'm mad. You're mad."

"How do you know I'm mad?" said Alice.

"You must be," said the Cat, "or you wouldn't have come here."

Alice didn't think that proved it at all; however, she went on: "and how do you know that you're mad?"

"To begin with," said the Cat, "a dog's not mad. You grant that?"

"I suppose so," said Alice.

"Well then," the Cat went on, "you see a dog growls when it's angry, and wags its tail when it's pleased. Now *I* growl when I'm pleased, and wag my tail when I'm angry. Therefore I'm mad."

"*I* call it purring, not growling," said Alice.

"Call it what you like," said the Cat: "Do you play croquet with the Queen to-day?"

5–10. LEWIS CARROLL. Alice's Adventures in Wonderland. *London, Macmillan and Co., 1866. Arents Collections*

John Tenniel's illustrations for Alice *are an example of "getting it right the first time." It is difficult to imagine that the story could be successfully illustrated by anyone else. Shown here is the first approved edition—Tenniel rejected the 1865 edition.*

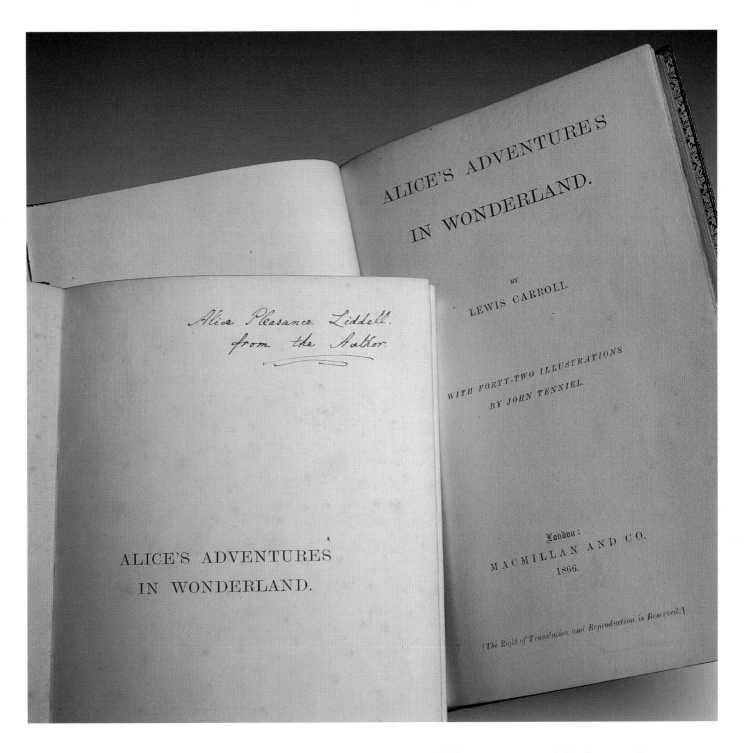

Alice Pleasance Liddell. from the Author.

ALICE'S ADVENTURES
IN WONDERLAND.

ALICE'S ADVENTURES
IN WONDERLAND.

BY
LEWIS CARROLL.

WITH FORTY-TWO ILLUSTRATIONS
BY JOHN TENNIEL.

London:
MACMILLAN AND CO.
1866.

[The Right of Translation and Reproduction is Reserved.]

obligingly did so, and the result was *Alice's Adventures in Wonderland.* When the first approved edition of *Alice* was published, the London *Times* pronounced it an "excellent piece of nonsense."

Unlike some other illustrators, Tenniel paid careful attention to how engravers translated his original drawings. An earlier edition had been withdrawn because both artist and author were dissatisfied with the quality of the printing, a judgment that may be checked in the Library's rare copy of that edition in the Berg Collection. The real Alice was presented with a copy of the first approved edition specially bound for her in blue morocco; it is also in the Berg Collection.

We are left to wonder what happened in 1863—when Alice was eleven years old—to cause a serious breach between Carroll and Alice's mother, who made the child burn all her letters from him, in effect ending their companionship. Dodgson continued with his professional duties at the university, but we may also

5–11. LEWIS CARROLL. Alice's Adventures in Wonderland. *London, Macmillan and Co., 1866. Berg Collection*

The idea of an "association copy" of a book is nowhere better represented than by the copy of Alice, *which Carroll presented to Alice Liddell, "his Alice."*

5–12. EDWARD LEAR. A Book of Nonsense. *London, McLean, 1846. Arents Collections*

An accomplished painter of landscapes and natural history subjects, Lear is thought to have originally written and illustrated these limericks for the children of a friend.

wonder how many readers have encountered and been won over by *Euclid and His Modern Rivals* (1879), considered the most valuable of his various mathematical treatises.

Shortly before Lear's book had appeared, Heinrich Hoffmann-Donner, a German physician, had opened a new psychological approach to illustrated picture books for children. Hoffmann-Donner was medical adviser for a lunatic asylum as well as an active general practitioner and, it seems, a compulsive doodler. In the Christmas season of 1844, he went shopping for a picture book for his very young son but could find nothing he considered adequate for a small child. He impulsively brought home a blank book and proceeded to fill it with his own spontaneous verses and sketches drawn from his clinical and parental observations of childhood behavior in all its phases, the bad with the good. He reports of "Cruel Frederick," one of his juvenile characters who:

> Caught the flies, poor little things
> And *one* by *one* tore off their wings!

The last episode is of Struwwelpeter (Slovenly Peter), which became the book's title when it was published in 1845.

5–13. HEINRICH HOFFMANN-DONNER. Struwwelpeter. *Frankfurt, Literarische Anstalt, 1845. Spencer Collection*
Hoffmann-Donner wrote the hair-raising stories that come under the title of "Slovenly Peter" for his children. Their violence and cruelty have resulted in their going out of favor among contemporary parents.

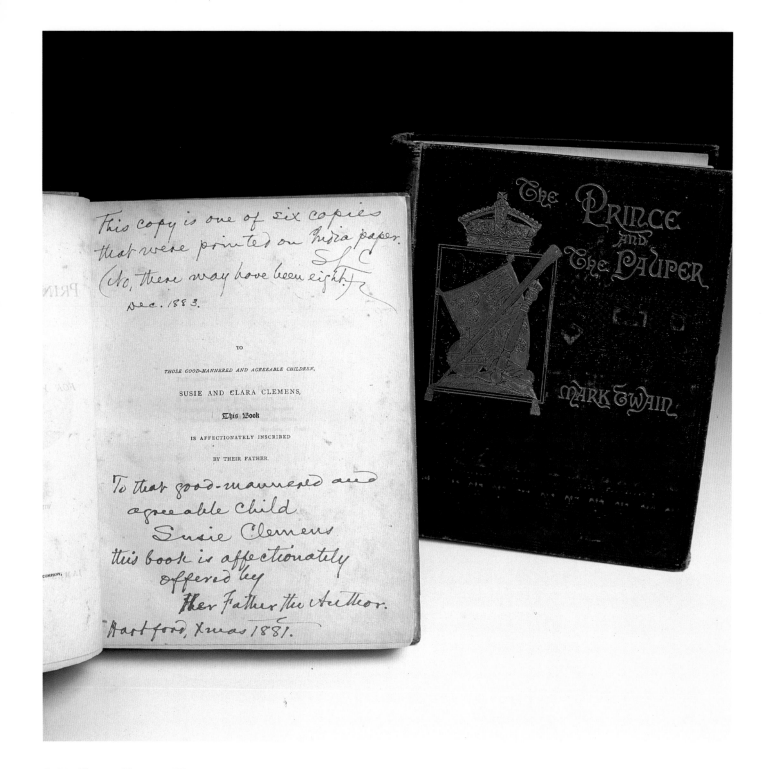

This copy is one of six copies that were printed on India paper. S.L.C. (No, there may have been eight.

Dec. 1883.

TO

THOSE GOOD-MANNERED AND AGREEABLE CHILDREN,

SUSIE AND CLARA CLEMENS,

This Book

IS AFFECTIONATELY INSCRIBED

BY THEIR FATHER.

To that good-mannered and agreeable child
Susie Clemens
this book is affectionately offered by
Her Father the Author.
Hartford, Xmas 1881.

5–14. M A R K T W A I N . The
Prince and the Pauper. *Boston,
J. R. Osgood, 1882. Berg
Collection*

*The caustic wit that charac-
terizes much of Twain's writing
masks his capacity for sentimentality and family feeling.
This copy of* The Prince and
the Pauper *was presented to one
of his daughters, Susie.*

Mark Twain (the pen name of Samuel Clemens) had a try at translating the book for the amusement of his beloved daughters, Susie, Jean, and Clara. In his version the title character is described with a proper measure of disdain:

See this frowsy "cratur" —
Pah! it's Struwwelpeter!
On his fingers rusty,
On his tow-head musty,
　　Scissors seldom come;
Lets his talons grow a year,
Hardly ever combs his hair, —
Do any loathe him? Some!
They hail him "Modern satyr" —
Disgusting Struwwelpeter.

Hoffmann-Donner's grown-up friends insisted that he publish the manuscript, which he did before the following Christmas. Hoffmann-Donner would not be rated highly as an artist, but he illustrated the first published copies from lithographs he drew himself on stone. The Library owns a rare handful of surviving copies of this first edition; the rest have been thumbed out of existence by childish readers. More than forty-seven editions followed in rapid order, however, probably totaling several million copies. In 1848, an American edition was published with the promising claim that these were "Pretty Stories and Funny Pictures for Little Children."

Few children's books of enduring popularity have been initiated less pretentiously than *Pinocchio*. The adventures of this little wooden puppet were conceived by the Italian author Carlo Lorenzini (the pen name of Carlo Collodi) to run as a series in the *Giornale per i bambini*, a Roman periodical. The first installment appeared in 1881 and was far from eye-catching; printed in small type on cheap paper in narrow columns and totally without illustrations, it might easily have been overlooked. However, it quickly caught on as successive episodes were added to the story, and in 1883, twenty-five of these were gathered together and published as a book, with, appropriately enough, stick-figure illustrations. In 1892, *Le avventure di Pinocchio* was translated into English, and edition after edition has been issued over the years since. It won special fame in 1940 when it was produced in a film version by Walt Disney, who gave us the image of the precocious puppet with which we are most familiar.

In the last quarter of the nineteenth century, four brilliant English artists — Kate Greenaway, Walter Crane, Randolph Caldecott, and Beatrix Potter — turned their talents to illustrating children's books. Each of them had a distinctive style; as a group, all helped create what are considered the first modern picture books for youngsters. From here on the pictures in a book for the young would be deemed at least as important as the accompanying text, sometimes bringing new life to old texts with the fresh spirit of those illustrations. The Library's collections include important examples of original watercolors and drawings by all of these artists. Through these original efforts we are able to get a special sense of their genius before the interpretive efforts of engravers and printers took over.

Kate Greenaway will ever be remembered for her delicately and colorfully drawn pictures of child life. Among other things, these images went far to set the styles of clothing for children of two continents — especially those images of her little maidens. With his all but irrefutable judgment, John Ruskin once wrote her, "I could contentedly and proudly keep you drawing nice girls in blue sashes

with soft eyes and blissful lips, to the end of—my poor bit of life." And he solemnly advised an Oxford audience, "In her drawings you have the radiance and innocence of re-instated infant divinity showered again among the flowers of English meadows."

One of the great treasures of children's literature in the Library is the manuscript containing the drawings and watercolors for her version of *Mother Goose*, which was published in 1883. Housed in the Arents Collection of Books in Parts because the manuscript consists of two small notebooks, this work reveals Greenaway's skill as a colorist, something that printers disguised through their use of darker tones than she originally intended. The manuscript is particularly important because it contains not only finished watercolors but also sketches and drawings in pencil, thus allowing the viewer to contemplate the workings of the creative mind.

This delight in the personal aspect of children's books in manuscript can also be seen in the Spencer Collection's original watercolors for Walter Crane's *Beatrice's Birthplace*. This is a book the artist, best known as a member of the Pre-Raphaelite movement, made for his daughter while they were on a visit to Rome in 1882–1883. It had been his habit to make the occasional book for her entertainment, and these tend to be rather more interesting than some of his commercially produced books. Abandoning his somewhat droopy medievalism, he displays in this work a talent for and a delight in fantasy that we find as captivating as his daughter must once have done.

Randolph Caldecott won an everlastingly high reputation with the pictures he rendered for such rhymes as "The House That Jack Built" (1878), "Hey Diddle Diddle" (1882), and "The Frog He Would A-Wooing Go" (1883). The imagination of little people is uninhabited by the censors that sober their vision as they grow older; cows that jump over moons and dishes that run off with spoons seem quite as plausible as the stories they may learn from the Bible or any that they may overhear from adult conversations. It was in appreciation of Caldecott's special genius that in 1936 the directors of the American Library Association inaugurated the Caldecott Medal as an annual tribute to an especially outstanding children's book.

The Library's collection of Caldecott's picture books is supplemented by six original drawings done for his *Diverting History of John Gilpin* (1878). The Arents Collection of Books in Parts has nine of the drawings for *Ride a Cock Horse to Banbury Cross* (1884). In these works directly from the artist's hand we may note his sureness of line and composition as he let his imagination give form to familiar stories.

The father of Beatrix Potter collected Caldecott's drawings, and his young daughter shared his admiration of them. She had an incipient talent of her own, albeit no intention of capitalizing on it. She was passionately fond of little animals and studied her many pets in the utmost detail. (She was, in fact, a serious amateur naturalist and once even addressed a meeting of the venerable Linnean Society of London on the rather formidable topic of the "Germination of the Spores of Agaracina Agaricina Agaracinae" with some highly individual observations.)

She wrote her young friends about her favorite pets and illustrated these letters with her drawings. One batch, addressed to a four-year-old, concerned her rabbits; it was published in 1902 as *The Tale of Peter Rabbit*. She was by this time in her mid-thirties, and the success of her trial publication dictated her activities for the next eight years, during which she produced thirteen successful books. Looking back, it seems altogether likely that the world of our imagination would not have been completely shaped without the abiding presence of Peter. So it is with all the

5–16. KATE GREENAWAY.
Mother Goose. *Original manuscript with watercolor drawings,
ca. 1880. Arents Collections*
   *In two small notebooks, Kate
Greenaway painted her delicate
watercolors, which later appeared as a popular children's
book epitomizing the idealized
sweetness of Victorian bourgeois
attitudes toward childhood.
Here, "Mary, Mary Quite Con-
trary" is illustrated.*

Opposite
5–17. WALTER CRANE.
Picture Books, *1873–1874.
Central Children's Room, Donnell Library Center*
   *Among the artists who con-
tributed to the great flowering
of illustration for children's
books in England in the second
half of the nineteenth century,
Walter Crane stands out for his
innovative designs. Here "Puss
in Boots" is illustrated.*

"No, Master," said Puss, "give me boots to my feet—
A pair of top-boots—and please leave me alive,
And you shall just see how we'll flourish and thrive."

She went to the tailor's
    To buy him a coat,
But when she came back,
    He was riding a goat.

She went to the cobbler's
    To buy him some shoes,
But when she came back,
    He was reading the news.

best juvenile books. We keep going back to them even as we age, renewing old acquaintanceships with new refreshment.

While the English picture book tradition was flourishing, American illustration for children was also beginning to display a distinctive national character. If one were to risk a broad generalization on the nature of the differences, it would be that American illustration focused on drama and action, while English illustration was a matter of fantasy and coziness.

These were the years when the American writer Howard Pyle was creating his popular stories of chivalry and adventure, such as *The Merry Adventures of Robin Hood* (1883), to the everlasting delight of generations of readers. He also created his own illustrations in a highly personal style that still excites the imagination. This style may be examined up close in the complete set of highly finished pen-and-ink drawings for *Robin Hood* that were given to the Central Children's Room by the book publishers, Charles Scribner's Sons. In these drawings, the figures are packed closely into their frames as if bursting to get out. They successfully conveyed a sense of vigor and heartiness, which in certain circumstances some might find alarming.

Not without good reason has Pyle been called "the dean of American illustrators"; he was probably the first to win recognition overseas. With unbecoming condescension, the prominent English poet, artist, and designer William Morris expressed surprise that such worthwhile work could have been produced in America. That condescension was all the more undiscerning since it was such books that were moving America into the forefront of this genre. One important factor in the rising quality of these books was the improvement in printing techniques, especially in color reproduction, which had earlier been a tedious and expensive process—all but prohibitively so for illustrating children's books. Children, and the elders who bought the books for them, had never before been exposed to such brightly colored pages as were becoming available at a reasonable price.

This page and opposite
5–18. RANDOLPH
CALDECOTT. Hey Diddle
Diddle *and* Baby Bunting.
*London, G. Routledge & Sons,
1882. Arents Collections*
   *The series of picture books
that Caldecott illustrated in the
1880s brought an almost sur-
real quality of imagination and
playfulness into the genre.*

5–19. RANDOLPH
CALDECOTT. Ride a Cock
Horse to Banbury Cross.
*Original pen-and-ink drawing,
1884. Arents Collections*
*The simplicity of Caldecott's
approach to illustration is best
shown in his uncolored preparatory drawings, where his sureness of line and adroit sense of
composition are seen to full
effect.*

Another very practical factor in the wider circulation of such books was the
progressive development of the publishing industry into something like the compet-
itive business we know today. With better organized control of production and
distribution of their stocks, as well as more ample financing, such firms could
promise writers and artists more dependable rewards for their efforts. Meanwhile,
a growing, literate middle class and a proliferation of public libraries provided
a more substantial market for books of all sorts.

Never in the past had there been so many strong inducements to produce attractive books for the young, and they rolled off the presses in a profusion that continues to mount. New titles mushroomed and old tales were reissued, with or
without adaptations, in new formats, and with fresh illustrations, increasingly
reproduced in full color. Thus, N. C. Wyeth, Pyle's most eminent pupil, produced

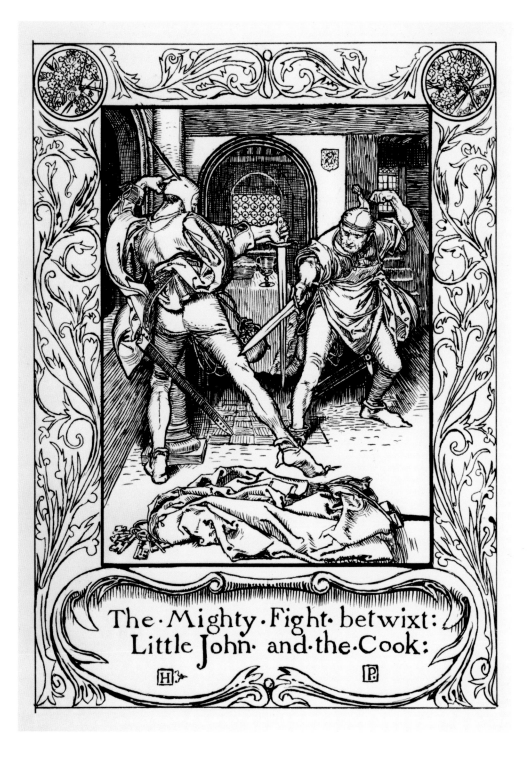

The·Mighty·Fight·betwixt:
Little·John·and·the·Cook:

unforgettable illustrations for such books as Robert Louis Stevenson's *Treasure Island* and *Kidnapped*. It is through Wyeth's renderings that thousands of readers have visualized Stevenson's bold pirates and hapless castaways. The original paintings for a number of those dramatic scenes are in the Central Children's Room. "Paintings" is the correct word, for Wyeth conceived his illustrations on a bold scale, about 3 × 2½ feet in size. They were then reduced in scale when photomechanically reproduced in books such as *Treasure Island* (1911), *Kidnapped* (1913), and *Robin Hood* (1917).

The years since Wyeth and Pyle have been a golden age for children's books. Millions of copies of old and new titles have been produced every year; a great many of them in the United States. Some fair number of them will no doubt earn a place among the classics of such literature. With that wealth to choose from,

5–20. HOWARD PYLE. *Original drawing for* The Merry Adventures of Robin Hood, *ca. 1883. Pen and ink. Central Children's Room, Donnell Library Center*

Pyle wrote as well as illustrated this story of medieval derring-do. His work marks the rise of a distinctly American tradition of children's illustration, which can stand comparison with contemporary work produced in England.

5–21. N. C. WYETH. The
Treasure Cave, *ca. 1906. Oil
on canvas. Central Children's
Room, Donnell Library Center*
   *Wyeth executed full-scale
paintings of an elaborate finish
such as this for a number of
children's books. His paintings
were reduced and then photomechanically reproduced. The
Treasure Cave appeared in the
1911 edition of Robert Louis
Stevenson's Treasure Island,
published by Charles Scribner's
Sons.*

it might seem all but hopeless to single out what may be the best and most lasting.
It is, perhaps, institutional prejudice that brings us to highlight one work from
among these many thousands of titles, but James Daugherty's retelling of the story
"Androcles and the Lion" in his *Andy and the Lion* (1938) has special meaning
for the Library since its Fifth Avenue facade figures in the book's imagery, and the
lion whom the hero heals and by whom he is befriended bears a striking re-
semblance to the pair of stone lions that guard the front steps of the building.
Recognizing the special relationship of this book to the institution, the Spencer
Collection acquired the original preparatory and finished drawings for the work.
   Every country in the world treasures its children's books. What is probably
more important, the children of almost every country treasure the good books that
have reached their own country from other lands. Through that international
exchange of ideas and images, the literature of childhood has become a widely
shared experience of each generation of youngsters wherever they may be. As
one example, *Robinson Crusoe* has been translated into Arabic, Maori, Bengali,

5–23. EL LISSITSKY. Pro dva Kvadrata [About Two Squares]. *Berlin, Verlag Skythen, 1922. Spencer Collection*
    The Russian Revolution set in motion artistic as well as political changes. In this striking Constructivist children's book, a highly sophisticated graphic concept is employed to tell a simple story of conflict between a red square and a black one.

5–24. ALEXANDER PUSHKIN. Skazky Pushkina [Pushkin's Fairy Tales], *illustrated by Ivan Bilibin. St. Petersburg, 1907. Slavonic Division*
    Pushkin's story of "the golden cockerel" with its distinctly Russian flavor was illustrated by Ivan Bilibin in a style that reflects the influence of folk art.

5–25. JAMES
DAUGHERTY. Andy and the
Lion. *New York, Viking, 1938.*
Spencer Collection
The lion in Daugherty's story
was rather freely based upon
one of the lions that guard the
front entrance to the Library.

Syrian, Hebrew, Yiddish, Armenian, and Persian, not to mention all the European
tongues, and there have been Australian, South African, and Canadian editions.
With this one tale of adventure, Daniel Defoe has traveled the wide world and
thrilled continuing generations of readers.

The Library's juvenile collections include more than 100,000 books, in scores
of different languages. Some of these titles have, in translation, won audiences
far beyond the lands where they originated, as *Robinson Crusoe* did. To realize this
we have only to recall *Aesop's Fables*, *Mother Goose*, *Pinocchio*, and, more recently,
the *Babar* stories, to name but a very few examples. It is said that in the early
eighteenth century, when Antoine Galland was translating *The Arabian Nights*
into French—a book that still enchants people of all ages and nationalities—
impatient readers rapped on his windows, pleading for the tale of the next night.
It reminds one of the children who so eagerly await the next week's very popular
storytelling hours at the Library.

CHAPTER SIX

MAPS AND VOYAGES

The Map Division of The New York
Public Library has in its collections
some 360,000 maps, 11,000 atlases
and 4,000 books about mapmaking.
But as we have seen, just as no one division of the Library has a monopoly on
rare materials in English and American literature, so, too, there are rare maps
also to be found in a number of the Library's departments, among them the Rare
Books and Manuscripts Division, the Wallach Division of Art, Prints and Photographs, and the Arents and Spencer Collections.

At the core of these collections are the nineteenth-century holdings of the Lenox
and Astor libraries. Lenox's profound interest in the history of the Americas led
him to collect maps that showed the evolution of the exploration of the New World
in a particularly graphic way. The results of the continuing series of European
voyages of the fifteenth, sixteenth, and seventeenth centuries can be vividly traced
in the successive maps that were produced and disseminated with the written
reports of the travelers on their return home. For Lenox, maps were not simply
aids for travel, they were documents that revealed to the researcher where European man stood at a particular time in relation to his world.

The Astor Library collected maps as an aspect of its mission to serve as the
reference library for the people of the City of New York. Joseph Green Cogswell,
its long-time superintendent and animating spirit, collected the best maps of
the period in order to provide standard and authoritative works for the use of his
readers.

When the physical consolidation of the Astor and Lenox libraries took place
in 1911 in the new building at Fifth Avenue and Forty-second Street, the Map
Room, as it was then called, held fewer than thirty thousand maps. Since that time,
it has grown more than tenfold, sharing, with the rest of the Library, the burden
of the explosion of knowledge and information that has been one of the characteristics of this century. The variety of its collections may prove astounding to those
of us who primarily use maps simply to find the quickest route from, say, New York
to Washington or from Petaluma to La Jolla. For maps are available here that
can tell us a great deal about the nature of the society, the planet, and the universe
we inhabit. To note but a few examples, the Map Division has astronomical and
lunar maps, maps of New York State assembly districts, and U.S. geological survey
maps.

The plethora of types of maps and the uses to which they may be put belie
the fact that strictly accurate or scientific mapmaking is a relatively young branch

of knowledge. The foundations of this knowledge were laid in the sixteenth century and were brought to fruition in the seventeenth century in Holland, during the golden age of mapmaking. Today, satellites and radio telescopes have enabled us to achieve a never-before-dreamed-of accuracy in determining the geography of our planet and the shape and extent of our solar system and galaxy.

Just where and when the first maps were made is not known, but they appear to have been a universal phenomenon, in some cases even antedating the development of writing. The earliest surviving maps evidence long-practiced conventional patterns that had become traditions. While the ancient Babylonians were probably the first to produce a map of the world, it is with the emergence of classical Greek civilization in the centuries before the Christian era that philosophers and mathematicians began their searching inquiries into the nature of the earth that ultimately led to the science of cartography.

By the fourth century B.C., Aristotle and his enlightened contemporaries had concluded, with unquestionable logic, that the earth was spherical, but none of them had a clear idea of how large it was or what lay beyond their own relatively

6–1. CLAUDIUS PTOLEMAEUS. Geographia. *Illuminated manuscript on vellum. Florence, ca. 1460. Rare Books and Manuscripts Division*

Elaborate manuscript copies of classical works continued to be produced after the invention of printing. The text was written by Nicholas Germanus.

limited horizons. Within a century after Aristotle's death, however, the Greek scholar Eratosthenes, by ingenious experimentation, highly informed speculation, and some luck, measured the probable size of the globe with astonishing accuracy; his figures were unfortunately largely forgotten or ignored for long years afterward.

Eratosthenes did not venture to speculate about the world beyond the limits known to and reported by seamen and other travelers. But not long after Eratosthenes made his calculations, Seneca boldly prophesied in his *Medea:* "An age will come after many years when the Ocean will loose the chain of things, and a huge land will lie revealed; when Tethys will disclose new worlds and Thule no more be the ultimate." (In Greek mythology Tethys was a sea goddess, both sister and wife of Oceanus; Thule was an island at the northernmost region of the habitable world.) Fifteen hundred years later, Columbus, who read the classics, may have seen and pondered that suggestive passage with some wonderment. In any case, his son, Ferdinand, noted in his family copy of the book, "This prophecy was fulfilled by my father the Admiral, in the year 1492."

The thought and research of the Greek philosophers and scientists of the classical era served to inform and inspire the work of the man whose vision of the world was to remain the dominant one in European mapmaking for over a thousand years. This was Claudius Ptolemaeus, or Ptolemy, who has been called "the indisputable father of modern geography." He was a Graeco-Egyptian who, in the second century A.D., was one of the foremost scholars pursuing studies at the incomparable library in Alexandria. Ptolemy defined geography as "a representation in figures of the whole known world together with the phenomena which are contained therein."

Ptolemy wrote two memorable books. One, on astronomy, best known by its Arabic title *Almagest* (The Greatest), was in fact an impressive compendium of his scientific theories and of the learning of that time. The other was his famous *Cosmographia,* or *Geography.* The basic assumptions and conclusions of this work went largely unchallenged for almost fifteen hundred years—this although the book perpetuated a crucial error. Ptolemy divided the known world into three parts, Europe, Africa, and Asia. Disregarding the calculations of Eratosthenes, he estimated the earth to be only about three-quarters of its actual size. He also extended the Asian coast much farther to the east than it actually is.

Whatever his miscalculations (or however fortuitous they may have been), Ptolemy's positive contributions to the science of mapmaking and the art of navigation were enormous. He adopted and developed a coordinated system of numbered lines of latitude and longitude, a grid of intersecting meridians and parallels extending from east to west and from north to south over the surface of the known earth. On this grid the degrees were divided into minutes (') and seconds (").

Ptolemy apparently did not travel far in any direction. Aside from his encyclopedic knowledge of studies of his distinguished ancient predecessors, he had to rely for documentation on reports of contemporary mariners, travelers, and leaders of Roman military expeditions to Great Britain, northern Europe, and elsewhere. In his measurements, he knew all too well how imprecise these sources could be and deplored such handicaps. It would take centuries—indeed, not until the 1760s—before enough reliable data were compiled so that a system of coordinates could be applied with precision. But, that grid did provide the vital framework into which increasing knowledge could be incorporated.

The oldest maps in the collections of The New York Public Library are contained in a manuscript of Ptolemy's *Cosmographia* in the Rare Books and Manuscripts Division. Known as the Ebnerianus Codex, it was written and illuminated in northern Italy in about 1460. The man responsible for editing the text was Nicolaus

Germanus, but the artist who drew its twenty-seven exquisitely colored maps is unknown. With rich gold and vivid blue, he traced out the shapes of the countries then known to him, shapes and images that had not changed significantly for centuries.

The editor's last name suggests that he was German, or at least of German descent, an interesting coincidence when we compare this manuscript with an edition of the *Cosmographia* printed at Ulm in 1482, a copy of which, printed on vellum, with hand-colored maps, is in the Spencer Collection. If one were to place the two volumes side by side, one would be hard pressed to tell which was the manuscript and which the printed book. For it is clear that the Ptolemy printed in Ulm was based on the same sources as the Italian manuscript of some twenty years before. Great care was taken by the printers not only to produce what is almost a facsimile of a handwritten book but also to provide its readers with maps of an accuracy comparable to those available in manuscript sources.

This early application of the then-new technology of printing to the production of maps was of crucial importance in disseminating cartographic information quickly and widely in the age of discovery and exploration that was dawning. Although manuscript maps would continue to be drawn and used in the age of printing, the printed map transmitted new information more rapidly and accurately than the hand-drawn tradition could ever have hoped to accomplish.

The technology seemed to come along at a particularly fortuitous time, for the late fifteenth century saw an increasingly robust Europe attempting to find new routes to the Indies. With the fall of Constantinople to the Turks in 1453, easy access to the termini of the Oriental trade routes in the Middle East was halted. In Portugal, under Prince Henry the Navigator, and in Spain, under King Ferdinand and Queen Isabella, thought was being given to securing new trade routes unencumbered by Moslem fleets or armies.

In 1493, there was published, first in Barcelona and later throughout Europe, a small and rather unprepossessing pamphlet. It consisted of four folio-sized pages, and its message was a simple and dramatic one: Christopher Columbus announced to his patrons at the Spanish court that he had discovered a new world. We can only understand the impact of this message by considering what our own reaction would be if on television one evening a newscaster were to announce the discovery of humanoid life forms on another planet in an adjacent galaxy.

The Library owns the only surviving example of the first printing of Columbus's letter. It is, beyond all question, one of the most precious documents of Americana in existence. It reads, in part:

> Since I know that you will be pleased at the great victory with which Our
> Lord has crowned my voyage, I write this to you, from which you will
> learn how in thirty-three days I passed from the Canary Islands to the
> Indies, with the fleet which the most illustrious King and Queen, our
> Sovereigns, gave to me. There I found very many islands, filled with innu-
> merable people, and I have taken possession of them for their Highnesses,
> done by proclamation and with the royal standard unfurled, and no op-
> position was offered to me.

The introduction that Columbus carried to the Great Khan from Ferdinand and Isabella did him little good here, for the naked islanders fled from the strange white intruders—and, in any case, had never heard of the Great Khan. But on the not-so-very-distant mainland, when once it had been reached, Columbus believed there would be "great commerce and profit." "This is a land to be desired,"

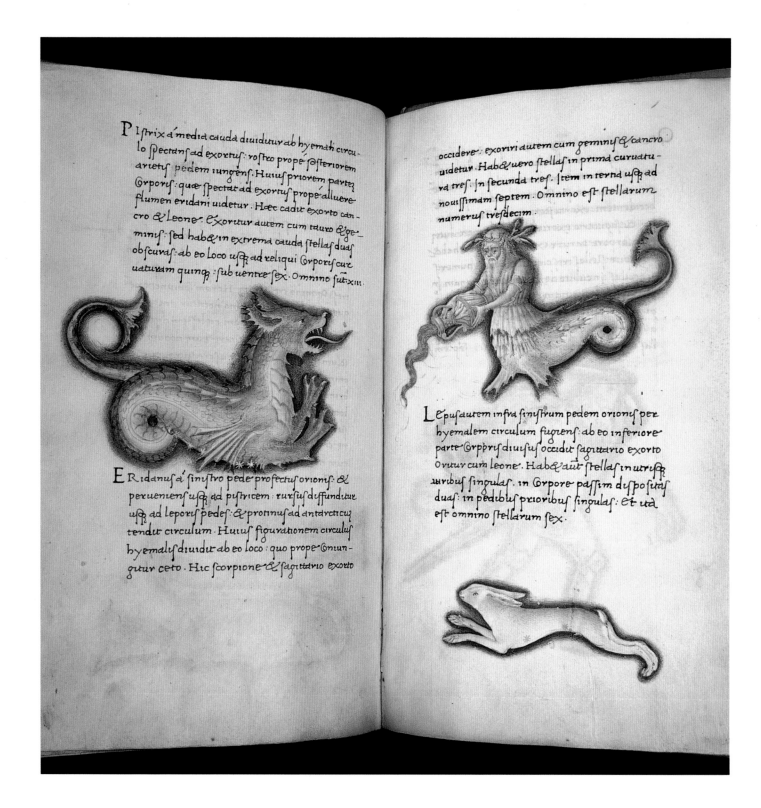

P Istrix á media cauda diuidítur ab hyemalí circu-
lo spectans ad exortus: rostro prope posteríorem
arietís pedem iungens. Huíus priorem partem
corporís: quae spectat ad exortus prope alluere
flumen erídani uidetur. Haec cadit exorto cancro & leone. Exorítur autem cum tauro & gemínís: sed habet ín extrema cauda stellas duas
obscuras: ab eo loco usq ad relíqui corporís cur
uaturam quinq: sub uentre sex. Omnino sut xiii.

E Rídanus á sínístro pede profectus orionís: &
perueníens usq ad pistrícem: rursus diffundítur
usq ad leporís pedes: & protinus ad antarcticum
tendít circulus. Huíus figuratíonem circulus
hyemalís diuidit ab eo loco: quo prope coníun-
gítur ceto. Hic scorpíone & sagíttarío exorto

occídere: exorírí autem cum gemínís & cancro
uidetur. Habet uero stellas ín príma curuatu-
ra tres. In secunda tres. Item ín terná usq ad
nouíssímam septem. Omnino est stellarum
numerus tresdecím.

L Epus autem ínfra sínístrum pedem oríonís per
hyemalem circulum fugíens: ab eo inferiore
parte corporís diuísus occídit sagíttarío exorto
Oritur cum leone. Habet aut stellas ín utrísq
auríbus singulas. In corpore passím dispositas
duas: ín pedíbus príoríbus síngulas: et ita
est omníno stellarum sex.

6–2. CAIUS JULIUS
HYGINUS. De Sideribus
Tractatus. *Illuminated manuscript on vellum. Italy, ca.
1450. Spencer Collection*
 *The characters that represent
the constellations in this manuscript are accompanied by a
text whose ultimate source is
the ancient Greek astronomer,
Eudoxios.*

he reported, "and once seen, never to be relinquished." That letter was immediately pirated. The Library has copies of six of the nine separate editions published in several different European countries within a year's time.

The import of that sensational message could not, of course, be quickly understood. Until his death in 1506, Columbus himself remained convinced that he had indeed sailed into the costal waters of the Orient; he never realized the magnitude of his real discovery. Within the year following his death, the acclaim for having found a new world had passed to another.

In one respect surely Columbus failed—the new world he discovered was not to be named after him but after an Italian adventurer, Amerigo Vespucci, who characterized himself as "more skillful than all the ship-masters of the world." There is some dispute about that claim and about some of the voyages described in his *Mundus Novus* (1504). Indeed, it is only his "third" voyage to Brazil, under the patronage of King Emanuel of Portugal, that seems to be accurately described in the form of a letter to Vespucci's former employer, Lorenzo di Piero Francesco de Medici.

But this was ignored by Martin Waldseemüller, a cartographer who, in the course of editing a new edition of Ptolemy's *Cosmographia* in 1507, added a map of the newly discovered fourth continent. He called that continent "America," in honor of Vespucci, adding the note: "I do not see why anyone should object to its being called after Americus the discoverer, a man of natural wisdom, Land of Americus or America since both Europe and Asia have derived their names from women." Subsequently, he had a change of heart, or of information, and he removed Vespucci's name from later maps. But by then it had become so widely accepted that the name was fixed forever in the minds of men and on their maps.

While editions of Ptolemy were being updated with maps that gave readers a general sense of the location and outline of the New World, another device was being developed to give people a true view of their planet. This was the globe, of which several Greek examples are known, but which appear in the early sixteenth century after Columbus's discoveries. One of these sixteenth-century efforts

6–3. CHRISTOPHER COLUMBUS. Letter to Sanchez (in Latin). Basel, Jakob Wolff, 1493. Rare Books and Manuscripts Division

The importance of the invention of printing to the spread of contemporary information is best exemplified by the printing of the letter in which Columbus announced his discovery of the New World. It appeared in nine editions in 1493. Shown here is the woodcut image of a ship bound into the printed edition.

at presenting a three-dimensional image of the world in line with Eratosthenes' theories and Columbus's voyage is one of the great treasures of the Library's Rare Books and Manuscripts Division. This is the Hunt-Lenox globe, named for Richard Morris Hunt, the architect who bought it in France in 1850 for the proverbial "song." He presented it to Lenox for his library after it was determined that this small copper sphere (about 5 inches in diameter) was apparently the earliest post-Columbian globe. It has been dated to about 1510. Although it contains no signature or date and no degrees of longitude or latitude, it does contain the earliest representation on a globe of North and South America. North America is shown as a group of scattered islands, one of which appears to be Newfoundland. South America appears as a large island, with three regional names: Mundus Novus (the New World), Terra Sanctae Crucis (the Land of the Holy Cross), and Terra de Brazil (the Land of Brazil).

Globe making also took forms other than that of laborious engraving. Employing the still relatively new technology of printing, mapmakers in the sixteenth century produced printed world maps in tapestry-like strips called "globe gores." These would show all the sides of the globe on a flat surface and were meant to be cut up and pasted onto a wooden sphere to create a three-dimensional globe. A set of such globe gores in the Library's collections, probably produced about 1530, not only shows a strait at the tip of South America, but also traces the route Magellan's expedition followed on his phenomenal adventure around the world. To add to its special interest, this set has been related to the globe pictured in Hans Holbein's famous painting, *The French Ambassadors* (now in the National Gallery, London).

6–4. The Hunt-Lenox Globe, ca. 1510; SIR THOMAS MORE. Utopia. Basel, 1518; AMERIGO VESPUCCI. Mundus Novus. Augsburg, 1504. Rare Books and Manuscript Division

More's novel was inspired by the western discoveries of Vespucci, whose travels were better reported than those of Columbus. The Hunt-Lenox Globe includes one of the first cartographic representations of the New World.

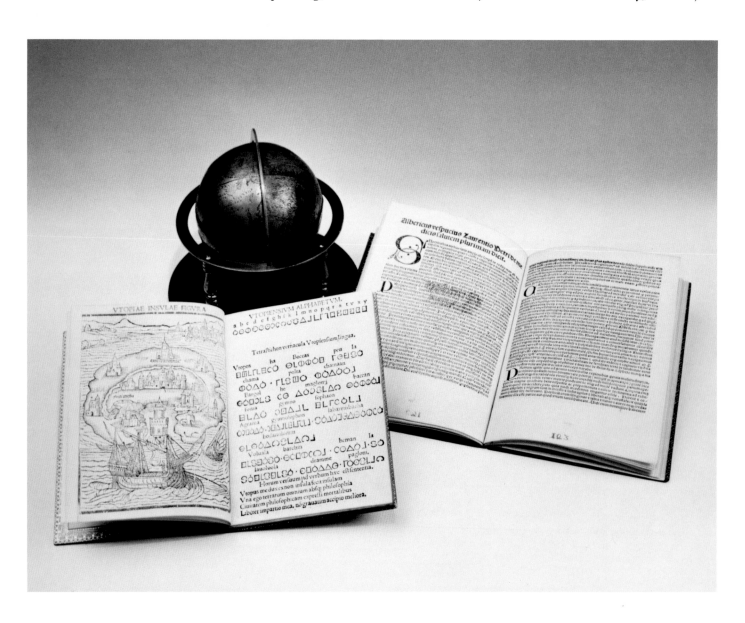

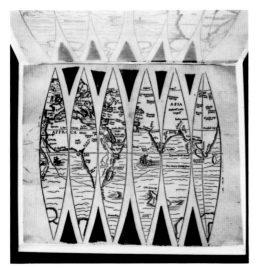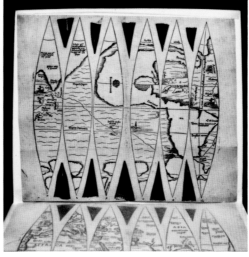

The New World began to work its way into the European literary imagination as well as into its geography books. In 1516, St. Thomas More published his *Utopia*, the Latin edition of which was overseen by the great humanist scholar Erasmus of Rotterdam. In this tale, the narrator, Raphael Hythloday, relates that he had sailed with Vespucci, journeyed overland to the far west of America, and there discovered Utopia. In this remote area he claims to have found a community refreshingly different from any known in Europe—a cooperative society; an eight-hour working day; a system of justice that needed no lawyers; and a people who enjoyed "free liberty of mind" with education for all. That book gave the world a new word and ideas that are still revolutionary. "Utopia" means "nowhere land," but for centuries to come, a utopian vision led a long file of flesh-and-blood pioneers westward to such a haven in America.

These discoveries shattered the Ptolemaic world view by adding a fourth continent for cartographers to cope with. But they did not eliminate the abiding influence of Ptolemy on mapmaking or quickly clarify the image of America for the rest of the world to ponder. One reason for the erratic progress of mapmaking lay in the technical difficulties of reproduction. Printing from woodcuts required laborious carving of the image and did not lend itself to delicate lines or corrections. Also, the wooden block was liable to warp or break. Copperplate engravings were more durable but also more expensive. Many prints continued to be pulled from plates with obsolete information simply because they were available and the cost of replacement was deemed to be too high. In addition, since it was an intaglio process, it required a separate printing from the letterpress of the text.

If the Americas were indeed a fourth part of the world, no one yet knew what might intervene between its western boundaries and the Orient. The conventional wisdom of the day, supported by the works of Ptolemy and by Marco Polo, extended the shores of China far out into the sea beyond. Japan, with its reputation for great wealth in gold, was placed in about the actual position of Mexico, as it was still shown on Waldseemüller's map.

In 1519, after a heroic march across the Isthmus of Panama, Vasco Núñez de Balboa discovered the shores of the Pacific and, with the banner of Castile aloft, waded out into the surf to claim this "Southern Sea," as he termed it, for his Spanish sovereigns. But it was not until a few years later, when Ferdinand Magellan passed through the straits that bear his name and ventured westward, that the world would begin to realize the immensity of that watery wilderness (which he

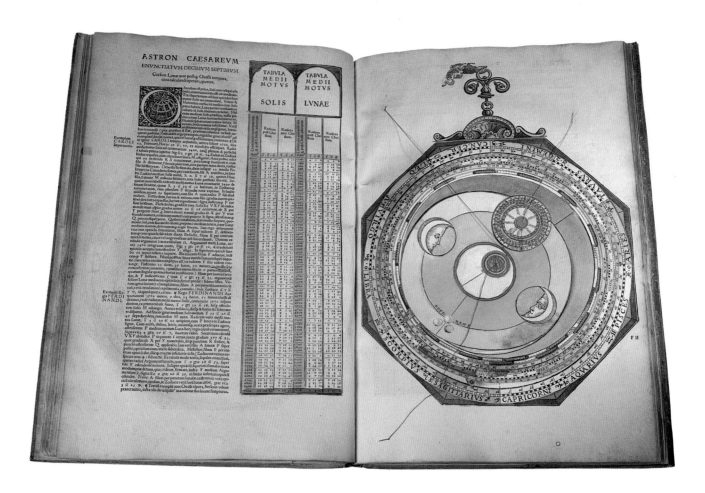

6–6. PETRUS APIANUS.
Cosmographiae Introductio.
Venice, Ioannes Antonio, 1540.
Rare Books and Manuscripts
Division

*Astronomer, mathematician,
cartographer, and printer, Apianus based his work on earlier
geographical treatises by Martin
Waldseemüller and Johannes
Schoner, a Nuremberg globe
maker. In use for more than a
century, the book appeared in
fifteen editions and was translated into five languages.*

named the Pacific Ocean). The Pacific was three times the width of the Atlantic, which Columbus had crossed from Europe to the eastern shore of America.

Magellan never did complete his planned circumnavigation of the globe. On April 27, 1521, he was killed by tribesmen on the tiny island of Mactan in the Philippines. However, the expedition was not abandoned. In September 1522, the remnants of his fleet and crew returned to Spain after nearly three years at sea. One semiseaworthy ship of the original five vessels and thirty-five of the crewmen had survived.

When the results of the Magellan expedition were made known, the true size and scope of the earth were documented for the first time with eyewitness testimony. All existing world maps would have to be radically revised to indicate that the Americas were indisputably oceans apart from Europe and the Orient.

The maps of the skies would also have to be revised to accommodate newly visible heavenly bodies that would emerge as unfamiliar areas of the globe were explored, and to compensate for celestial landmarks that could no longer be seen. For sailors could still accurately determine their place on earth—more exactly, at sea—only by consulting the stars. "Here it is," the Koran points out, "who hath appointed for you the stars that ye guide yourselves thereby in the darkness of land and sea; we have made the signs distinct for a people who have knowledge."

When navigators sailed farther south than they ever had before, they lost sight of Polaris, the North Star, that had so constantly and importantly served to guide them in northerly climes. The sea routes that would now serve the traffic between West and East most often led voyagers through southern waters.

Throughout history, the night skies have provided an awesome spectacle for earth dwellers to witness and interpret as best they might. From most ancient times, the patterns of stars in different constellations have been construed as representations of mythological and other figures, such as Hydra, Osiris, the Pleiades, the Big and Little Dippers, and countless others. That the position and movements of these nightly apparitions influence human affairs is a belief that has never been abandoned, as the horoscopes printed in our daily newspapers clearly show.

Celestial mechanics is a wondrously complicated study. To simplify matters for noblemen who were not accomplished mathematicians, in 1540 Petrus Apianus designed a spectacular book filled with plates that have movable parts (called "volvelles") for easy calculations. The Library's copy of that adjustable reference is a prime example of this work. According to some evidence, Apianus not only conceived the format of this book but, in addition, made the drawings and printed and hand-colored it. Charles V, Holy Roman Emperor, was so impressed by the accomplishment that he made Apianus a nobleman and rewarded him with a substantial amount of gold.

Countless generations of mariners have kept nautical records of their journeys, with accounts of the routes they followed, the winds they had fought or caught en route, landmarks they had spotted, their ports of call, distances from one point to another, and whatever else would be helpful to seagoers like themselves. Often enough, these were accompanied by roughed-out charts to supplement their notes. Marco Polo, for instance, wrote that he learned what he knew of the Ceylon coast from mariners' charts. Out of such evidence evolved the so-called "portolan charts," the first accurate coastal charts. They were working tools for sailors and bothered little about what lay beyond the coastal areas, prototypes of the pilot books still being issued by major coastal nations to guide and regulate seaborne traffic to and from and in and out of their major ports.

With the dawning years of the fourteenth century, portolan making had become an increasingly important craft, and the chart makers who turned them out were active wherever maritime activity flourished. (The craft was frequently a family matter with traditions that were handed down from one generation to the next.) From relatively rudimentary beginnings, their products became progressively more elaborate, fit material for the cabinets of royalty. The Library owns a superb illuminated example, by one of the later practitioners of this traditional craft, produced in an atlas by Battista Agnese at Venice in 1552. It is notable less for the new geographical information it contained (although it does trace Magellan's voyage of thirty years earlier) than for the quality of its illustrations and for the fact that it

6–7. BATTISTA AGNESE. Portolano. *Illuminated manuscript on vellum. Venice, 1552. Spencer Collection*

The development of the portolan atlas as an art form coincided with increased European interest in exploration. Battista Agnese, a native of Genoa who worked in Venice between 1536 and 1564, was the greatest portolan maker of the sixteenth century. Many of his atlases were made for presentation to royal patrons; this one, for example, was made for Charles V, the Holy Roman Emperor.

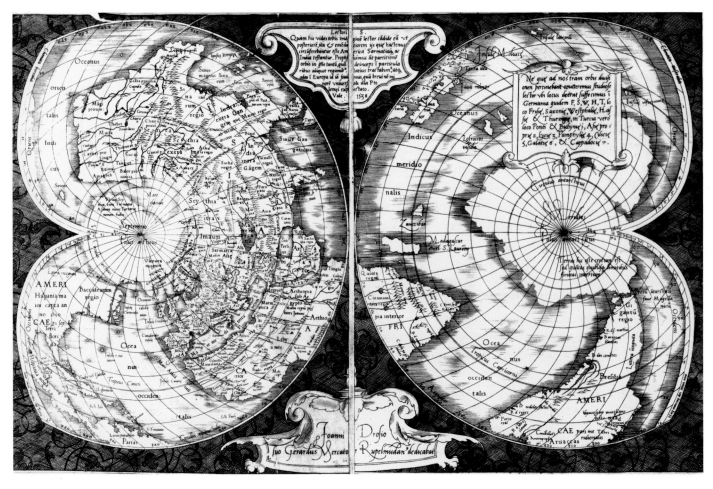

TYPVS ORBIS TERRARVM.

QVID EI POTEST VIDERI MAGNVM IN REBVS HVMANIS, CVI AETERNITAS
OMNIS, TOTIVSQVE MVNDI NOTA SIT MAGNITVDO. CICERO:

has been preserved in its original red morocco binding. Agnese began his atlas for Charles V, the Holy Roman Emperor who intended it as a gift to his son, the future King Philip II of Spain.

The first map to apply the name "America" to *both* southern and northern continents was issued in 1538 by the Flemish cartographer Gerhardus Mercator. Aside from the Library's copy, only one other example of this map is known. In designing it, Mercator used a double cordiform (or heart-shaped) projection, with the world sphere broken into halves. The equator works as the common base, thus making it possible to show both polar regions. With its elegant cartouches and border decorations, it is a handsome example of Renaissance engraving on copper. Mercator was the foremost cartographer of the sixteenth century and one of the greatest in the history of mapmaking. He was among the most determined to update maps in an effort to keep pace with the new information revealed by a growing swarm of explorers and discoverers. Wherever he could, he eliminated errors that had misguided navigators in the past.

Mapmakers have always been challenged by the problem of projecting the spherical shape of the earth onto a flat surface. If a sailor wanted to be able to lay a course on a world map—let us say, between England and America—and be able to follow a straight course, a simple, flattened globe created a problem of distortion: the lines of longitude would curve. Mercator computed a system allowing for this distortion, thus enabling global navigators a greater degree of precision in charting their courses than they had heretofore enjoyed.

In his later years, Mercator devised an ingenious scheme that bears his name; with modifications, it has been more generally used than any other for navigators' maps of the world. Mercator introduced his new kind of projection in a map of the world (*Orbis Imago*) issued in 1569, a work that demonstrated the great progress in exploration that had been made since Waldseemüller's map of 1507. While he was working on his own map, Mercator was helping a younger friend, Abraham Ortelius, with the publication of his *Theatrum Orbis Terrarum* (The Picture of the World). This appeared in the spring of 1570 and constituted the first modern atlas. It was printed at Christophe Plantin's prestigious press in Antwerp (after ten years of work) and at once became a best-seller. Within the next thirty-two years, editions were issued in at least seven different languages, bringing Ortelius fame and fortune.

Contemporary navigators had not found Mercator's system easy to understand or practical to use, sophisticated as it was, and all but ignored it. But in 1599, when the English scholar Edward Wright refined it and clearly explained its significance, the result was one of the most important advances in nautical history. Wright's observations were published with the title *Certain Errors in Navigation*. In this very important book, he provided mathematical tables that would enable navigators to rectify errors in using their instruments. Wright's own version of a world map is commonly referred to as the "Wright-Molyneux Map" because the geography as shown is based on a globe engraved in 1592 by Edward Molyneux, a prominent London globe maker.

Wright's world map was reproduced in 1600 in *Hakluyt's Voyages*. Much that we know about early voyages to America derives from the material brought together in the late sixteenth and early seventeenth centuries by Richard Hakluyt, an English scholar and speculator passionately interested in such matters, especially in English colonization. By the time he had published his voluminous papers, a number of nations of the Western world—first the Spanish and Portuguese, then the Dutch, French, and English—were all battling in both Americas to establish their authority in at least some parts of those unimaginably rich lands. The center

Opposite above
6–8. GERALDUS MERCATOR. Orbis Imago. *Louvain, 1538. Rare Books and Manuscripts Division*
    Mercator's engraving of the world in two hemispheres was the first map to identify the separate continents of North and South America. The great cartographer boasted that it was "more correct than those which have been published before."

Opposite below
6–9. ABRAHAM ORTELIUS. Theatrum Orbis Terrarum. *Antwerp, Ostelins, 1570. Rare Books and Manuscripts Division*
    This compendium of maps and topographical descriptions is recognized today as the first modern atlas. The collection proved so popular that forty-one folio editions were produced between 1570 and 1612.

6–10. RICHARD
HAKLUYT. The Principal
Navigations of the English
Nation [Hakluyt's Voyages].
*London, George Bishop et al.,
1598–1600. Rare Books and
Manuscripts Division*

   *Hakluyt's work contains the
first appearance of the Wright-
Molyneaux world map, based
on Mercator's concept of
projection.*

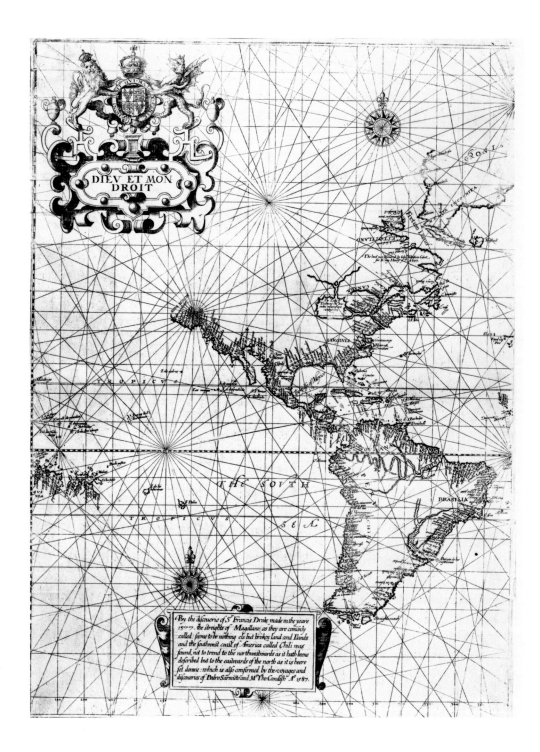

of European history, which for so long had been in the Mediterranean and the Levant, was now shifting to the Atlantic and its distant shores. The gradual realization of large worlds not before touched by Western civilization seemed to present opportunities to mankind unprecedented in history. For a time and by impressive conquests, Spain lay claim to a large share but in the end virtually bled herself to death in an effort to secure her advantages and maintain her authority.

Spain suffered some of her deepest wounds from the forays of the intrepid English Sea Dogs who spread terror over both coasts of the Americas and preyed upon the Spanish ships returning home with their spoils. Francis Drake was knighted when he arrived in England after rifling, among others, the great treasure ship *Nuestra Señora de la Concepcion*, "the chief glory of the whole South Sea," and entertaining its amazed and defeated admiral with violin music and "all possible kinds of delicacies" served on a silver plate.

Such was the way England opened a right of way to the American empire. It was almost the last of the great colonizing powers of Europe to swing into action. By then, the exploitation of America had become a matter of commercial speculation, with chartered companies organized to tap the public purse for investments. Thus the Virginia Company of London was formed in 1606, and Jamestown was founded in Virginia the following year. The promotional advertising of this very dubious venture was shameful. At a time when famine and exposure had decimated the population of the settlement, a booklet entitled *Nova Britannia* was issued in London, extolling in the most extravagant terms the benefits of joining the little colony. Here, it was claimed, were delights and resources of every description and "mountains making a sensible proffer of hidden treasure." The natives, it was added, were "generally very loving and gentle, and do entertain and relieve our people with great kindnesses. . . ." Not many years later, after those same natives had all but annihilated the Jamestown settlers, John Donne, the poet and dean of St. Paul's, was given a parcel of stock in the company for preaching a sermon boosting the colony in the name of God and King.

6–11. Virginia Company of London Chart. *Original drawing on vellum, ca. 1607. Wallach Division of Art, Prints and Photographs*
In 1606, the Virginia Company of London was formed by a group of investors to sponsor English settlements in North America. The first colony they founded was "James Cittie" (now known as Jamestown) in 1607. This chart defines in green ink the Company's territory along the Atlantic seaboard.

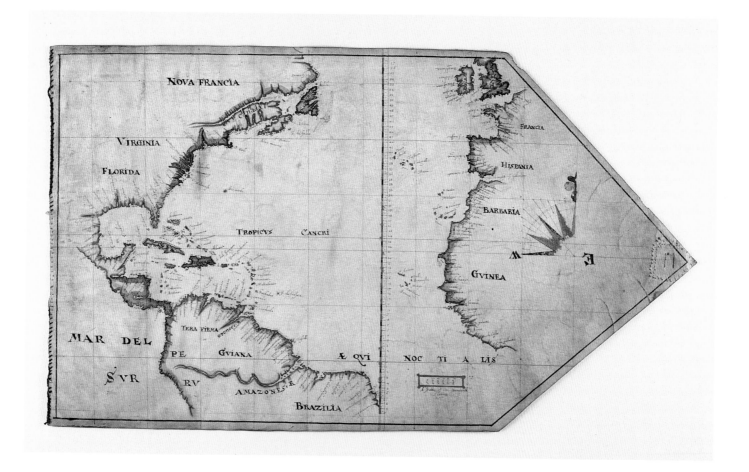

Fortunately, Captain John Smith was among the earliest settlers, and largely thanks to his practical services, the colony did not perish. Smith did even more. In 1614, he explored, mapped, named, and described New England. For these contributions he has been called a "founder" of that region. When the time came for their own journey to those parts, Smith claimed the Pilgrims declined to use his services as guide, "saying my books and maps were much better cheape to teach them than myselfe." Smith presented Prince Charles with a map of New England that he had charted, requesting him to change the "Barbarous names" of the New World locations to English ones so that "posterity may say, Prince Charles was their Godfather."

The Dutch in the seventeenth century were also active in the search for foreign colonies. Massive cartographic surveys of the entire world testify eloquently to Dutch power and wealth, which derived from the great trading groups: the Dutch East India and West India companies. Among the brilliant cartographers of this Dutch Golden Age, Willem Janszoon Blaeu stands out for his productions, in quality as well as in quantity. With his son, Joan, he produced thousands of maps documenting the age of discovery.

Their monumental *Tooneel des aerdriicx ofte nieuwe Atlas* (Theater of the World), 1648–1659, in eight volumes and their *Grooten Atlas* (Atlas Major) 1648–1664, in nine volumes, are unequaled in scope, with their combination of technical skill and artistic quality. The large copper-engraved, hand-colored maps, bound in vellum into massive folio volumes, totaled some six hundred different plates. Various editions, with Dutch, French, Latin, or German texts, were published over several decades. Hand-colored in outline, with decorative cartouches and legends, their beauty at times belies the hard-won knowledge therein revealed. Their achievement in mapmaking may be compared to that of Rembrandt in the most brilliant century in Dutch history.

The eastern coastal areas of what was to become the United States of America were quickly becoming well mapped. Only two of the early examples from the Library's exceptional collections can be mentioned here. In 1657, Nicholas Comberford drew on vellum a handsome and colorful representation of the southern part of Virginia, which, he explained, is "now the north part of Carolina." In it he introduced a number of English place-names that are still used in modified form, such as Knot Ile (Knott's Island), Machepungo River (Pungo River), and Pamylico River (Pamlico). It is of special interest as a document in that it was signed and dated by Comberford and then mounted on hinged oak boards.

Another totally different map, the first to be drawn, engraved, and printed in America, was made from woodcuts by John Foster and appeared as an illustration in the Reverend William Hubbard's narrative of King Philip's War, published in Boston in 1677. It was planned to serve as a guide to the campaigns of that very bloody fracas between the colonists and the natives, and was keyed to indicate the sites of the battles and massacres that took place until the slaughter finally ceased with the defeat of the natives.

In spite of a growing body of evidence, few Englishmen were reliably informed about the geography of the New World or the real conditions of life there for long years to come. Ecstatic reports that issued from the English press were often enough uninformed. America was a continent "of a huge and unknown greatness," and the truthful reports about it, which at best were partial, were hardly distinguished from the false. Early instructions from the royal council to one set of adventurers in America advised them to "settle along the river reaching farthest inland," or its branch that "bendeth most towards the northwest." "For that way," they

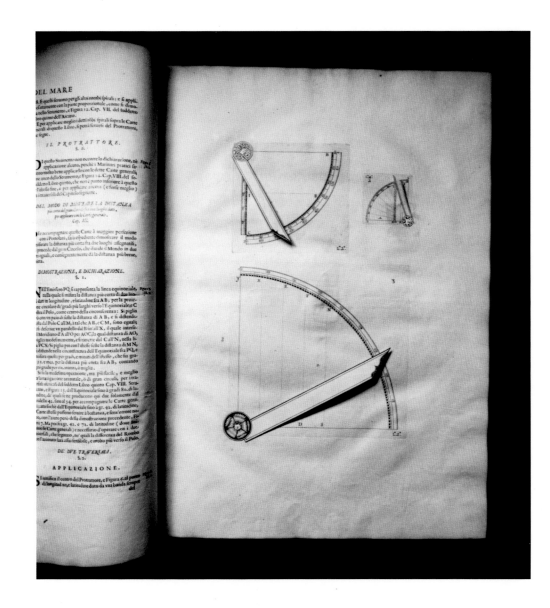

6–12. R O B E R T   D U D L E Y.
Arcano del Mare. *Florence,
1646–1647. Map Division*
    *This is the first marine atlas
in which all the charts were
drawn on the Mercator projection. The engraver worked for
twelve years to make the plates
used for printing the maps and
used some five thousand pounds
of copper in the process!*

were told, "you shall soonest find the other sea," that is, the Pacific, shown as
being "ten days' march . . . from the head of the James River" in a map published
in London in 1651. (Even a half century after the Glorious Revolution, hopeful
Englishmen were still applying to the British Colonial Office for passage to "the
Virginia Plantation" of which they had heard glowing reports.)

    What lay between the two coasts was better known to the French, who had
established their base for an American empire on a rocky eminence of Québec
in 1608, a site visited much earlier by the explorer Jacques Cartier. From that
majestic height were deployed explorers, traders, hunters, and Jesuit priests
through the midwestern wilderness to its southernmost limits at the Gulf of Mexico.

    Accounts of their adventures included some of the most popular travel books
of the seventeenth century. One of them, Louis Hennepin's *A New Discovery of
a Vast Country in America* (first published in English in 1698), ran to thirty-five
editions in four languages before it finally went out of print. In that very widely
read publication, the author concluded that, "situated between the Frozen Sea and
New Mexico," there was nothing wanting "to lay the foundations of one of the
Greatest Empires in the World." The author was not above gross hyperboles. He
was the first white man to see Niagara Falls, which he described as the "vast,
prodigious Cadence of Water which falls down after a surprising and astonishing
manner, insomuch that the Universe does not afford its Parallel." In the first

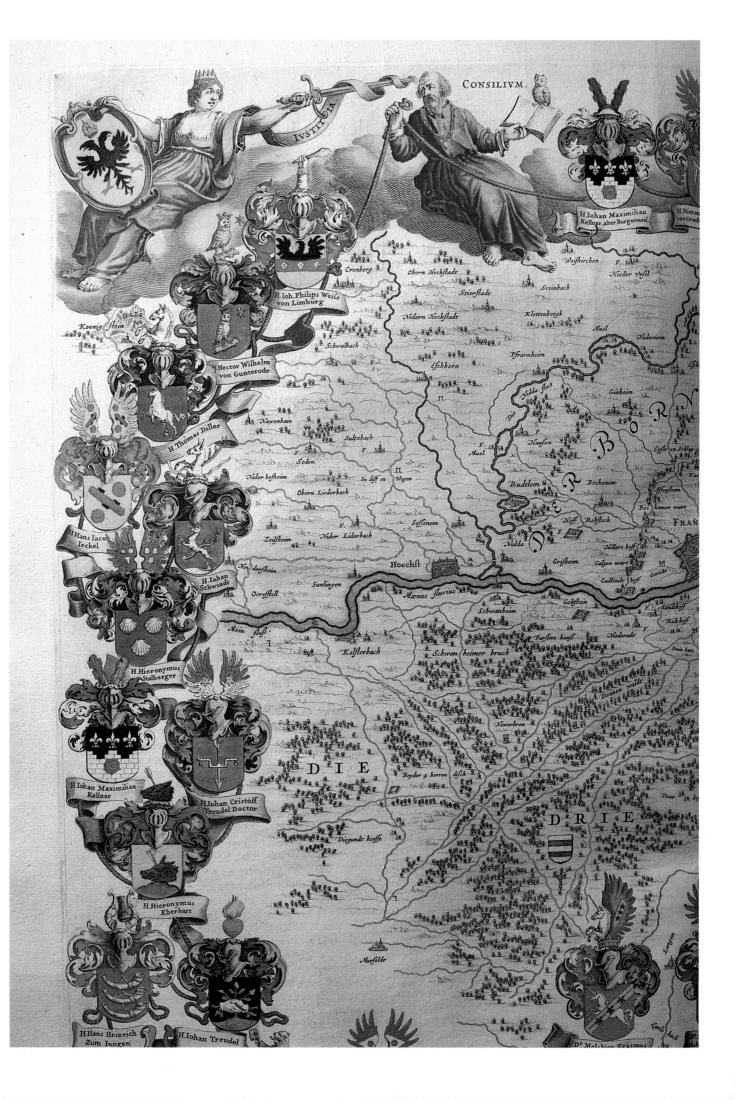

IVSTITIA

CONSILIVM.

H.Iohan Maximilian
Kellner alter Burgermeif.

H.Hieron
von Cronf

Koenigstein

Cronberg

Obern Heckstadt

Weiskirchen

Nider Vsfel

H.Ioh.Philips Weiß
von Limburg

Stierstadt

Steinbach

Nidern Heckstadt

Klettenbergk

Muel

Hedernem

Schwalbach

Pfravnheim

Ginheim

BORN

H.Hector Wilhelm
von Gunterode

Nawenhain

Eschborn

Ndda flus

Die

Hausen

Eyfen Schlag

F.

Muel

Sultzbach

H.Thomas Diller

Soden

F.

Rudtlem

Bockenem

Affenftein

Nider hofheim

In diff en

Wegen

Boc kemer wart

Obern Liederbach

Hoff

Rehftock

FRAN

H.Hans Iacob
Ieckel

Zeisheim

Nider Liderbach

Soffenem

F.

Nedda

Vollers hoff

Calgen wart

Griheim

Coriche

H.Iohan
Schwindt

Nerdersheim

Hoechst

Cullende hoff

Mænus fluuius

Golftein

F.

Sandthoff

Ocroftell

Sunlingen

Schwanheim

Ridhoff

H.Hieronymus
Stalberger

Mein fluß.

Kelfterbach

Schwan heimer bruch

Furftors hauß

Niederadt

Steen knie

Golftein

H.Iohan Maximilian
Kellner

Dennen waldt

Newerbron

H.Iohan Cristoff
Treudel Doctor

DIE

Beyder 4 herren difch

Door

H.Hieronymus
Eberhart

Diegundt hoeffe

DRIE

Murfeldt

H.Hans Heinrich
Zum Iungen

H.Iohan Treudel

D. Melchior Erasmus

Opposite and this page top
6–13. JOAN BLAEU.
Grooten Atlas. *Amsterdam,
Blaeu, 1648–1664. Map
Division*

*The elaborate borders and
cartouches that accompany the
maps in Blaeu's great* Atlas *are
thematically related to the regions described in the maps.*

*The nine volumes that make
up this work are one of the glories of the Dutch Golden Age.
In their combination of scientific accuracy and aesthetic sensitivity they are without peer in
the history of mapmaking.*

6–14. The Comberford Map.
*Original drawing on vellum,
1657. Rare Books and Manuscripts Division.*

*Nicholas Comberford drew
this chart of the North Carolina
coastline between Cape Henry
and Cape Fear in 1657. Intended for navigational purposes, the vellum map was
hinged on wooden panels for
convenient storage aboard ship.
Comberford was one of a group
of seventeenth-century chartmakers called the Drapers or
Thames School, after the district of London in which they
lived.*

6–15. ARNOLD
MONTANUS. *America.*
*London, Ogilby, 1671. Arents
Collections*
  *Ogilby, who held the title of
"His Majesty's Cosmographer,
Geographick Printer and Master
of the Revels," pirated Mon-
tanus's work and added maps
based on his own knowledge of
the English colonies.*

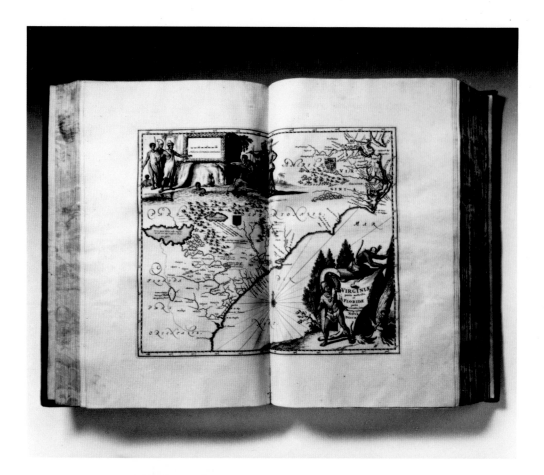

6–16. VICTOR COLLOT.
Voyage dans l'Amérique
septentrionale. *Paris, Bertrand,
1826. Rare Books and Manuscripts Division*
  *Collot, who died in 1805,
completed his description and
account of the French territories
of North America before the
Louisiana Purchase.*

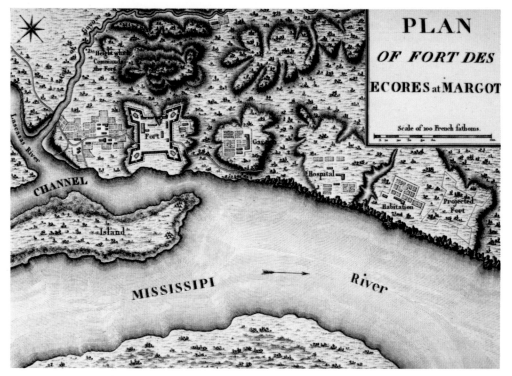

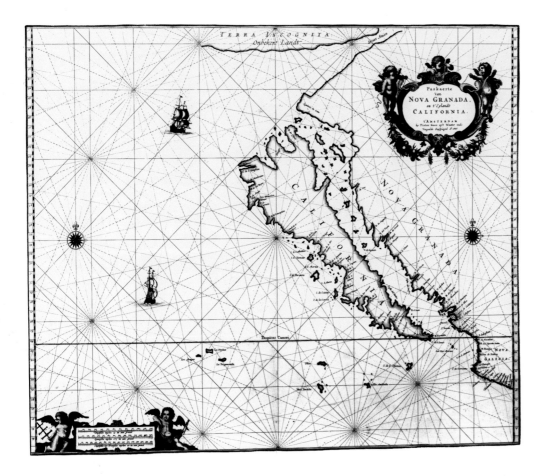

6–17. PIETER GOOS. De Zee Atlas. *Amsterdam, Goos, 1668. Map Division*

Until the eighteenth century California was thought to be an island off the Pacific coast of North America and not an integral part of the continent.

editions of his book, he reported that it was five hundred feet high, about three times the actual height. In a subsequent edition he revised the figure to six hundred.

In spite of their crucial defeat by the British on the Plains of Abraham, and then the colonists' victory over the British in their War of Independence, the French persisted in their vision of gaining firm control over the immense region beyond the Mississippi. Barely a dozen years after the conclusion of the American Revolution, the French minister to the United States commissioned General Victor Collot, a French veteran of the American Revolution, to supply "a minute detail of the political, commercial and military state of the western part of the United States and of the Ohio and Mississippi Valleys." The Directory, then governing France, apparently had every intention of containing the new nation within its bounds by taking over the Louisiana Territory (among other areas of the continent). For that purpose, Collot's handsome work provided invaluable reconnaissance. However, his maps were not published until 1826, years after Napoleon had sold to the United States his rights to those vast lands that reached as far as the Pacific Ocean.

In the eighteenth century, Spain reached up from its settled bases in Mexico and laid claim to much of the western coast to the north. For years, California had been presumed to be an island. That misconception was clarified in 1705 with the publication of a map by the Jesuit missionary Eusebio Kino, which clearly demonstrated that it was a part of the northern mainland (as Ortelius had so long before shown it to be) that could be reached by a land passage from Mexico's Sonora Valley. It was with this understanding that the leather-armored *soldados*, sandled Franciscans, and Christianized natives worked their way up into California along what was to be called the Camino Real to Los Angeles, Monterey, and San Francisco, where they built the northern outposts of Spanish sovereignty.

Before the end of the eighteenth century, American ships had rounded the Horn to reach those distant shores. The first to reach them overland from the eastern parts of the United States was the heroic band that accompanied Lewis and Clark on what was the most memorable expedition in American history, an unrivaled epic of discovery. Before they returned to their eastern base, these incomparable explorers had in nearly two and a half years covered almost eight thousand miles of wild country. (Most Americans had by then given up any hope of their return and had all but forgotten about the enterprise.)

What had been a vast territory of "rumor, guess, and fantasy," they turned into a land of observed reality. They had opened the way overland to the Pacific. Following the instructions of Thomas Jefferson, whose inspired vision had conceived such an expedition, every member of the valiant crew kept notes of his experience to document the findings of their venture. After several years of intensive homework with his assembled notes, Clark drew a monumental map depicting the character of the regions through which his route had led, a map of the area west of the Great Lakes that was not significantly improved upon for many years to come. When his manuscript was finally published in 1814, the immense breadth and nature of America was finally and clearly realized for the first time. It became the reliable source of a whole new generation of maps of the United States that progressively sharpened its accurate and complete image.

Opposite
6–18. Mapa de la Sierra Gorda. Manuscript on vellum, ca. 1763. Map Division
Jose de Escandon's map depicts the area of New Spain that bordered on the eastern coast of the Gulf of Mexico. Escandon, a general who supervised the settlement of the area, was later named count of Sierra Gorda for his achievements.

This page
6–19. MERIWETHER LEWIS. History of the Expedition Under the Commands of Captains Lewis and Clark. *New York, Inskeep and Maxwell, 1814. Rare Books and Manuscripts Division*
Lewis and Clark traveled to the sources of the Missouri River, across the Rocky Mountains, and down the Columbia River to the Pacific Ocean, setting the stage for the future westward expansion of the United States.

CHAPTER SEVEN

ORIENTALIA

A recent report named
The New York Public
Library one of the five
"mega-libraries" of the
world (along with the Library of Congress, the Harvard Library, the British Library, and the Bibliothèque Nationale). If The New York Public Library is one of the world's mega-libraries, then its Oriental holdings constitute one of its mega-divisions; indeed, it is one of the most extraordinary collections of Oriental literature in the world.

BY DR. JOHN M. LUNDQUIST,

CHIEF OF THE ORIENTAL

DIVISION, NEW YORK

PUBLIC LIBRARY

The privilege of access to the Oriental materials housed in The Research Libraries of The New York Public Library is to know the ongoing experience of discovery in its deepest and most thrilling sense. The collection illustrates and represents perhaps the greatest breadth and depth of Oriental languages and literatures — from the discovery of the Oriental cultures by the West to the present — of any library in the world. The roots of the division's collections go back into the nineteenth century, to the vision of two of the greatest librarians in American history, Joseph Cogswell and Wilberforce Eames, and to the philanthropy of Jacob Schiff.

It is particularly to Cogswell, John Jacob Astor's librarian, that we owe the division's present breadth of coverage in Oriental languages and cultures. Cogswell turned his attention to the problems of producing a book catalogue of the Astor Library's holdings soon after that library opened to the public. It was his intention to publish the catalogue by departments, and it was the department of Oriental and American linguistics that was chosen as the subject for the first catalogue, which was published in 1854 in an edition of one hundred copies. Printed at the "Astor Library Autographic Press" in two volumes, the catalogue is one of the treasures of the Oriental Division's holdings today. In it one can see the foundations of The New York Public Library's present Oriental and Jewish divisions and their holdings, the sources for the breadth and depth of these collections, as well as the vision of collecting responsibility, public service, and scholarship that is represented there. It is extraordinary to see the superb quality and breadth of Oriental materials that were made available to the public in mid-nineteenth-century New York. This in itself must rank as one of the most interesting and important intellectual achievements of American civilization, and one that has been overlooked.

The catalogue was divided into two sections, Oriental Philology and Oriental Literature. By "Oriental" was meant the now little-used sense of "Eastern," or general Asiatic, encompassing all the languages and cultures of what we today distinguish as the Middle East, South Asia, and East Asia. No library in America at that time, and certainly no public library, set forth to collect Oriental materials on so ambitious and wide reaching a scale as the Astor Library. A look at the contents of the catalogue, in addition to documenting the vision of Cogswell in things Oriental, also provides a view of some of the rare holdings of The Research Libraries today in these areas.

It was the intention of Cogswell to offer "one or more standard Grammars and Dictionaries in every leading language and a great part of the Dialects of Asia, Africa and the Oceanic Islands. . . ." And indeed, the extent of language coverage in the collection at that time is vast. Almost fifty languages and dialects of the Orient are represented in grammars, dictionaries, and readers. This is not counting Hebrew and the American Indian languages, both of which were included within this collection, but which now are collected by other divisions of the Library. Cogswell himself presumably purchased most of these books during his many book-buying trips to Europe during the 1830s and 40s, on commission from John Jacob Astor and in preparation for the collection of the not-yet-finished library. The late eighteenth and early nineteenth centuries saw the beginnings of the study of the Oriental languages and cultures by Western scholars. Most of the great

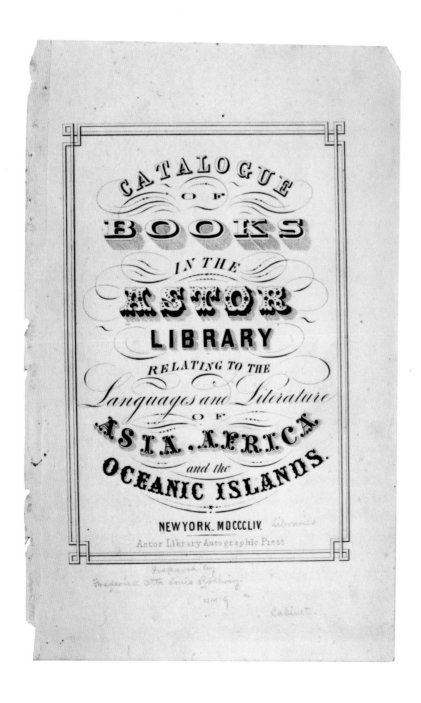

7–1. FREDERICK OTTO LOUIS ROEHRIG. Catalogue of Books in the Astor Library Relating to the Languages and Literature of Asia, Africa and the Oceanic Islands. *New York, Astor Library Autographic Press, 1854. Two volumes. Edition of 100 copies. Oriental Division*

This is the title page of the first published catalogue of the holdings of the Astor Library. The catalogue represented the holdings of the Department of Oriental and American linguistics. The contents provide an excellent view of the founding works of Oriental scholarship in the Western world.

7–2. ATHANASIUS KIRCHER. *Oedipus Aegyptiacus. Rome, Ex Typographia Vitalis Mascardi, 1652. Volume I, "Elogium 27."* Oriental Division

Athanasius Kircher was a noted Jesuit Orientalist who helped revive interest in the West in the Coptic language. Kircher's theories on the meaning of the hieroglyphics were fanciful. Here we have an imaginative obelisk, with equally imaginative hieroglyphic inscription rendered in Latin, in honor of Frederick III of Austria.

works of these decades are represented in the Astor Library catalogue, and in the collections of The Research Libraries today.

The Oriental Division and The Research Libraries in their other collections have long been known for one of the world's leading collections of Egyptology. It is easy to see the origins of this tradition of collecting from the Cogswell catalogue. All of the major early works are listed. This includes the important, as well as the eccentric, attempts to decipher the Egyptian hieroglyphics and to explain Egyptian culture that preceded the decipherment by Jean Jacques Champollion. Among these are works by Thomas Young, Horapollo—an Egyptian who lived in the fifth century B.C.—and Athanasius Kircher. Then there is the magnificent work that resulted from the invasion of Egypt by the army of France under Napoleon, beginning in 1798. This work, *Description de l'Egypte*, in twelve folio volumes of text and ten elephant-folio volumes of beautiful original engravings by French artists such as Pierre Joseph Redouté and Dutertre, was the end product of the work of the small army of scientists and artists who accompanied Napoleon into Egypt. The first edition of this work, published at Paris between 1809 and 1828, gave the impetus to the rise of scientific Egyptology as well to the whole Orientalist school of painting and design. Eight plates were devoted to the recording of the Demotic text of the Rosetta Stone, the ancient text that proved to be the key to the decipherment of Egyptian hieroglyphic writing. In the first editions of this work, such as the one held in the Oriental Division, many of the plates are hand-painted.

One of the most famous works of Egyptology, Champollion's *Lettre à M. Dacier* of 1822, in which he announced his decipherment of the Rosetta Stone to the French academy of literature and inscriptions, is today housed in the Rare Books and Manuscripts Division of the Library; it bears an Astor Library stamp of 1872, and is not listed in the Cogswell catalogue. Otherwise, the first editions of Champollion's grammar and dictionary are in the Oriental Division, as well as his studies of the Egyptian pantheon, which was the first study of the Egyptian gods published after the decipherment of the hieroglyphics. A very rare work of the early nineteenth-century treasure hunter Belzoni, *Narrative of the Operations and Recent Discoveries within the Pyramids, Temples, Tombs and Excavations in Egypt and Nubia*, published in London in 1820, is listed in the Cogswell catalogue. Accompanying this work is an atlas of elephant-folio-size plates, also published in 1820. However, an additional atlas of plates, bound with the previously mentioned work of 1820, and titled *Six New Plates Illustrative of the Researches and Operations of G. Belzoni in Egypt and Nubia*, published in 1822, had never received its own cataloguing within the Library cataloguing system. This exceptionally rare work emerged from the obscurity of the Library's stacks only recently when the National Geographic Society, assuming that the division had the work, inquired about the possibility of using one of the Belzoni plates as an illustration for a book on ancient engineering.

As the wealth of early Egyptological materials in the Cogswell catalogue has already been mentioned, it will be interesting as well to call attention to the breadth of other Oriental languages represented in the collection that stem from the important researches into these cultures by French scholars in the late eighteenth and early nineteenth centuries. Chief among these was Silvestre de Sacy, one of the greatest linguists of all time, and a pioneer in the introduction of Arabic studies to the Western world. The Astor Library, and the Oriental Division today, have housed a number of his important works on Arabic grammar and lexicography, as well as linguistic works dealing with the then premier linguistic problem of the decipherment of Egyptian hieroglyphics.

French Orientalism was given a major impetus by the desire to spread the ideology of the French Revolution into the East. An extraordinary example of this in the Oriental Division today is a copy of the Declaration of the Rights of Man, in French and Arabic on facing pages, translated by P. Ruffin, under the

7–3. Commission des Monuments d'Egypte. Description de l'Egypte . . . publié par les ordres de sa majesté l'Empereur Napoléon [Commission of Egyptian Monuments. Description of Egypt . . . published by order of His Majesty Emperor Napoleon]. *Paris, Imprimerie Imperiale, 1809. Vol. I, Pl. 49. Drawn by Dutertre, copper engraving by Dutertre and Beaugean. Oriental Division*
This plate, from the series on monuments, shows a view of the Great Temple.

THEBES . BYBAN EL MOLOUK .

Pl. 91.

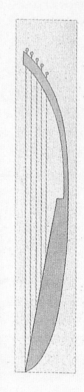

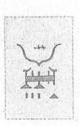

1. 2. TABLEAUX DE LA SALLE DES HARPES DANS LE 5.ᵉ TOMBEAU DES ROIS A L'EST. 3. 8 PEINTURES DES TOMBEAUX

direction of the great French Orientalist L. Langles, who was keeper of Oriental language manuscripts in the Bibliothèque Nationale. There were also a number of other works in the Astor Library by Langles, including dictionaries and grammars of the Manchu language, travel accounts, and a catalogue of an Orientalist library in Paris. A special set of type fonts for Oriental scripts had been developed by the Parisian publishing firm of Didot, and it was this publisher whose imprint appears on many of these books.

Cogswell's *Autobiography* is filled with references to his numerous book-buying trips to Europe, and the names of many libraries that he either purchased outright or in part, or unsuccessfully attempted to purchase, are mentioned. At one point, in a letter written from London to the editor of the New York *Literary World* in 1849, he proudly named the titles of several of the ten thousand books that he had by then accumulated for the Astor Library, "among them many costly works, of which few or no copies as yet are found in our libraries." Among these was *Monumenti del Egitto*, (*Monuments of Egypt*), one of the seminal works of Egyptology by the first Italian Egyptologist, Niccolo Rosellini, who led the Tuscan delegation to Egypt as a part of Champollion's expedition to Egypt of 1828–1829. This work, along with most of Rosellini's other works, is now in the Oriental Division. The color on the exquisitely hand-painted elephant-folio plates of ancient Egyptian tomb paintings that accompany the *Monumenti del Egitto* text is as fresh today as when the work was published between 1832 and 1844. Here again, we see how up-to-date, discriminating, and brilliant Cogswell was as the builder of the first great public library in America.

The Astor Library was also very strong in books on East Asia, particularly China and India. Many of the works of the first Protestant missionary to China, Robert Morrison, are presently in the collection and figure prominently in the Cogswell catalogue. These include his *View of China for Philological Purposes*, published in Macao in 1817, *Grammar of the Chinese Language*, published in Serampore (India), in 1815, a vocabulary of the Cantonese dialect published in Macao in 1828, a multipart Chinese-English dictionary published in Macao between 1815 and 1823, and a comparative study of two Chinese-English dictionaries, written with Antonio Montucci and published in London in 1817.

One of the strongest areas of the Oriental Division collection and of The Research Libraries in general has always been the languages, religions, archaeology, and art history of India. It is readily apparent from the Cogswell catalogue that strength in these areas was a high priority for Cogswell as he built the collection for the Astor Library. The collection is particularly strong in the works of the pioneers of Indo-European philology, and in Sanskrit, which played such a great role in the development of the science of Indo-European linguistics.

The division has long had an interest in collecting grammars and dictionaries of the language of the Gypsies, technically known as Romani, which is an Indic language related to Punjabi. The Astor Library held an unusually large number of grammars and dictionaries of this language, and of studies of the people themselves.

A particularly important example of a major acquisition of the Astor Library in the field of Indian linguistics is a seven-volume Sanskrit dictionary in folio size, mentioned by Cogswell in his report on library holdings, published in the *Home Journal* in 1854. This dictionary, the *Sabda kalpa druma*, by Rajah Radhakant Deb, was never printed for sale, but was "intended only for presents to the native and English pundits."

The strength of the Astor Library in books published in India in earlier centuries was highlighted in 1986 during the Festival of India celebrations in the United

7–5. Commission des Monuments d'Egypte. Description de l'Egypte . . . publié par les ordres de sa majesté l'Empereur Napoléon [Commission of Egyptian Monuments. Description of Egypt . . . published by order of His Majesty Emperor Napoleon]. *Paris, Imprimerie Imperiale, 1809. Vol. I, Pl. 11. Drawing and copper engraving by Gouguet. Oriental Division*

This plate, from the series on Egyptian wildlife, pictures a vulture.

7–6. Commission des Monuments d'Egypte. Description de l'Egypte, . . . publié par les ordres de sa majesté l'Empereur Napoléon [Commission of Egyptian Monuments. Description of Egypt . . . published by order of His Majesty Emperor Napoleon.] *Paris, Imprimerie Imperiale, 1809. Vol. I, Pl. 5. Drawing and copper engraving by Tavernier. Oriental Division*

This plate, from the series on Egyptian wildlife, pictures an aspic.

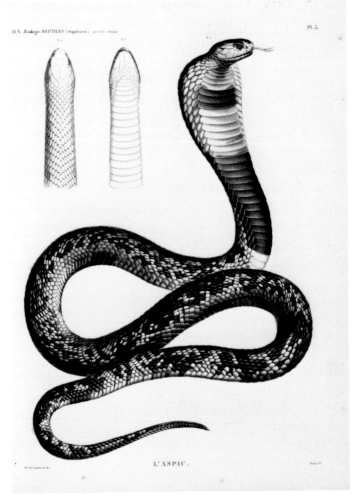

States. The New York Public Library staged an exhibition called "The Printed Book
in India, The First 300 Years," with sixty-four items taken largely from collections
of the Oriental Division and the Rare Books and Manuscripts Division. Included
were the earliest Bibles published in various Indian languages, such as Tamil,
as well as numerous grammars of Indian languages published in the great missionary center of Serampore. There was the earliest grammar of Chinese published
in India, written by Joshua Marshman, with its wonderful foldout plates on "The
Elementary Characters of the Chinese Language," and, most remarkably, the
earliest Hebrew grammar published in India, *The Rudiments of Hebrew Grammar
in Marathi*, by the Reverend John Wilson, published in Bombay in 1832. Also
for the Festival of India, the Library staged an exhibition called "The World of Jai-
nism." This exhibition, organized by Dr. Elizabeth Rosen, highlighted the important group of illuminated manuscripts in the Spencer Collection from the Jain
religion in India.

  The Astor Library laid the foundations for the Oriental Division's extraordinary
strength in the religions of India. The Library has thousands of volumes of Sanskrit
texts, commentaries, and translations, and dozens of series of texts, some of
which, such as the Bombay Sanskrit Series and the Harvard Oriental Series,
began to be collected by the Astor Library and were carried over into The New
York Public Library. A volume from the Astor Library that can serve as a representative of this literature is a translation into Greek of the *Bhagavad Gita* by De-
metrios Galanos, published in Athens in 1848. Another example, although in this

مجمع الملّة

المعروف باسم

قونوانسيون ناسيونال الى

قوم الفرانساوي

علن في مجلس يوم الثامن عشرين من شهر والندسيبر لسنة الثالثة عن تاريخ
الجمهور الواحد لا ينقسم
مترجم من اللغة الفرانساوية الي العربية ومطبوع بامر الفونوانسيون

في باريس

بدار الطباعة الجمهورسنة ٣ عن تاريخ الجمهور الفرانساوي
١٢٠٩ عن تاريخ السهجرة

ADRESSE

DE LA

CONVENTION NATIONALE

AU

PEUPLE FRANÇAIS,

DÉCRÉTÉE DANS LA SÉANCE DU 18 VENDÉMIAIRE,

AN III.e DE LA RÉPUBLIQUE FRANÇAISE, UNE ET INDIVISIBLE;

Traduite en Arabe par *P. Ruffin*, secrétaire-interprète
de la République;

IMPRIMÉE PAR ORDRE DE LA CONVENTION NATIONALE,

Par les soins de *L. Langlès*,

Sous-garde des manuscrits de la Bibliothèque nationale pour les
langues Arabe, Persane, Tatare-mantchou, &c.

A PARIS,

DE L'IMPRIMERIE DE LA RÉPUBLIQUE.

AN III.

Opposite above
7–8. G. BELZONI. Six New Plates Illustrative of the Researches and Operations of G. Belzoni in Egypt and Nubia. *London, John Murray, 1822. Pl. 2. Hand-colored lithograph. Drawn by A. Aglio. Oriental Division*

Belzoni was one of the best-known early-nineteenth-century adventurer/explorers in Egypt. He was trained in hydraulics, made many major discoveries, and supervised the removal and shipment to Europe of many major monuments. Here he shows how the colossal head of Memnon was transported from its original site; it ended up in the British Museum!

Opposite below
7–9. Adresse de la Convention Nationale au Peuple Français, Decrétée dans la Séance du 18 Vendemiaire, An IIIe de la République Française, Une et Indivisible [Address to the national convention of the French people, decreed during the meeting held on 18 Vendemiaire, the third year of the French Republic, one and indivisible]. *Traduite en Arabe par P. Ruffin. Paris, Imprimerie de la République, An III. Oriental Division*

The title page of a translation into Arabic of the Declaration of the Rights of Man.

This page
7–10. IPPOLITO ROSELLINI. I Monumenti dell' Egitto e della Nubia [The Monuments of Egypt and Nubia]. *Pisa, Presso Niccolo Capurro, e C., 1832. Pl. 118. Hand-colored lithograph. Oriental Division*

Menphtah, successor of Rameses II, of the Nineteenth Egyptian Dynasty, pictured at his tomb (No. 8) in the Valley of the Kings at Thebes. The scene shows him (on the left) before the deity Re'-Harakhti.

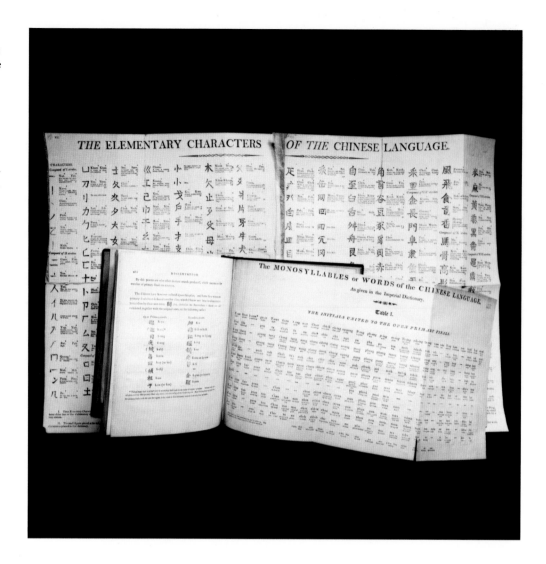

7–11. JOSHUA MARSHMAN. *Dissertation on the Characters and Sounds of the Chinese Language, Including Tables of the Elementary Characters, and of the Chinese Monosyllables.* Serampore [India], N.P., 1809. Oriental Division

The earliest grammar of Chinese published in India, a product of the Christian missionary work, which had publishing centers in Serampore, Calcutta, and Bombay.

case not a book that was in the Astor Library, is a Sanskrit edition of the *Bhagavad Gita,* with Latin commentary, by A. G. Schlegel, published in Bonn in 1823.

The Oriental Division's extraordinary strength in Tibetan, Bhutanese, and Nepalese languages and religious literature is also presaged in the Astor Library. Particularly important are dictionaries and grammars by the great Orientalist Alexander Csoma de Koros, as well as the German Tibetan expert J. J. Schmidt, whose works were published in St. Petersburg and Leipzig. Somewhat after the printing of the catalogue, the Astor Library acquired the *Alphabeticum Tibeticum* of the Augustine monk Antonius Georgi, published in Rome in 1762. This interesting work gives a synopsis of Tibetan history and culture, a grammar of the language, a comparative grammar in which he compared Tibetan with Hebrew, and a translation of Church creeds into Tibetan.

The Oriental Division has few peers in its collection of books in Arabic and Persian language and literature, Islamic law, and Islamic subjects in general. These fields, too, of course, are well represented in the Cogswell catalogue of Oriental Languages and Literatures. The collection was particularly strong in seventeenth-, eighteenth-, and early nineteenth-century grammars and dictionaries of Arabic, Persian, and their dialects. The Astor Library collection, as well as that of the Oriental and the Rare Books and Manuscripts Division and the Spencer Collection, are particularly rich in manuscript and printed Korans, translations of the Koran (for example, into Chinese, Russian, and Latin), Arabic poetry, numerous editions of the *Thousand and One Nights* in many translations, the ancient

Persian Avesta, Persian poetry, particularly the *Shahnameh,* and Sufi literature. An interesting and very representative example of an early Arabic book in the Astor Library is the *Specimens of Arabic Poetry* by J. D. Carlyle, published in Cambridge in 1796. It gives the Arabic and an English translation. The frontispiece has several bars of musical notation, meant to illustrate the musical nature of Arabic poetry, but the bars were printed upside down!

A remarkable work of Iranian cultural history and contemporary travel is the *Tour to Sheeraz by the Route of Kazroon and Feerozabad . . . ,* by Edmund Waring, published in London in 1807. This work can stand as a symbol for the richness of collections of early travelers' accounts of visits to the Orient contained in the Oriental Division in particular, and generally in The Research Libraries. Numerous editions can be found of Middle Eastern travelers Musil, Philby, Doughty, Palgrave, M. Niebuhr, and many others. The division holds superb editions of the *History of Japan* by Engelbert Kaempfer, published in London in 1727, supplied with important maps and engravings showing Japanese customs, architecture, and contemporary life. This work, in its first edition of 1727, was the first attempt by a European to describe Japan and Japanese culture in depth. Among the many early travelers' accounts of visits to China, mention should be made of *An Authentic Account of an Embassy from the King of Great Britain to the Emperor of China,* by Sir George Staunton, in the first edition of 1797, which describes the first British embassy to China. Other important travel accounts held in the library are the *Travels in Georgia, Persia, Armenia, Ancient Babylonia, 1817–20,* by Robert Ker Porter, in the first edition of 1821, and J. Morier's *A Journey through Persia, Armenia and Asia Minor to Constantinople,* in its first (London) edition of 1812.

7–12. S. C. BELNOS. The Sundhya or the Daily Prayers of the Brahmins, Illustrated in a Series of Original Drawings. *London, N.P., 1851. Plate 10. Hand-colored lithograph. Oriental Division*

After purification in the sacred stream, the Brahmin assumes a fixed posture, and recites devotional verses on Siva, Vishnu, etc., with varied hand and finger gestures (mudras). This particular mudra is the Kurma mudra (tortoise, one of the avatars of Vishnu).

7–13. Scenes from the lives of
Krishna and others. *18 miniature paintings mounted into a
folding album. Jaipur, Ra-
jasthan, 18th century. Spencer
Collection*

*This painting illustrates
Saraswathi, goddess of learning
and of music. She is the consort
of Brahma, presides over knowledge, and carries the musical
instrument veena. The peacock
is her vahanam, or vehicle.*

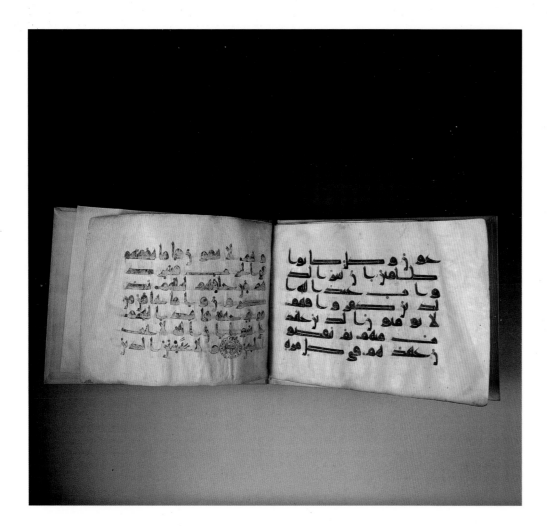

One of the treasures of the Oriental Division, which was added to the Astor Library after the Cogswell catalogue was printed, is the three-volume *Reisebeschreibung nach Arabien und andern umliegenden Ländern* (*Travels in Arabia and in Surrounding Lands*) by Carsten Niebuhr, published between 1774 and 1837. There are dozens of engravings in this work, consisting of maps and scenic views of the cities he visited, illustrations of modes of dress, industrial and technical machinery, and charts of numerous scripts, including those of the then still undeciphered Egyptian hieroglyphic and several of the cuneiform scripts. Niebuhr's work was the first really comprehensive view of the East by a European, and it paved the way for the spectacular discoveries that would occur during the nineteenth century. In particular, it was his survey of the ancient Persian site of Persepolis, and his publication of clear copies of the Old Persian inscriptions from the site, that made deciphering this language possible.

Both the Astor and Research Libraries boast many of the works of Richard F. Burton, with numerous editions of his *Personal Narrative of Pilgrimage to El-Medinah and Meccah,* the most notable of these being the richly illustrated three-volume edition of 1855–1856. The Library also holds the collected works of the great Central Asian and Tibetan explorers, including Sven Hedin and Aurel Stein. Stein's various publications are in the Oriental Division and consist of several multivolume sets of sumptuous folio-size tomes published by Oxford University Press. The Library also has two copies of the rare subscriber's edition of T. E. Lawrence's *Seven Pillars of Wisdom.* One of these belonged to Mrs. George Bernard Shaw.

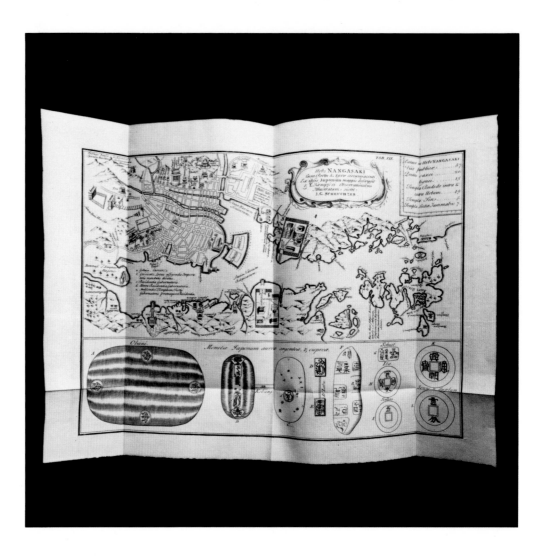

Mention was made above of the many editions of the *Thousand and One Nights* that are in the Oriental Division today. The editions in English by Scott, Lane, Hole, and others that were in the Astor Library have been increased many times over. The division tries to acquire all editions that are published and can offer editions translated into many languages, for example, into Gaelic. Additionally, the division holds many limited-print-run subscriber editions of this work, for example, in the translations of Burton and Payne.

Another example of Middle Eastern literature that is collected exhaustively in the Oriental Division is the poetry of Omar Khayyam. Although no editions of this famous poet's work were listed in the Cogswell catalogue, several editions were later added to the Astor Library. Over forty languages are currently represented in translated editions.

The Oriental Division's strong commitment to Armenian builds upon the foundation laid in the Astor Library, which also collected Georgian (a Caucasian language spoken in the Soviet Union), one of the Oriental Division's responsibilities today. The Cogswell catalogue lists a number of grammars, dictionaries, and other linguistic works dealing with these two languages published in the seventeenth through nineteenth centuries. Among these are some very rare works, including an Armenian grammar published in Rome in 1675, an Armenian grammar by Johann Schroeder published in Amsterdam in 1711, and a number of editions of the English and Armenian grammatical and lexicographical works of Father Paschal Aukerian, of the Armenian Academy of St. Lazarus in Venice (one of the most important centers of Armenian publication at the time outside of Armenia itself).

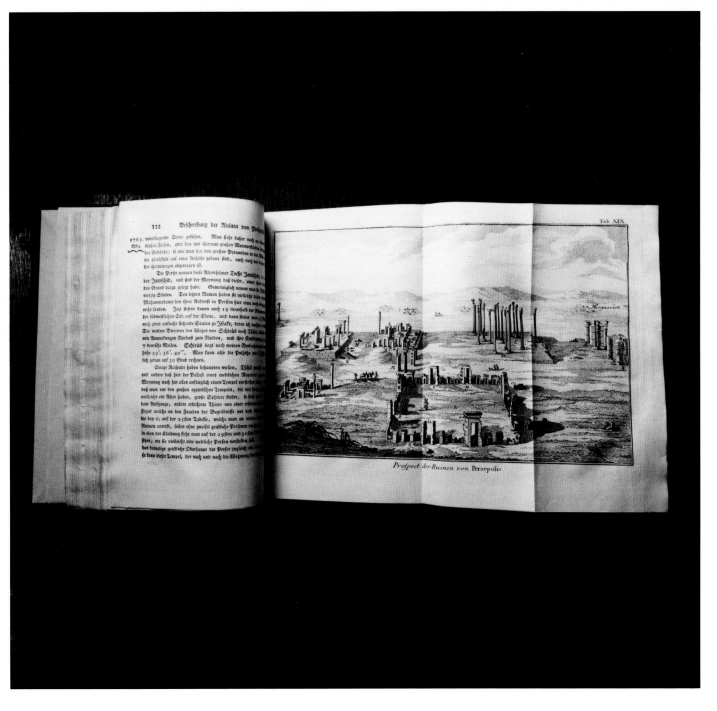

7–16. C. NIEBUHR.
Reisebeschreibung nach
Arabien und andern
umliegenden Ländern
[Description of a trip to Arabia
and other nearby lands].
*Kopenhagen, Nicolaus Möller,
1778. Vol. II, Pl. 19. Oriental
Division*

This engraving shows the cit-
adel area of Persepolis, the capital of the Achaemenid Persians
after 522 B.C. The view is to
the west and is based on
Niebuhr's visit in March of
1765. The large building in the
foreground is the Hundred-Col-
umn Hall.

These works were published by the Academy at Venice in the early nineteenth century. An additional important publication of the Academy of St. Lazarus at Venice is the complete works of the tenth-century Armenian mystic Gregorius Narekatzi, published in 1840. Another quite extraordinary Armenian work from the Astor Library is the *Essai sur la langue Arménienne*, by Bellaud. This work was published in Paris in 1812 by the Imprimerie Imperiale; the corresponding year of the Armenian calendar, 1261 is also noted. The division also holds many Bibles and lectionaries in Armenian, in addition to literary and historical works, and has an ongoing commitment to excellence in this very important area of world culture.

There is one additional area of the Oriental Division and The Research Libraries strength that is represented in the Cogswell catalogue, and that remains a noteworthy area of collection responsibility in the division today: the cuneiform cultures of ancient Western Asia, the Sumerians, Babylonians, Hittites, and Persians. These languages were deciphered one by one from the early nineteenth century to the early twentieth century (in the case of Hittite). The brilliant, but generally unrecognized, decipherment of the Old Persian script by G. F. Grotefend in 1802, based on inscriptions from Persepolis published earlier by Carsten Niebuhr, is represented in the Astor Library collection by Grotefend's work of 1837 *Neue Beiträge zur Erläuterung der persepolitanischen Keilschrift* (*New Contributions to the Clarification of the Persepolis Cuneiform*). The decisive decipherment of Assyro-Babylonian cuneiform by Rawlinson, Hincks, Oppert, and others is well represented in publications that were collected by the Astor Library. In addition, the magisterial volumes of mid-nineteenth-century Mesopotamian exploration, each set with many exceptional engravings, are well represented. There are the *Monuments of Nineveh* by Layard, the *Voyage en Perse* by Flandin, the *Monuments de Ninive* by Botta, with the magnificent drawings of Eugène Flandin, and the Victor Place *Ninive et L'Assyrie*, of 1870, with its wonderful suggested reconstruction of the ziggurat at Sargon II's ancient capital of Dur-Sharruken (modern Khorsabad) in seven multicolored stages. A publication series of great importance that was in the Astor Library is the British Museum *Cuneiform Inscriptions of Western Asia*, edited by Rawlinson, the publication of which began in 1861. Also in the British Museum series of publications is the famous work by George Smith, the *Chaldaean Account of the Deluge* of 1874, which contained the photographs of the original Nineveh tablets of the Gilgamesh epic, along with Smith's translation. The publication of this text, with its remarkable parallels to the biblical account of the Flood, opened up the era of the study of biblical and Mesopotamian parallels, a study that continues to this day.

Before leaving the Cogswell catalogue and the Astor Library, something should be said about the collection of periodicals, since it is the strength of a library's periodical literature that determines that library's overall standing as a research library. The Astor Library catalogue lists a large number of the most important Oriental periodicals of the time, many of which are exceptionally rare today. It is these titles, when combined with the hundreds that have been added since then, that give the Oriental Division its depth as a research collection, enabling readers to search the literature of a given subject back to the beginnings of that subject as a scholarly discipline. And the articles contained in these early journals do not have merely antiquarian value. Many of the articles contained in such journals as the *Royal Asiatic Society* in its various branches, the *Journal asiatique*, the *Zeitschrift der deutschen morgenländischen Gesellschaft*, the *Journal of the American Oriental Society*, and the *Chinese Repository* contain valuable contemporary observations, editions of language texts, and photographs or drawings of now de-

CHAMBER C. PLAN 4.

BRICK PLAN 3.

FROM NORTH WEST PALACE (PLAN 3).

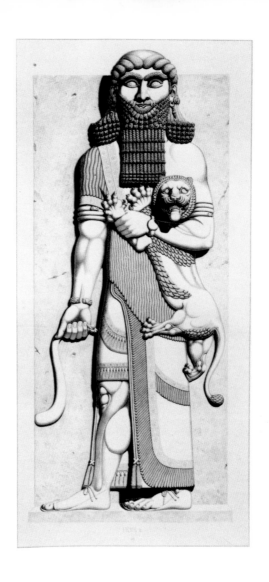

7–18. P. E. BOTTA.
Monument de Ninive. *Mesuré et
dessiné par E. Flandin. Paris,
Imprimerie Nationale, 1849.
Vol. I, Pl. 47. Copper engrav-
ing. Oriental Division*

*This figure was a protective
genius or hero, a "master of the
animals," part of a sculptural
relief façade in the palace of
Sargon II (721–705 B.C.) at
Khorsabad, ancient Dur-
Sharukkin, in Iraq.*

stroyed archaeological ruins or dramatically changed cities or social customs
that are of inestimable value to the contemporary scholar.

Also of immense importance are the early translation series, such as the *Oriental Translation Fund*, published in London after 1828. This series contains original
texts of Oriental epics, poems, histories, and grammatical works, with English
and Latin translations. Other major early series of texts and translations are the
Collection orientale, published in Paris after 1838, with editions of major Arabic,
Persian, and Indian texts with French translations in magnificent folio volumes;
the *Sacred Books of the East*, edited by F. Max Muller after 1879; the some three
hundred volumes of the *Bibliotheca Indica*, published by the Royal Asiatic Society
of Bengal from 1878; and the *Pali Text Society*, which has published translations
of over three hundred volumes of Buddhist texts from Pali originals since 1881.

These publications—the periodicals and the series of texts and translations—
continue to add to the strength of the division. The Oriental Division now subscribes to almost one thousand periodicals in close to twenty languages. In addition
to all of the main journals of the learned societies, and the major journals of linguistics, archaeology, history, the social sciences, and the humanities, the division
subscribes to a large number of very specialized and rather obscure but extremely
important journals, which one would only rarely find in another Oriental collection.
Additionally, many ongoing series of texts and translations in numerous Oriental
languages are received in the division. The Oriental collection in the Astor Library
grouped the diverse languages and cultures of the Orient together in one

collection, rather than segregating them, as is the custom in most libraries today, and thus the reader can come to the Oriental Division and examine various subjects in the periodical literature, as well as many languages in the original and in translation, over the entire range of Oriental cultures.

The extent of books on Oriental subjects in the Lenox Library cannot be known as readily as it can be for the Astor because these materials were not published in a separate catalogue. There are many books in the collection today that bear the Lenox Library stamp, but they have never been counted or isolated as such. The section on the Oriental Division in the 1975 *Guide to the Research Collections of The New York Public Library* gave the figure of 3,321 volumes on Oriental subjects in the Astor Library as of 1867. As of 1911, when the central building was opened, the Oriental collections numbered fifteen thousand volumes. (The division now holds approximately two hundred fifty thousand volumes.) Thus it is not known how many volumes on Orientalia the Lenox Library contributed. But whatever their number, the significance and quality of that contribution is quite extraordinary. There are a number of early Korans that bear the Lenox Library stamp, including a translation into French of 1847, and a very early English translation by George Sale, published in London in 1734. The Oriental Division holds a number of Sale translations of the Koran, mostly published in the late eighteenth and early nineteenth centuries.

7–19. P. E. BOTTA. Monument de Ninive. *Mesuré et dessiné par E. Flandin. Paris, Imprimerie Nationale, 1849. Vol. II, Pl. 151. Oriental Division*
    Flandin's drawing shows the bronze lion discovered at the entrance to the city.

7–20. WILLIAM
BROCKEDEN. Egypt and
Nubia. *From drawings made on
the spot by David Roberts, with
historical descriptions by
William Brockeden. Litho-
graphed by Louis Haghe.
London, F. G. Moon, 1846–
1849. Vol. I, Pl. 22. Oriental
Division*

*The exquisite hand-colored
lithographs made from Roberts's
drawings are among the treasures of nineteenth-century records of Egypt. This plate is
entitled "Thebes: The Colossal
Statues of Amunoph III."*

7–21. VICTOR PLACE.
Ninive et L'Assyrie [with essays
on the restoration by Felix
Thomas]. *Paris, Imprimerie Im-
periale, 1867. Vol. III, Pl. 37.
Colored engraving. Oriental
Division*

*Victor Place replaced Botta
as excavator of Khorsabad in
1852. Here we see a proposed
restoration of the ziggurat (a
staged temple tower) at Khorsabad, ancient Dur-Sharukkin,
in Iraq.*

ESSAI DE RESTAURATION

OBSERVATOIRE

ÉLÉVATION

Echelle de 0.005 P.M.

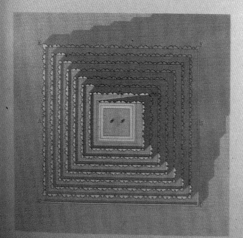

PLAN   COUPE SUR A.B.

Echelle de 0.001 P.M.

A.Bordes, sc.

Imp.ted Lemercier, Paris.

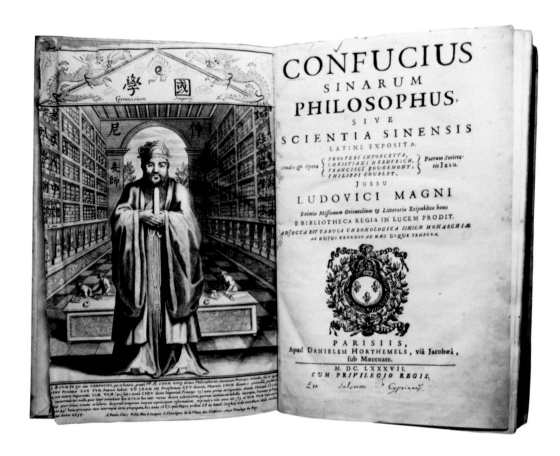

7–22. Confucius Sinarum philosophus, sive Scientia Sinensis Latine exposita [Confucius, Philosopher of the Chinese, or Chinese Wisdom Set Forth in Latin]. *Studio et opera P. Intorcetta, C. Herdtrich, F. Rovgemont, P. Couplet, jussu Ludovici Mangi. Paris, D. Horthemels, 1687. Oriental Division*

This is a Latin translation of the Ssu-shu, *the Four Books, the most basic of the Confucian classics. It is one of the earliest translations of Confucius into a Western language and is an example of the well-known Jesuit missionary and cultural activity in China in the seventeenth century.*

Another very important series of books presently in the Oriental Division and in the Wallach Division of Art, Prints and Photographs that were originally in the Lenox Library is the series of magnificent color lithographs of scenes in Egypt and Nubia, "from drawings made on the spot," by David Roberts, published in London in the 1840s. There are two sets of his *Egypt and Nubia* in the Oriental Division alone that came from the Lenox Library. The bringing together into one library collection of three libraries, the Astor, Lenox, and Tilden, created some very interesting, and most welcome, duplication in the Oriental Division. The division presently has two sets of the 1849 edition of Layard's *Monuments of Nineveh*, the set dedicated to Sir Stratford Canning and signed in facsimile on the dedication page by Layard. One set of this beautifully illustrated and historically important work came from Tilden's library, the other from the Lenox. Then there is an edition of the second series of the same title, from the Astor Library. An important addition to the division's Armenian collection from the Lenox Library is a Bible in Armenian printed at the Mission Press in Serampore, India, in 1817. Finally, the impact of the Lenox Library on the Chinese collection of the Oriental Division can be seen in a Latin translation of the works of Confucius, published in Paris in 1687. This work bears the stamp of what appears to be the Ducal Library of Gothenburg, Sweden, indicating that it was a duplicate, presumably deaccessioned and sold in the nineteenth century. The translation was the work of four Jesuit missionaries to China, and is thus an example of the important Jesuit missionary work in China during the seventeenth century.

The impact of Wilberforce Eames (chief librarian of the Lenox Library when it was incorporated into The New York Public Library) on the Library's Oriental collections is seen primarily in two forms: first, through the collection of cuneiform tablets that he collected and that came into the Library after his death; and, second, through the purchase by the Library of Chinese books from his collections. There are about four hundred cuneiform tablets and clay cones inscribed in Sumerian of the Neo-Sumerian period (about 2100–2000 B.C.) and Babylonian. They are mainly records of business transactions involving Sumerian temples around the area of ancient Ur. They were catalogued by the late Professor A. Leo Oppenheim in 1948.

It is the Chinese books collected by Eames, which he sold to the Library in 1909, that form the basis for the Chinese collection in the Oriental Division today. Many of the approximately two hundred titles of Chinese rare books housed in The Research Libraries were purchased by Eames from the library of the great nineteenth-century British Sinologist James Legge. His library was listed for sale in 1899 by the London bookseller Luzac and Co. The Library still has Eames's signed personal copy of the catalogue of this sale, with his copious notations in the margins, noting books that were already sold and books he had ordered. There are some truly remarkable books and manuscripts in this collection, including Legge's personal manuscript concordance to his famous bilingual editions of the Chinese classics, annotated in his own hand in both Chinese and English. These form an invaluable research aid to the understanding of the production of one of the most famous and enduring English translations of the classic Chinese literature. Another important volume in this set of materials is a manuscript annotation of the Chinese *Book of Poems*, prepared by Legge's close personal friend, the Chinese scholar Wang T'ao. And yet one more item of exceptional interest is Legge's personal, signed copy of the famous and very rare (but not quite com-

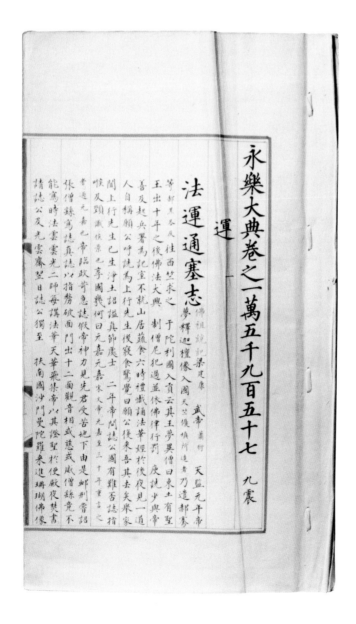

7–23. Yung-lo Ta-tien. *Originally compiled in 1408. This edition is a copy made before 1572. Chapters 15957 and 15958. Rare Books and Manuscripts Division*

With a total of 917,480 pages in 11,100 volumes, the Yung-lo Ta-tien *is the largest encyclopedia ever attempted. It was compiled at the order of Emperor Yung-lo, 1403–1425, of the Ming Dynasty.*

plete) set of the pamphlets issued by the Chinese Christian/messianist rebels in the Taiping Rebellion of 1850–1864. This collection of Chinese books and manuscripts also contains many Ming and Ching dynasty items. Of these surely the most important is the *Yung Lo Ta Tien*, which the Library purchased from Eames in 1913, and which today is housed in the Rare Books and Manuscripts Division. This work constitutes several sections of a copy made before 1572 of a Chinese encyclopedia originally written in the early fifteenth century. Recent reprintings of the encyclopedia in the People's Republic of China did not include these sections, as they were unaware of the existence of this copy.

While on the subject of the Chinese collections in the Oriental Division, it is important to mention yet another interesting and unique collection, the Mason collection of Chinese Mohammedan materials. This collection of several hundred books, pamphlets, and periodicals, in Chinese, Arabic, Arabic transliterated into Chinese, as well as other Middle Eastern languages, was collected early in this century by Isaac Mason, a Fellow of the Royal Geographical Society and expert on the Chinese Muslim community. It was Mason who introduced the West to this important but neglected literature, and he published a translation of the first Chinese Life of Muhammed. The Oriental Division continues today to have a strong commitment to collect materials from the Chinese Muslim community, including the Turkic languages of the Muslim minorities of Chinese Turkestan (the Xinjiang Autonomous Region in the People's Republic of China): Uighur, Kazakh, and Kirghiz.

The final pillar in the foundation for the greatness of the Oriental Division, and of the Oriental collections in The New York Public Library, was laid by the beneficence of Jacob M. Schiff, a wealthy New York banker who had long been interested in the development of a circulating library in New York City. He was, for example, a trustee of the New York Free Circulating Library until 1901. Beginning in 1897, Schiff gave The New York Public Library a gift of $10,000 for the purchase of Semitic literature. These gifts were continued into the early decades of the twentieth century. In 1934, funds from the Schiff gifts paid for the purchase of two hundred fifty Arabic manuscripts (which are now housed in the Rare Books and Manuscripts Division). Although the Schiff Fund for Semitic Literature was separated from the Oriental Division after the First World War, thereafter to be used for the benefit of the Jewish Division, the materials purchased that are now housed in the Oriental Division and in the Rare Books and Manuscripts Division provide the basis for the greatness of the collections in this area of scholarship.

Although the exact number of items purchased by the Schiff Fund for the Oriental Division is not known, an estimate would place it at around five thousand. Thus, many examples of outstanding acquisitions from this fund could be given. There is the 1835 publication of a Turkish translation of the charming Persian tale *Kalilah and Dimnah*, the 1847 Calcutta lithographed edition of the early manuscript copy of the Arabic story of *Yusuf and Zulaikha*, and the 1850 publication of an Arabic-Persian dictionary, edited by the German scholar Wetzstein. Of exceptional importance are two early works, one a digest of Arabic philosophy translated into Latin and provided with a commentary and a dedication to Cardinal Richelieu by the Lebanese Maronite Christian Abraham Ecchellensus, published in 1641, and a Persian manuscript featuring selections from early Islamic history, published in Bombay in 1827. This copy bears the signature of the famous Persian language expert James Darmesteter, many of whose translations of Persian classics appear in the *Sacred Books of the East*.

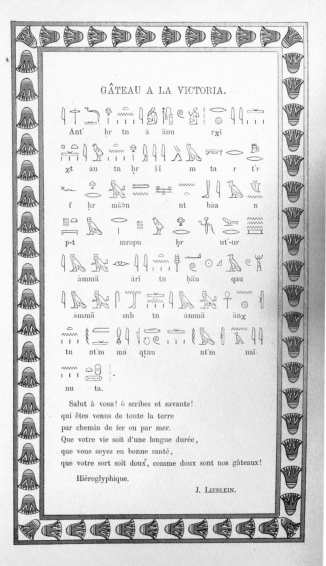

GÂTEAU A LA VICTORIA.

Ant´   ḫr   tn   à   ānu   r´χī

χt   áu   tn   ḫr   īī   m   ta   r   t´r

f   ḫr   mā´ən   nt   bàa   n

p-t   mropu   ḫr   ut´-ur

àmmā   árī   tn   ḫàu   qau

àmmā   snb   tn   àmmā   ānχ

tn   nt´m   mà   qtnu   nt´m   naī

nu   ta.

Salut à vous! ô scribes et savants!
qui êtes venus de toute la terre
par chemin de fer ou par mer.
Que votre vie soit d'une longue durée,
que vous soyez en bonne santé,
que votre sort soit doux, comme doux sont nos gâteaux!

Hiéroglyphique.

J. LIEBLEIN.

7–24. Menu du Diner Offert au VIIIe Congrès International des Orientalistes. Stockholm, le 7 Sept. 1889. *Leiden, E. J. Brill, n. d. Oriental Division*
This is the title page and the "Gâteau à la Victoria," rendered in Egyptian hieroglyphics, romanized transliteration, and a French translation by the Egyptologist J. Lieblein.

The Schiff Fund was not restricted to the purchase of texts. One of the division's most important works is the two-volume study of the Islamic Ummayad period castle of Kuseir 'Amra, in Jordan, which was published in 1897 by the great Orientalist and explorer Alois Musil. The plate volume contains exquisitely colored engravings of the paintings of the castle's interior. One of the division's most fascinating and charming holdings was also purchased from the Schiff Fund. This is the menu of a dinner served at the Eighth International Congress of Orientalists at Stockholm on September 7, 1889. But this is no ordinary menu. Each dish or drink, from the soup to the dessert, was announced by a poem or paean in one of the Oriental languages, with its script, composed for the occasion by one of the great Orientalists of the time. There are twenty in all—twenty languages represented. The "Salmon Imperial" is introduced with a poem in Sanskrit, the pâté in Manchu, the salad in Akkadian, the "Gâteau à la Victoria" in Egyptian hieroglyphic, the "Dessert International" in classical Japanese. The menu is a veritable guide to the scripts of the Oriental languages!

Gifts have always played a major role in the development of the collections of the Oriental Division. In addition to those already mentioned, many others are noteworthy. In 1898, the king of Siam gave the division a thirty-nine-volume edition of the Buddhist Tripitaka (the canon of the Buddhist scriptures) in the Pali language, using the Siamese script; then, in 1921, the Siamese prince of Chantaburi gave the Library a twelve-volume Siamese commentary on the Buddhist Tripitaka (the Oriental Division holds complete editions of the Buddhist Tripitaka in Chinese, Mongolian, Tibetan, Pali, and Thai and partial editions in Sanskrit and Manchu); in 1922, J. P. Morgan gave the division a set of fifty-seven folio volumes containing photographs of Coptic texts in the Morgan Library; more recently, Professor Alex Wayman of Columbia University gave the Library a very important set of books on Indian art from his personal library. Included in this gift was a complete set of the important journal of Indian art, *Rupam*. A gift of great charm, as well as scholarly value, was given to the division in 1956 by Secretary of State John Foster Dulles. A hotel in Miyanoshita, the Fujiya Hotel, issued brief descriptions of many aspects of Japanese culture on menu cards. These cards were subsequently compiled and published in three volumes under the title *We Japanese* (between 1937 and 1949). The volumes, which taken together comprise a very interesting encyclopedia of Japanese popular culture, are inscribed "To Ambassador John Foster Dulles," from the president of the hotel, H.S.K. Yamaguchi.

The Japanese collection of the Oriental Division, while not of the same depth as the other areas of the Orient (this was the case as well in the Astor Library), nevertheless has a number of unique and important features. The Astor Library did have a number of very important early grammars and dictionaries, as well as seventeenth- through nineteenth-century histories of Buddhism in the Japanese language. The division also has some early and rare books on various aspects of the martial arts, on Japanese folk culture, Japanese erotica, and the tea ceremony. An important work of Japanese erotica is the 1907 publication of Dr. Friedrich S. Krauss's *Das Geschlechtleben in Glauben, Sitte und Brauch der Japaner (Sexual Life in the Beliefs, Customs and Habits of the Japanese)*. This work was published in a very small print run, of which the division's copy is number thirty-one. The division just recently acquired the very rare trilogy of works by Lawrence E. Gichner, published in the late 1940s and early 1950s, *Erotic Aspects of Japanese Culture, Erotic Aspects of Chinese Culture*, and *Erotic Aspects of Hindu Sculpture*. The division has also emphasized Japanese publications on science and technology, and holds over two hundred current periodicals on these subjects. Additionally, the division's collecting interests in Japanese culture focus on the tea ceremony, archaeology, and serious literature. The Library's Music Division collects the Japanese popular music form known as "Kara Oke," which is words and music made available to amateurs, usually in bars, who sing along with the recorded music. The Spencer Collection holds one of the world's most important collections of Japanese prints and scrolls. These were highlighted in an exhibition organized by Dr. Miyeko Murase, called "Tales of Japan." The Research Libraries collections in Japanese art rank among the best in the world.

Here then we have the foundations for the collections of the Oriental Division. The division today is an expansion of what it was when the Astor Library opened in 1854. It has essentially the same strengths, the same collecting emphases, the same breadth, the same depth. While no library can collect everything, today or at any other time, the Oriental Division has attempted to remain an outstanding research collection in the areas of Egyptology and ancient Near Eastern languages and archaeology, Oriental religions, the ancient and modern languages and the cultural history of India, Arabic and Persian languages and their literatures, the Turkic languages of the Islamic peoples of inner Asia, certain aspects of Chinese literature and culture, and Tibetan language and culture.

To bring matters up-to-date, and to bring them full circle from the days of the Astor Library, it will be interesting to mention a number of very recent outstanding acquisitions by the Oriental Division. These include a Bible in Urdu (the language of Pakistan) containing the Gospel of John, one of the earliest editions of any part of the Bible in Urdu, published in Calcutta or Serampore in the early nineteenth century; a dictionary of Manchu, Mongolian, Tibetan, and Chinese, published in Beijing around 1700; the two-volume *Literature of Egypt and the Soudan* by Ibrahim-Hilmy, the most important work of Egyptological bibliography of the nineteenth century (published in London in 1886), in a rare, mint-condition, engraved red morocco binding; a magnificent two-volume, folio-size, full-color edition of Tibetan painted Mandalas, published in Tokyo in a limited edition of three hundred copies in 1983; *The Battle Reliefs of King Sety I*, published by the Oriental Institute of the University of Chicago in 1986; and the *Lughat Wanquli*, a Turkish-Arabic dictionary published in Istanbul in 1729, the first book printed by a Muslim, and the first book printed in Arabic script in an Arabic country. This work was part of an edition of one thousand copies. We see here publications that are unusual, rare, even unique to American research libraries, but which are only the latest link in a long chain of collecting interest and strength in these fields of Oriental studies by the Oriental Division.

Given the extraordinary range of collecting interests detailed above, the Oriental Division and the Oriental collections of The Research Libraries continue to be a collection of last resort for readers from around the world. The editor of the *Swiss Air Gazette* in Zurich had searched a number of European libraries to find photographs from *The Drawings and Paintings of Rabindranath Tagore*, published in Delhi in 1961. She was able to find a copy in the Wallach Division. A member of the Philippine Mission in New York needed to find a line of poetry from the *Rubaiyat* of Omar Khayyam, which contained the phrase "the moving finger." The librarian found the verse through a translation that had a first-line index. A reader in Malaysia wrote, requesting photocopies of parts of English translations of two novels by Chinese women writers, published in 1930 and 1940. After having searched twelve libraries in Southeast Asia without success, he wrote the Oriental Division, and we were able to fill the request. A California publisher wanted to reproduce parts of a book of poems by the French poet Victor Segalen, called *Steles*, published in Peking, China, in 1912. And finally, a New York choreographer, a speaker of the Kannada language of India, requested a paraphrase of

7–25. Dai Hannya Haramittakyō
[The Greater Sutra of the
Perfection of Wisdom].
*Frontispiece, Chapter 544. Late
Heian Period, ca. 1125. Hand-
scroll, gold and silver ink on
dark blue paper. Spencer
Collection*
 This is a section from the
opening chapter of the Tripitaka, the Buddhist canon of
scriptures, copied in Japan for
deposit in a temple. The blue
paper was meant to give the
appearance of lapis lazuli. The
Buddha is seated on a lotus
pedestal, flanked by bodhisatt-
vas, with four laymen dressed
as Chinese officials in front of
him.

a poem by a prominent Kannada poet, which she wanted to incorporate into a dance she was creating. The Oriental Division was able to supply the original, an English translation, and an English synopsis.

In its ninth decade as a named division, and approaching its one hundred fortieth year as a collection, we can now suggest a slight, but basic, modification to a statement found in the preface to Cogswell's catalogue of Orientalia: "Now, the Oriental apparatus *is* sufficient to supply the wants of scholars engaged upon the profoundest investigations into the language, literature and philosophy of the East."

7–26. RAMANANDA CHATTERJEE, ED. The Golden Book of Tagore. *A Homage to Rabindranath Tagore in Celebration of His Seventieth Birthday. Calcutta, The Golden Book Committee, 1931. No. 575 of an edition of 1500 copies. Hand-written note of Tagore in facsimile laid in.* Oriental Division

The portrait is after a photograph by Martin Vos, New York. The book contains poems, printed drawings and paintings, photographs, scholarly articles, tributes, and letters of congratulations from many of the major cultural and political figures in the world at that time.

CHAPTER EIGHT

AMERICANA

As the son of Scottish immigrants who had prospered mightily in New York, James Lenox felt that he owed the city a debt of gratitude. Quietly and unobtrusively he used his inherited wealth to found a hospital, an old-age home, and a research library. James Stevens, the Vermont-born London bookseller who acted as Lenox's agent for book purchases for over twenty-five years, wrote of him: "He was a man of few words and few intimate friends, but of varied information, much studious reading, extensive correspondence and many books."

These "many books" formed the core of the Lenox Library, which was incorporated in 1870 and opened to the public on January 15, 1877. The library building, at Fifth Avenue and Seventieth Street, where the Frick Collection is now located, was designed by Richard Morris Hunt, who also designed the main section of New York's Metropolitan Museum of Art and Harvard's Fogg Art Museum. Its contents, which included paintings and porcelains as well as books, were the reflection of Lenox's personal interests. Upon his death in 1880, the Lenox Library's trustees eulogized him:

> This library is the lasting monument of his devotion to history, literature
> and art. Its rich collections are literally personal memorials of his loving
> and faithful labors in those perennial fields of noblest culture. It was
> the charm of his youth, the delight of his manhood, the comfort of his
> age; and, as he has given it his name, it will be the glory of his memory
> hereafter. Of all his public works, it is the noblest and most conspicuous
> which he has intrusted to our watchful care and guardianship. In its charter
> and establishment he has clearly indicated the principles which should
> govern its administration; and the fidelity with which his trusts continue
> to be secured and protected will prove the permanent measure of its value.

The library is indeed his lasting monument, but the beautiful building that housed it did not, unfortunately, last very long. The Lenox Collection was incorporated into The New York Public Library in 1895, and the building itself was torn down to make way for Frick's palace. Today, the Lenox Library remains the heart and soul of The New York Public Library's Rare Books and Manuscripts Division.

Lenox's primary collecting interests were the Bible, the works of John Bunyan and John Milton, and Americana. The last of these is a field of continuing collecting interest to the Library in many of its divisions. In this it honors Lenox's intention that the American experience should be documented in the most comprehensive manner possible. He defined as "Americanum" any work that referred to either the North or South American continent in any way. Thus a book or manuscript that has as its primary focus the history of trade between England and Spain would count as an Americanum by reason of its reference to some product of American origin, such as tobacco.

Americana comprise, therefore, the records of our hemisphere's experience, from its discovery in 1492 down to the present day. Like many children of immigrants, Lenox was fascinated by the question of the separate identity of those descendants of Europeans, Africans, or Asians who were to become something else entirely, something new and distinctive: Americans, with a character and language all their own.

The first stop on the researcher's tour of these vast holdings will be the United States History, Local History and Genealogy Division with its 125,000 volumes specifically related to the American past. Next, the General Research Division will be consulted for the literature and anthropology of the Americas. The Wallach Division of Art, Prints and Photographs will provide not only information about the history of art in the New World but also thousands of views of America. American literary rarities and manuscripts will be found in the Berg Collection of English and American Literature and in the Rare Books and Manuscripts Division. The Arents Tobacco Collection documents the history of this American plant. The experience of black Americans is the concern of the Schomburg Center for Research in Black Culture. Moreover, there are 145,000 pieces of nineteenth-century American sheet music and thousands of letters and composers' holograph compositions in the Americana Collection of the Music Division at the Performing Arts Research Center at Lincoln Center.

Documents relating to the American experience either directly or tangentially are the province of many of the Library's divisions and special collections, and one may indeed wonder if it is possible to comprehend clearly the scope of such varied resources. In one short chapter we certainly cannot presume to explore fully so vast an area, but we hope that by presenting a few key examples we will be able to hint at the variety of works the Library preserves as records and evidence of our history and our culture.

We begin, as inevitably we must, with the voyage of Christopher Columbus, or rather with a small, somewhat badly printed pamphlet. It's nothing much to look at, really. The paper is not the best available in the year it was printed, 1493. Indeed, placed next to the great incunabula produced in Germany or Italy, it would be dismissed as a rather sloppy and amateurish work. But it changed the face of the world. Known as "The Columbus Letter," this pamphlet was written by the explorer as he returned home on the *Nina*. In it he reports to his patrons, the king and queen of Spain, on the results of his voyage, telling them that he had "so far found no human monstrosities as many expected . . ." and that the people he had so far seen "all go naked, men and women . . . although some of the women cover a single place with the leaf of a plant." This "letter" (the original manuscript does not survive) went through nine editions in 1493; the Library owns six of them, including the unique copy of the very first edition, which was printed in Barcelona (reproduced here), and the only complete copy of the edition printed in Basel, which has a woodcut image of a ship very much like the one in which Columbus sailed (reproduced in the earlier chapter entitled Maps and Voyages).

As we contemplate the incredible impact on Europe of the discoveries of Columbus and his successors, we may forget that those whose history was most profoundly changed—indeed, sometimes brought to a close—were the native inhabitants of this new-found land. For Columbus came across the Atlantic as a conqueror determined to possess what he discovered. Displaying the flag of Spain and carrying the cross as his ensign, he was totally convinced of the justice

of his task and unwilling to permit any obstacle to remain in his path. He prepared the way for an empire, and empires are built on theft, exploitation, and murder. There was to be no question of coexistence; the Native Americans of New Spain were to submit to their Most Catholic Majesties or they were to die.

While the intent of the European conquerors was to change or destroy the native cultures they encountered, they did not completely disregard their achievements. They began to document the strange appearance of these seemingly otherworldly creatures, the reports of whose habits and demeanor were warped by fantasy. In a woodcut of around 1505 in the Spencer Collection we see a conflated image of Native American life guaranteed to shock its intended European audience. The inhabitants of the New World are portrayed as cannibals, who are also rather exhibitionistic in their sexual practices and primitive in their dress and domestic arrangements.

In the Columbus Letter and this woodcut we have the earliest documents in the Library's collections of materials relating to Native Americans. There are well over twelve thousand volumes relating to the original inhabitants of both North and South America. They range from archaeological findings and anthropological studies to drawings and photographic surveys of surviving tribesmen and records of their lingering cultural heritage, from the first reports of the conquistadores, whose novel agents of terror—horses that "swallowed the ground with fierceness and rage" and cannon that manufactured thunder and lightning—so ruthlessly annihilated the Aztecs, to the hardly less lurid tales of massacres and captivities farther north. The Library houses formal studies of more than three hundred Indian languages and dialects, and an unusual collection concerning Indian place-names.

With these resources in hand, the researcher may review the early history of the Americas from a variety of vantage points: that of the native peoples themselves, that of the Spanish conquerors, and that of later researchers. Among them, of course, none can really speak to us with the same immediacy as the

8–2. A New World Scene. Woodcut. German, ca. 1505. Spencer Collection
This colored woodcut is one of the earliest ethnographic portrayals of the inhabitants of the New World.

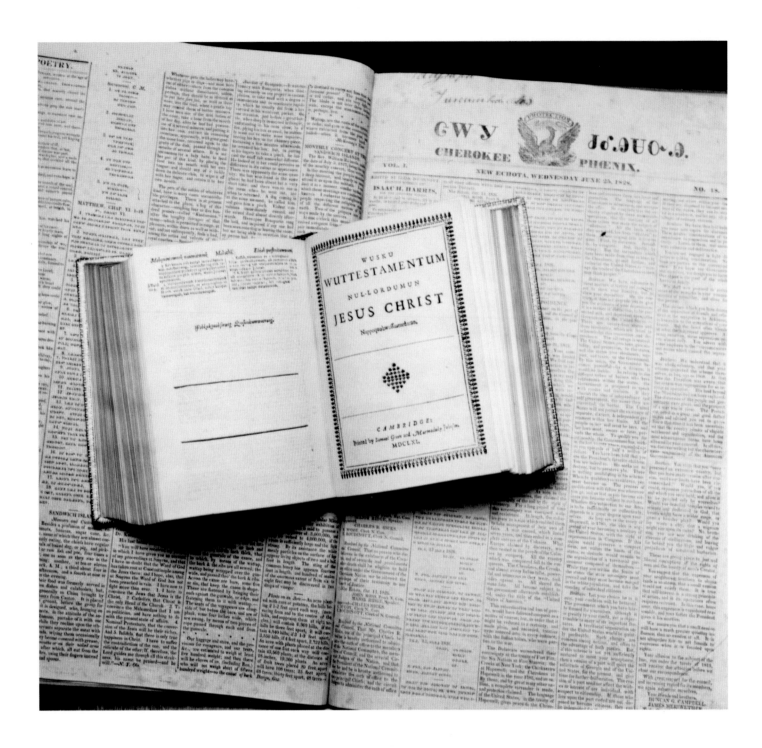

8–3. The Holy Bible: Containing the Old Testament and the New . . . translated by John Eliot. *Cambridge, Massachusetts, Green and Johnson, 1663. Shown with a Cherokee newspaper. Rare Books and Manuscripts Division*

John Eliot, a Puritan divine, prepared this translation of the Bible into Algonquin to proselytize for Christianity among Native Americans. The gradual near-total extinction of autochthonous American cultures was accompanied by the occasional expression of deference to their customs and language.

voices of the native inhabitants themselves. Such records are the historian's basic and most precious tools. When we read such reports—or even merely look upon them—we sense the reality of the past more vividly than we could in any other way.

A manuscript in the Spencer Collection offers a moving sense of that immediacy. It is called "The Council House of Santa Maria Toluca," and it was written around 1535 in the province of Toluca in Mexico. In both form and content it is a distinctly New World production, for it is written (in the Roman alphabet) in Nahuatl, one of the native Mexican languages, on a coarse clothlike fibrous paper made from the maguey plant, itself native to Central America. The text deals with the division of the Aztec empire by the Spaniards, while the naive watercolors that accompany it show us scenes from the natives' daily life. It is likely that this manuscript was compiled by a Mexican at the orders of Spanish authorities who wanted a record of their subjugation of the Aztec empire in a native language.

What were the thoughts of the artist-scribe as he wrote and decorated this work? He might have been old enough to remember the days of Montezuma before the humiliation of defeat at the hands of a few soldiers of fortune. One senses from the drawings that this was a conscious effort to show life as it once was and would never be again, and one cannot help but be touched by the effort.

While the Spanish were assiduously attempting to obliterate the culture and religions of the inhabitants of Mexico, they were also laying the foundations for a new culture, one that was originally intended to be merely an extension of Spanish life across the seas. To this end, new cities were established and churches and schools were built—and in their wake came the printing press.

As in the Old World, printing in the conquered territories was the result of an international collaboration. Juan Cromberger was a German printer who had set up a press in Seville. In 1539 he obtained from Charles V, Holy Roman Emperor and king of Spain, the exclusive rights to print books and government ordinances in New Spain. As the latter was a garrison state, this contract would prove to be a lucrative one. Cromberger did not come himself to Mexico but sent Juan Pablos, one of his master printers, who was born in Brescia in Italy. Juan Pablos's status as agent can be confirmed by the fact that the books he printed appeared not under his own name but as *en casa de Juan Cromberger* (at the shop of Juan Cromberger).

The earliest surviving complete book printed by Juan Pablos is in the Rare Books and Manuscripts Division of the Library (only a fragment of an earlier book survives—in the Biblioteca Nacional in Madrid). It is an edition of Juan de Zumarrága's *Doctrina Breve*, and it was printed in 1543–1544. Zumarrága was the bishop of Mexico, and in this work, used no doubt to instruct prospective native converts to Catholicism, he sets out the basic tenets of Christianity. While the text of this work may not strike us as particularly significant, the fact of its being the second book printed in the Western Hemisphere (and, we may note, appearing one hundred years before the first book printed in English North America) is crucial, for it indicates the priority given to the cultural transformation of the conquered by their conquerors.

The Spaniards moved south from Mexico through Central America and along the Pacific coast, where they subdued the Inca empire. They also moved north, adding the west coast of North America to their vast holdings. This empire, comparable in size only to that of Genghis Khan, was administered by the Council of

8–4. Council House of Santa Maria Toluca. *Manuscript on paper. Mexico, ca. 1535. Spencer Collection*
    This Aztec manuscript, written in Nahuatl and Latin characters, contains an account of the division of land by the Spanish invaders in Mexico. It was written on paper made from the maguey plant.

the Indies, an efficient bureaucracy whose records survive in the Archives of the Indies in Seville. Records of the conquest also are held in 149 volumes of manuscripts in the Obadiah Rich collection of the Rare Books and Manuscripts Division.

Rich was an American diplomat of the early nineteenth century who was also active as both a collector and bookseller in London. In 1830 he acquired from a French collector, Henri Ternaux de Compans, an important collection of manuscripts relating to New Spain. These in turn had come from the collection of Juan Bautista Muñoz, who had been appointed in the late eighteenth century by King Charles III of Spain to write a history of the Indies based on material in Spanish archives and libraries. Muñoz employed scribes who, with him, made transcripts of the relevant documents for his work, which he never completed. These transcripts, along with original documents added by Campans and Rich, provide an important resource for the study of Spain's conquest in the New World. It is also a convenient one, since they gather together in one place materials that are scattered throughout Spain. For this reason James Lenox, whose interest usually was in primary materials and not copies, acquired the collection from Rich in 1848 and passed it along to his library when that opened; it came to The New York Public Library as part of the Lenox collections.

These manuscripts offer not only a portrait of conquerors and their conquests, they also offer some insight into those individuals active in the subjugation of the New World. For the conquistadores were more than just violent freebooters hypocritically cloaking their greed with a veneer of religious purpose. They seem to have been possessed by a tremendous unrest, an almost pathological need for movement for its own sake. In one letter (an original and not a transcript), Diego Columbus, the oldest son of Christopher, writes to Ferdinand II, king of Spain, of his ambition to sail around the world. This was written on July 19, 1511, only nineteen years after his father had first laid eyes on land no European had ever seen before—and this was well before the conquest of the New World was completed or its vastness fully explored. There is no precedent for this compulsive wanderlust, but it strikes a contemporary chord, for a similar impulse appears to be leading us to travel to other planets and to explore the origin and nature of other solar systems.

While the Spanish were busy building cities and converting the native peoples, other Europeans were barely beginning to colonize the Americas. It was not until late in the sixteenth century that France and Britain made serious efforts to establish footholds in the Western Hemisphere; these efforts were at first tentative and their life span short.

In 1564 the French sent out an expedition to Florida under the command of René Goulaine de Laudonnière. With him there went an artist named Jacques Le Moyne de Morgues whose assignment was to record the people and places he saw and to provide maps for the use of future explorers. He made forty-two gouache drawings on vellum, only one of which survives. This is in the Library's Wallach Division of Art, Prints and Photographs. It shows "Laudonnière and Chief Athore of the Timucua Indians at Ribaut's Column," a monument erected by the French explorers. The figure of the chief, commanding and impressive, is the most distinctive element of this little work. He seems so self-assured and dignified, the gracious but regal host to people who are at least as strange to him as he to them. Clearly, he was oblivious of the intent of these foreign gentlemen, who were ultimately to be the agents of the extinction of himself and his kind.

Chief Athore is the pictorial embodiment of the concept of "the noble savage," an idea that enjoyed a certain vogue in the eighteenth century. It ascribed great

virtue to people raised in a "natural" state who thus lacked those constraints of European custom that stifled creativity. Whatever the merits of this concept, it highlights the fact that it took Europeans a very long time to come to terms with Native Americans and their culture, or at least with those they had not completely obliterated. Well into the sixteenth century, Native Americans were still being portrayed with little or no understanding; they were pictured not only as a race apart, they appear to be another species altogether.

The largest body of graphic images of Native Americans produced in the sixteenth century was published by Theodore De Bry in Frankfurt. Called *Les Grands Voyages*, they were published in several languages in the 1580s and were reprinted well into the seventeenth century. Along with the published accounts of explorers like Laudonnière, they comprise the major sources for contemporary European impressions of what and whom they saw in the New World. One of the volumes, Thomas Hariot's *A Briefe and True Report of the New Found Land of Virginia*, appeared in 1590. It resulted from the voyage Hariot undertook, at the direction of Sir Walter Raleigh, to document the experiences of the first English colony in North America. Beautifully illustrated with engravings after John White's drawings, the work was written to encourage others to join the rather small and frightened band of adventurers who were already there. We are shown images of "noble savages" as well as neat and orderly native villages, with fields of sprouting crops surrounding them; among the plants identified in the text is tobacco. It calls to mind the description of Virginia by the seventeenth-century English poet Michael Drayton as "Earth's only paradise."

8–5. JACQUES LE MOYNE DE MORGUES. Laudonnière and Chief Athore of the Timucua Indians at Ribaut's Column. *Watercolor on vellum, 1564. Wallach Division of Art, Prints and Photographs*

Depicted are the French explorer René Goulaine de Laudonnière and his companions and the Floridian Timucua Indians with their chief, Athore. Le Moyne de Morgues had accompanied Laudonnière on his voyage to record the sights and map out the lands they visited.

This toehold in Virginia was later matched in New England by the Plymouth Colony, settled by the Pilgrims in 1620. Their initial experience would seem to offer the necessary balance to Virginia's "paradise," for half of them died in the first year of the settlement and the remainder lived in fear occasioned in part by the natives who were, according to William Bradford, the Pilgrims' leader, "readier to fill their sides with arrows than otherwise." The Rare Books and Manuscripts Division owns a copy of the little book in which their experience in the first year of their "plantation" is recorded. In *A Relation or Journal of the Beginning and Proceedings of the English Plantation Settled at Plimoth*, published in London in 1622, we have a firsthand account of their daily lives, of their fears on the eve of debarkation, their response to the first sightings of the natives of New England, and their ideas for a harmonious division of labor among the settlers.

It was to be eighteen years before they were sufficiently settled to set up a press and begin printing books for themselves. In 1640 there appeared *The Whole Booke of Psalmes Faithfully Translated into English Metre*, printed in Cambridge, Massachusetts, by Stephen Day. Commonly known as the "Bay Psalm Book,"

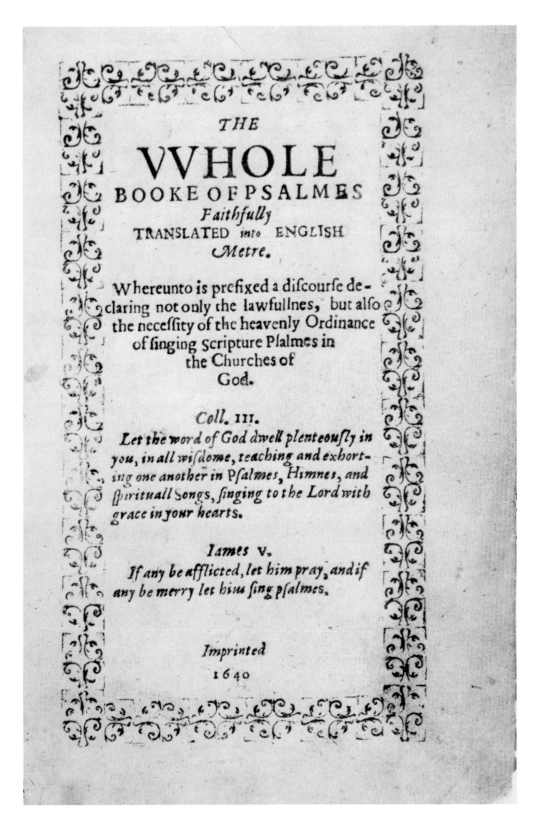

THE
VVHOLE
BOOKE OF PSALMES
Faithfully
TRANSLATED *into* ENGLISH
Metre.

Whereunto is prefixed a difcourfe declaring not only the lawfullnes, but alfo
the neceffity of the heavenly Ordinance
of finging Scripture Pfalmes in
the Churches of
God.

Coll. III.
*Let the word of God dwell plenteoufly in
you, in all wifdome, teaching and exhort-
ing one another in Pfalmes, Himnes, and
fpirituall Songs, finging to the Lord with
grace in your hearts.*

Iames V.
*If any be afflicted, let him pray, and if
any be merry let him fing pfalmes.*

Imprinted
1640

8–7. The Whole Booke of
Psalmes Faithfully Translated
into English Metre. *Cambridge,
Massachusetts, S. Day, 1640.
Rare Books and Manuscripts
Division*

Known as The Bay Psalm
Book, this was the first book
printed in North America. It
was preceded (by over one hundred years) by books printed in
the major cultural centers of
South and Central America.

it is one of the great rarities of Americana, surviving in only eleven copies. One
of these was acquired by James Lenox in 1855.

The Bay Psalm Book is poetry of a sort, a makeshift metrical translation from
the Hebrew of David's Psalms, designed to fill the need for divine songs in religious
meetings. Richard Mather was one of the translators. In the minds of most Puritan
men of learning, Hebrew was considered the "mother of languages," and it was
a subject diligently studied. "If . . . the verses are not always as smooth and ele-

gant as some may desire or expect," the venerable Mather wrote in a preface, "let him consider that Gods altar needs not our polishings."

Insignificant as this volume may appear as a printed book or work of scholarship and literature, it marked a portentous beginning. The Puritans were a bookish people. Measured by the number of imprints, by 1700 Boston had become the second most prodigious publishing center of the Anglo-Saxon world after London, surpassing even Oxford and Cambridge. As just one token of the intellectual life of the colony, by as early as 1646 more than one hundred thirty university graduates had immigrated to New England. And in that life of learning the Mather dynasty—Richard, Increase, and Cotton—played a dominant role. As an old epitaph puts it:

> Under this stone lies Richard Mather,
> Who had a son greater than his father,
> Ane eke a grandson greater than either.

Among the three of them, they produced literally hundreds of books, a generous number of them represented in the Library by first or early editions. There has been nothing remotely comparable to this family output in the history of American literature.

For the most part, these works were important in their day and in ours indispensable to understanding that period of our history. But for most readers today they are indeed tedious in their lengthy exegetical preachments. ("The real Excellency of a Book," Cotton Mather explained, "will never ly on *saying of little*.")

8–8. JUDAH MONIS.
Grammar of the Hebrew Tongue. *Boston, Jonas Green, 1735. Rare Books and Manuscripts Division*

This was the first Hebrew grammar published in North America from the first complete font of Hebrew types in the colonies.

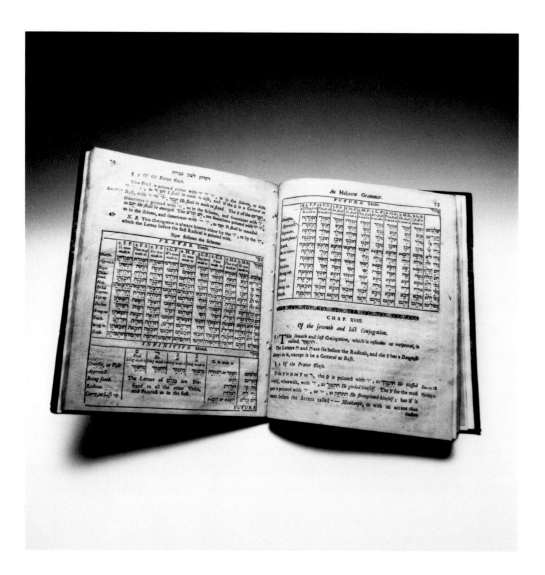

8–9. BENJAMIN
FRANKLIN. Letter to George
Washington. *Manuscript, June
21, 1776. Rare Books and
Manuscripts Division*
In this letter Franklin offers
to Washington his opinion that
England would probably not
send troops to quash an American rebellion. He also notes
that "A Declaration of Independence is preparing."

The fact that the first book printed in English North America was, like the
first book printed in the Spanish colonies a hundred years before, religious in
content, suggests the basic nature of both settlements. Yet the content of the two
books shows the divergent purposes of the English and Spanish. The latter set
out to claim the New World for their faith and for their king; they were seeking an
extension of their motherland. The Pilgrims were seeking an alternative to their
homeland, one in which they could practice their severe brand of Protestantism
without being persecuted for it. This is not to say that they were opposed to all per-
secution; their treatment of other religious groups does not strike the modern
observer as being particularly tolerant.

This yearning for a place in which to practice a religion freely also characterizes
the immigrants who settled in Maryland in the seventeenth century: English
and Irish Catholics. It also characterizes the Jews who came to New York from
Holland in the seventeenth century.

But it was not just freedom of religion that concerned the inhabitants of the
English colonies, it was also a basic desire for independence, in thought and
ultimately in politics. As the settlements along the Atlantic coast grew and prospered and as the native-born generations succeeded the nervous immigrants,
there arose a spirit of confidence and trust in reason and the value of individual
perceptions that was, in part, a reflection of the spirit of the Enlightenment that
informed European thought in the eighteenth century. But that spirit was also
a reflection of something uniquely American.

Perhaps no figure of the American eighteenth century better represents that
spirit than Benjamin Franklin. Born in Boston, he found work as a teenager in a
Philadelphia printing shop. He went on from that job to become, over the next

fifty-odd years, one of the most celebrated figures of the eighteenth century, universally honored for his wisdom and beloved for his genial nature by all except Louis XVI, who resented the affection shown "cher Papa" in his old age by the ladies of the French court. Everything Franklin produced deserves the attention it has long received, and he wrote on just about everything that affected the lives of his fellow men.

The variety of the contributions that came from Franklin's pen and his printing presses may be suggested by the Library's holdings. To choose any examples from these is bound to seem invidious, for each has its special fascination. One of the earlier manuscripts is a leaf, bearing Franklin's signature, of the "Memorandum of Agreement" between the directors of the Library Company of Philadelphia and Louis Timothee, its first librarian. In founding and operating a public circulating library in 1732 and in devising the curriculum for a liberal education, Franklin established principles that stand at the heart of The New York Public Library's purposes as an institution.

The Library also owns two signed letters in which Franklin explains the workings of his "smokeless chimney"—one of these was written to Dr. Ingelhousz, Physician to the Emperor, at Vienna. Another of the manuscript letters, dated June 21, 1776, and addressed to George Washington, noted that "a Declaration of Independence is preparing." Franklin continued his prodigious output until he died at the age of eighty-four, when he was still working on his memorable *Autobiography*.

The Declaration of Independence was indeed "preparing." In 1775 the members of the Second Continental Congress, who had assembled in Philadelphia, prepared and signed a petition to King George III requesting that the acts restricting colonial trade be rescinded and the efforts to collect taxes by armed force be discontinued. With this one final gesture they hoped to forestall a revolution. Because John Adams had referred to it as an earnest effort "to keep open the door of reconciliation, to hold the sword in one hand and the olive branch in the other," the plea became known as the Olive Branch Petition. But blood had already been spilled at Lexington and at Bunker Hill, and the king had little mind to compromise with these offensively independent-minded rebels. The letter went unanswered. The Library's copy of this futile petition is a sad reminder of man's hopes and follies at that critical point in history.

8–10. VICTOR HUGO. *Franklin's House at Passy. Watercolor, ca. 1836. Rare Books and Manuscripts Division*
The great French novelist was an accomplished draftsman. He donated this eerie representation of the house in which Franklin had lived during his nine-year sojourn in France to the U.S. Sanitary Commission in 1864. He hoped that it would be auctioned to raise money for the Commission's war-relief activities.

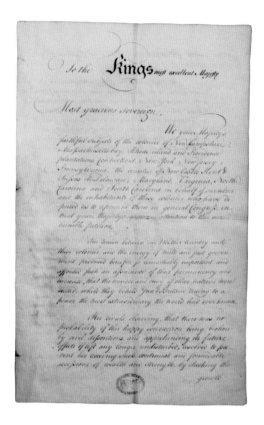
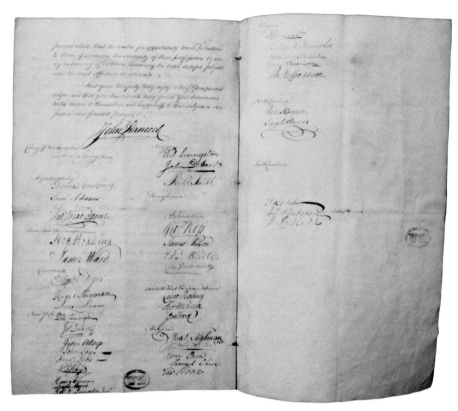

The colonists' response to this refusal of reconciliation was to declare officially their independence. This document was largely the work of Thomas Jefferson, who, after drafting it, made five "fair" copies in his own hand for circulation and comment. One of these five copies holds a place of honor in the Rare Books and Manuscripts Division. It was given to the Library not, for a change, by Lenox, but by Thomas A. Emmet, a noted collector of American historical documents who had joined with it a letter or signature by each of the men who signed it.

Jefferson was not only a man of letters. Like Franklin, Adams, Madison, and the other leading statesmen of the period, in all his writings he put the need to inform, argue, persuade, and elucidate above style as such. However, the literature of ideas as it was presented in the diverse writings of these philosopher-statesmen set a solid foundation for a national literature—a literature whose influence would in time cross back over the Atlantic and create new avenues of thought and expression overseas.

The Declaration resulted, of course, in the War of Independence from which the Library's collections provide some rather interesting documents. Through the *Diaries* and drawings of Archibald Robertson, we see the battles and battlefields of the war with a sense of immediacy that makes them come alive. In his entry for October 18, 1776, we find the "rebels" losing ground in a battle fought just north of New York City:

18th at Day Break the Grenadiers and Light Infantry moved to Stevens's point where they embark'd in the Flat Boats. The rest of the Army and Cannon went to Hunt's Point. About 8 o'clock the Flat Boats came up and landed under Cover of the Guns on Rodmans' Neck opposite Hunt's Point without any opposition. I was ordered to join the Light Infantry and Grenadiers under Lieutenant General Clinton. After moving on about a mile towards East Chester I was ordered by the General to the top of a Rising

8–11. The Olive Branch Petition. *Manuscript, July 8, 1775. Rare Books and Manuscripts Division*
The members of the Continental Congress sent this petition to King George III as a last gesture to avoid rebellion. They asked the king to direct his ministers to repeal the acts restricting colonial trade and to cease trying to collect taxes by force of arms.

A Declaration by the Representatives of the UNITED STATES OF
AMERICA in General Congress assembled.

When in the course of human events it becomes necessary for one people to
dissolve the political bands which have connected them with another, and to assume
among the powers of the earth the separate and equal station to which the laws of na-
-ture & of nature's god entitle them, a decent respect to the opinions of mankind re-
-quires that they should declare the causes which impel them to the separation.

We hold these truths to be self-evident; that all men are created equal; that
they are endowed by their Creator with inherent & inalienable rights; that among
these are life, liberty, & the pursuit of happiness; that to secure these rights, govern-
-ments are instituted among men, deriving their just powers from the consent of the
governed; that whenever any form of government becomes destructive of these ends,
it is the right of the people to alter or to abolish it, and to institute new government,
laying it's foundation on such principles & organising it's powers in such form as to
them shall seem most likely to effect their safety & happiness. prudence indeed will
dictate that governments long established should not be changed for light & transient
causes. and accordingly all experience hath shewn that mankind are more disposed to
suffer while evils are sufferable, ———, themselves by abolishing the forms
they are accustomed. but when a long train of abuses & usurpations, begun at a distin-
-quished period, & pursuing invariably the same object, evinces a design to reduce them
under absolute despotism, it is their right, it is their duty, to throw off such government
& to provide new guards for their future security. such has been the patient sufferance
of these colonies; & such is now the necessity which constrains them to expunge their
former systems of government. the history of the present king of Great Britain, is a
history of unremitting injuries & usurpations, among which appears no solitary fact
to contradict the uniform tenor of the rest; but all have in direct object the esta-
-blishment of an absolute tyranny over these states. to prove this let facts be sub-
-mitted to a candid world, for the truth of which we pledge a faith yet unsullied by falsehood

He has refused his assent to laws the most wholesome & necessary for the public good:

he has forbidden his governors to pass laws of immediate & pressing importance, un-
-less suspended in their operation till his assent should be obtained, & when so
suspended, he has neglected utterly to attend to them:

he has refused to pass other laws for the accomodation of large districts of people, unless
those people would relinquish the right of representation in the legislature,
a right inestimable to them & formidable to tyrants only:

ground in front with the Advance Guard of the Light Infantry to recon-
noitre, but we were immediately fired upon from behind Trees and heaps
of Stones where the Rebels lay concealed, and from which they were
very soon forced to retire. On the Batns [Batteries or Battalions] coming
up we had 10 men Killed and Wounded. Here we halted untill General
Howe came up. The Rebels appeared drawn up in our Front behind all the
Fences and high stone walls. The Grenadiers were ordered to march
in a Column on our Right. About 10 we advanced a little and halted till
12 when the 1st Battalion Light Infantry advanced on our left Flank.
Here they received a very smart fire from the Rebels from behind Trees
and Walls, but they soon forced them to retire. (We lost here about 12
Men Killed and Wounded and 3 Officers Wounded.) Our Grenadiers kept
advancing on our Right the Hessian Grenadiers in the Centre, and after
some Cannonading the Rebels entirely quited the heights. Few of them were
left on the field, but a good many were taken off wounded. We took our
Position on the heights of Pelham's Manner our left to East Chester Creek
and Right to New Rochelle, our Front extending about 2 miles facing
North or NNE.

8–12. THOMAS
JEFFERSON. The
Declaration of Independence.
*Manuscript, July 6–10, 1776.
Rare Books and Manuscripts
Division*
  *Jefferson prepared this draft
of the Declaration for a friend
in Virginia after Congress had
approved the text on July 2,
1776.*

Robertson's mention of the Hessian mercenaries employed by the British calls
to mind the cache of manuscripts relating to them in the collection of George
Bancroft, the American historian whose library was acquired by the Lenox Library
in 1894. Included are items such as a letter from a Hessian officer stationed on
Long Island in 1776. The Loyalists who remained true to England during the war
may be studied in detail in the volumes of American Loyalist papers in the Rare
Books and Manuscripts Division.

With the end of the war and the triumph of the colonists, George Washington
was elected our first president. His reflections on that experience and on the
future of the nation are summarized in his Farewell Address to his countrymen,
delivered in 1796. The manuscript of this document is, along with the Declaration
of Independence, one of the most revered objects in the Library's collections.

It is an awesome experience to gaze at the thirty-two heavily corrected pages
in which the Father of His Country painstakingly advised his fellow Americans to
"observe good faith and justice towards all nations; cultivate peace and harmony
with all and among all things, to steer clear of permanent alliances, with any portion of the foreign world." It was these very pages that he delivered to the Philadelphia printer David Claypoole for the public records, and that James Lenox
bought at auction in 1848, outbidding the Library of Congress.

As a brief aside to the rich story of Washington's career, the Library owns a
very rare copy of the fifth edition of *The Life of Washington the Great* by Mason
Locke Weems, a clergyman and the all-but-legendary author and peripatetic
bookseller. In this little book, Weems strayed from actual history to include his
invention of the hatchet-and-cherry-tree story and other "very curious anecdotes."
It is these that made his publication famous.

The Library owns two other patriotic documents of entirely different but singular
interest. One is the only surviving copy of the first American printing of "Yankee
Doodle" by Benjamin Carr in 1795. It is our earliest national song and is unique
among the patriotic songs of the world in that it makes fun of the very people
it celebrates. It was the first piece of American music to make a hit abroad, as
it did when it was sung in the streets of London on the eve of the Revolution—an
example, it would seem, of the pro-American propaganda that was then so active in
England.

8–13. ARCHIBALD
ROBERTSON. American
Scenes. *Pen-and-ink drawing
with wash, 1776–1780. Spencer
Collection*

    *An engineer in the British
army of occupation, Robertson
recorded the events of the American Revolution in a diary and
in a group of drawings that together evoke the era with a
striking sense of immediacy.*

The other document is the first sheet-music edition of "The Star-Spangled Banner," written by Francis Scott Key after the British bombardment of Fort McHenry in the War of 1812. These verses became immediately and lastingly popular. It was accepted everywhere in the young and robustly proud nation and in 1931 became the official national anthem.

The end of the War of 1812 saw the beginnings of the development of a national identity and the emergence of a distinctive American literature. The Library's collections contain many examples of the increasing attention Americans were beginning to pay to their own land and its native inhabitants, as well as to the flora and fauna of the wilderness they would soon conquer. In the first half of the nineteenth century men like John James Audubon, Robert Fulton, Washington Irving, and George Catlin pioneered in the creative and scientific efforts through which a colonial outpost became a thriving nation.

Less than a decade after the conclusion of the War of 1812 the French immigrant John James Audubon conceived and undertook work on his monumental *Birds of America*. When his drawings were first publicly exhibited abroad, one critic pointed out that these were more than ornithological studies on a brave new scale: they gave old Europe a fresh, poetic vision of America that fired the imagination. "Who would have expected such things from the woods of America?" exclaimed the fashionable Parisian artist François Gérard.

When the work was finally completed in 1838, it constituted one of the most audacious publishing enterprises in the history of that profession: four volumes, each weighing as much as a strong man could carry, comprised of 435 huge and meticulously prepared colorplates. The set sold for roughly a thousand dollars (equal to about $100,000 in today's currency). The "American woodsman"—as Aubudon was called—had provided the entire contents of the project and served as his own promotion agent, salesman, and publisher. With all the industry's elaborate apparatus for promotion and distribution, and its monetary resources, no publisher today would dream of launching such a venture. But Aubudon brought it off, gaining a small profit and lasting fame.

Americans have never lacked ample opportunities to see themselves as others have seen them. Throughout its history this land has been increasingly an object of Europeans' curiosity, especially in the years following the birth of the new nation. The Library has amassed a very substantial body of manuscripts and other documents recounting observations by those investigative visitors.

One unusual example is from the pen of Paul Petrovich Svinin, a young Russian who toured much of the eastern seaboard early in the nineteenth century and found much to admire and marvel at. Here, he reported, every muzhik was schooled side-by-side with bankers' sons, and there seemed to be labor-saving shortcuts to the production of almost everything. To him, Robert Fulton's new steamboats, which he viewed plying up and down the Hudson River, were things of wonder—as indeed they were to many sophisticated New Yorkers. Predictions were that the new invention would annihilate time and space and provide the essential cohesive force that would forever bind the widely scattered parts of the Union. It did, and it marked a turning point in history.

Fulton's inventive genius was many sided. He patented machines for sawing marble (which Svinin also commented on), spinning flax, and twisting hemp rope, and he instigated various improvements in canal construction and navigation, which were adapted in Europe as well as the United States. Before his success with the steamboat, he had worked on the development of submarine mines and torpedoes, which caught the attention of the governments of France, Britain, and later the United States.

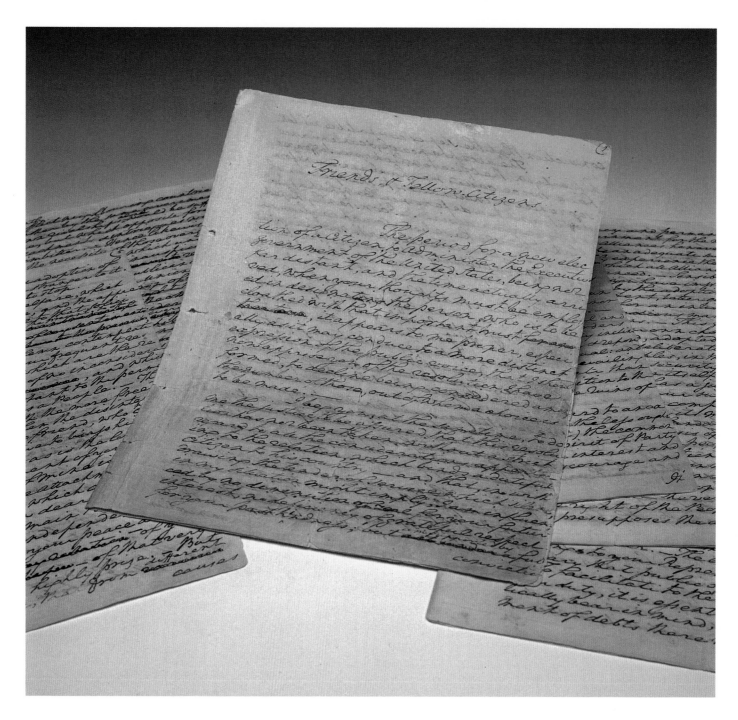

8–14. GEORGE
WASHINGTON. Farewell
Address. *Manuscript, 1796.*
*Rare Books and Manuscripts
Division*
   *The thirty-two page manu-
script of Washington's Farewell
Address was delivered to the
printer of* The American Daily
Advertiser *in Philadelphia on
September 19, 1796.*

THE LIFE

OF

WASHINGTON THE GREAT.

ENRICHED WITH A NUMBER OF VERY

CURIOUS ANECDOTES,

PERFECTLY IN CHARACTER, AND EQUALLY

HONORABLE TO HIMSELF, AND EXEMPLARY TO HIS

YOUNG COUNTRYMEN.

A life how useful to his country led!
How lov'd! while LIVING....how REVER'D! how DEAD!
Lisp! lisp! his name, ye children yet unborn!
And make your Father's virtues all your own!

THE FIFTH EDITION....GREATLY IMPROVED.

PRICE 50 CENTS.

BY M. L. WEEMS.
OF LODGE NO. 50....DUMFRIES.

AUGUSTA:

RE-PRINTED BY GEO: F. RANDOLPH.

....1806....

COPY RIGHT SECURED

LIFE OF WASHINGTON.

make so large a part of my happiness; but still I would give him up rather than see him a common liar.

"PA, (said George very seriously) do I ever tell lies?"

"No George, I thank God you do not, my son; and I rejoice in the hope you never will: at least, you shall never, from me have cause to be guilty of so shameful a thing. Many parents, indeed, even compel their children to this vile practice, by barbarously beating them for every little fault; hence, on the next offence the little terrified creature slips out a lie! just to escape the rod. But as to yourself, George, you know I have always told you, and now tell you again, that, whenever by accident you do any thing wrong, which must often be the case, as you are but a poor little boy yet, without experience or knowledge, never tell a falsehood to conceal it, but come bravely up, my son, like a little man, and tell me of it, and instead of beating you, George, I will but the more honor and love you for it my dear."

THIS you'll say was sowing good seed!—Yes, it was, and the crop, thank God, was as I believe it ever will be where a man acts the true parent, i. e. the Guardian Angel, by his child.

THE following anecdote is a case in point; it is too valuable to be lost, and too true to be doubted, for it was communicated to me by the same excellent lady to whom I was indebted for the last.

"WHEN George," said she, "was about six years old he was made the wealthy master of a hatchet! of which, like most little boys, he was immoderately fond, and was constantly going about chopping every thing that came in his way. One day, in the garden, where he often amused himself hacking his mother's pea-sticks, he unluckily tried the edge of his hatchet on the body of a beautiful young English cherry tree, which he barked so terribly that I dont believe the tree ever got the better of it. The next morning the old gentleman finding out what had befallen his tree, which by the by was a great favorite, came into the house, and with much warmth asked for the mischievous author, declaring at the same time that he would not have taken five guineas for his tree. No body could tell him any thing about it. Presently George and his hatchet made their appearance. George, said his father, do you know who killed that beautiful little cherry tree yonder in the garden? This was a tough question, and George staggered under it for a moment; but quickly recovered himself; and looking at his father, with the sweet face of youth brightened with the inexpressible charm of all-triumphant truth he bravely cried out, "I cant tell a lie, Pa, you know I cant tell a lie, I did cut it with my little hatchet." Run to my arms you dearest boy, cried his father in transports, run to my arms, glad am I George, that you ever killed my tree, for you have paid me for it a thousand fold. Such an act of heroism in my son, is more worth than a thousand trees though blossomed with silver and their fruits of purest gold.

B

8–15. MASON LOCKE WEEMS. The Life of Washington the Great. *Augusta, Maine, George Randolph, 1806. Rare Books and Manuscripts Division*

The many editions of "Parson" Weems's biography of Washington promulgated a number of popular myths about the nation's first president, among them the story of the cherry tree.

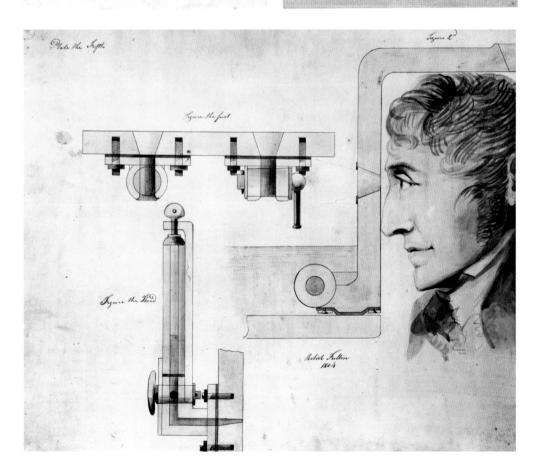

8–16. ROBERT FULTON. Drawing relating to his invention of a submarine. *Watercolor, 1804. Rare Books and Manuscripts Division*

In 1806, Fulton presented to the British government detailed plans for the development of an attack submarine. He had made twelve drawings to accompany those plans, seven of which are in the Library's collections.

Pl. 256.

8–17. JOHN JAMES AUDUBON. The Birds of America. *London, 1827–1838. Wallach Division of Art, Prints and Photographs*

The 435 hand-colored etchings (with engraving and aquatint) that comprise the "double elephant" folio edition of Audubon's greatest work are the major monument of American ornithological illustration.

Ivory-billed Woodpecker.

1 Male 2 & 3 Female.

Drawn from Nature by J.J. Audubon FRSFLS   Lith.d Printed & Col.d by J.T. Bowen Phil.

In pursuing these experiments, Fulton was motivated by his dual concern to assure peace on the high seas and to produce machines so devastating that they would make warfare unthinkable. His idealism was prescient; "deterrence" is a dream still very much with us. A number of manuscript letters and drawings elucidating these proposals are preserved in the Library. Fulton was also a competent professional artist, and his watercolors are of interest beyond the technical information they impart.

If Fulton's inventions show "Yankee ingenuity" at its best, the works of Washington Irving show another side of the nation's developing character. Writer, diplomat, and public figure, Irving was a cosmopolite, as much at home in the salons of Europe as in the boardroom of the Astor Library, whose first president he became. A New Yorker by origin, Irving helped to create some of the city's mythological history in his *History of New York . . . by Diedrich Knickerbocker.* He also explored the early history of the Americas in his *History of . . . Christopher Columbus.* He was a prime example of the man of letters — a species now almost entirely extinct.

8–18. JEAN LOUIS PREVOST. La nicotiane tabac. *Watercolor, ca. 1810. Arents Collections*
Before the discovery of the New World, tobacco was unknown to Europeans. As their settlement of North and South America developed, they turned this indigenous plant into a major element of their agriculture and commercial activities.

la Nicotiane Tabac.

Given his connections with one of the Library's parent institutions, it is fitting that a major collection of his manuscripts should be housed in its Rare Books and Manuscripts Division. It is called the Seligman-Hellman collection after its donors, Mrs. Isaac N. Seligman and Mr. George S. Hellman. Through its trove of original letters and literary manuscripts there emerges an image of a man at peace with himself and his era, a man with a sense of fun and of duty. Irving lived and wrote at a time when it was not necessary to be alienated from society to be an artist, and indeed, alienation would have seemed to him a sign of creative failure. For him the times were good, and he could find no reason not to enjoy them.

Times were somewhat less than good for the Native Americans of the western plains. The confidence and vitality that underlie the inventions of Robert Fulton or the writings of Washington Irving were soon to result in the pressure of expansion westward. With that expansion was to come the conquest of the natives and the end of their traditional way of life. Before that destruction was completed, a number of travelers had made records of these people that stand as monuments to a lost world.

Karl Bodmer was a Swiss artist who accompanied Prince Maximilian of Wied-Neuwied on a trip through the American West in 1832–1834. Like Le Moyne de Morgues or John White before him, his task was to provide a pictorial record of the new things the prince saw on his journey. His paintings of scenes of native life and of warriors in full regalia were reproduced in lithographs that offer us primary evidence of cultures now extinct.

George Catlin traveled through the West without the benefit of a prince's company. His travels were born of a passion for documenting the lives of "every tribe of Indians on the Continent of North America." In his *Souvenirs of the North American Indians as They Were in the Middle of the Nineteenth Century*, we find scenes

8–19. KARL BODMER.
Warrior with Dog Dance.
Lithograph, ca. 1840. Rare Books and Manuscripts Division
  Bodmer accompanied Prince Maximilian of Wied-Neuwied on his travels in the American West. His lithographs, made from drawings and paintings created on that tour, are among the most vivid documentation of the lives of the Plains Indians.

of native life and portraits of individuals drawn with the painstaking detail of
a modern ethnologist.

Before the final press westward and the destruction of its original inhabitants
could begin in earnest, however, the threat to the Union had first to be resolved.
The only resolution was found in war, the Civil War, the bloodiest conflict in history
to that date. No other war has been so minutely studied and restudied by buffs
and professional historians alike, domestic and foreign. The tragic record is exhaustively reported by material in the Library's collections, from both Confederate
and Union sources.

One very significant but lesser-known story to be found in those records is
contained in the papers of the United States Sanitary Commission that were given
to the Astor Library in 1878. The Commission was a private enterprise undertaken
early in the war to assist charitable organizations, the Union Army, and the Union
government to attend to the urgent needs of soldiers. In their efforts no detail
was overlooked, from attending to immediate, critical problems on the battlefield
to setting up, maintaining, and overseeing adequate hospitals and rest areas,
from studying camp conditions and delivering provisions to assuring humane conditions for prisoners of war. The work of the Commission signified a new concern
to ameliorate the miseries of war. It had a fruitful legacy in the subsequent charitable work of the Red Cross and the U.S.O.

After the assassination of Lincoln, the Commission published excerpts from
the firsthand report of this infinitely sad episode by Dr. Charles H. Leale who

8–20. GEORGE CATLIN.
Souvenirs of the North
American Indians. *London, the
artist, 1850. Rare Books and
Manuscripts Division*

George Catlin created suites
of drawings of American Indians using a template based
on his original sketches made
during his travels in the interior
of North America.

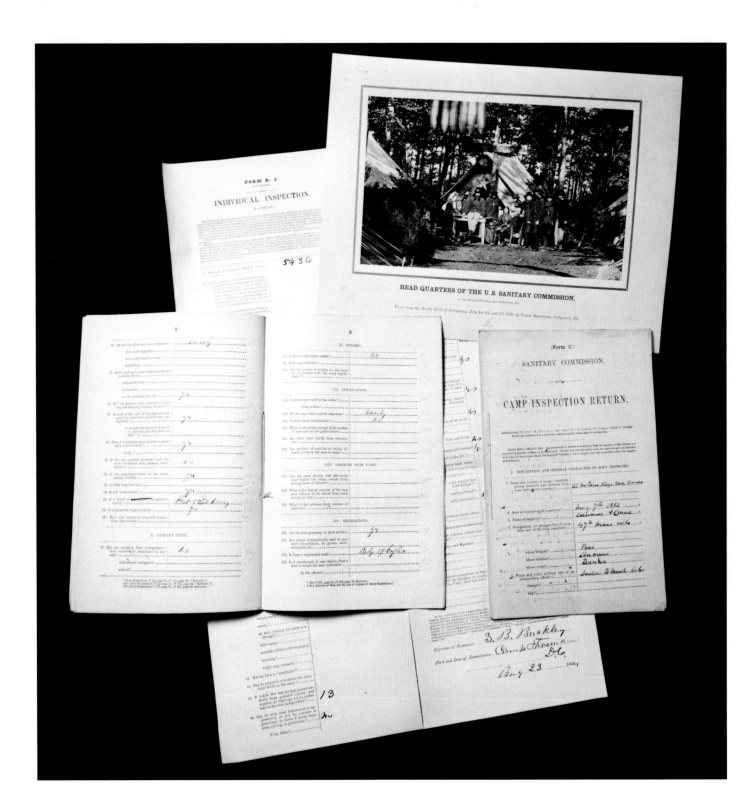

8–21. Headquarters of the U.S. Sanitary Commission, Gettysburg. *Photograph, ca. 1863. Rare Books and Manuscripts Division*

The U.S. Sanitary Commission, a volunteer group formed to provide medical aid to Union troops during the Civil War, grew out of the Women's Central Association of Relief. It was later to inspire the creation of the American Red Cross.

witnessed the shooting in Ford's Theatre and attended the president until his dying moment. The Library owns a manuscript copy of his full report. "When I reached the President he was in a state of general paralysis," the surgeon reported. "His eyes were closed and he was in a profoundly comatose condition while his breathing was intermittent & exceedingly stertorous. I placed my finger on his right radial pulse but could perceive no movement in the artery." At 7:20 the next morning Lincoln died.

With the end of the Civil War a new industrialized nation was born, destined for empire. Over the course of the next century the nation's population would soar thanks in part to the vast number of European immigrants "yearning to breathe free." Advances in science and technology would add fuel to this wild-

8–22. Menus, *19th and 20th century. General Research Division*

Miss Frank [sic] E. Buttolph was indefatigable in her pursuit of menus of every sort. She presented her collection to the Library in 1909 and continued to add to it until it totaled more than 20,000 items.

8–23. CHARLES H. LEALE. The Assassination and Death of Abraham Lincoln, President of the United States. *Manuscript, 1865. Rare Books and Manuscripts Division*

Leale was seated in the dress circle of Ford's Theater on the evening of April 14, 1865. When Lincoln was shot, he rushed to his side and supervised his removal to a bed in a nearby house where, the next morning, the president died.

The Assassination & Death of Abraham Lincoln, President of the United States.

By Charles. H. Leale. Assist. Surgeon. U.S. Vol. Executive Office "Armory Square" U.S. Genl Hospt. Washington, D.C.

Having been the first of our profession who arrived to the assistance of our late President & after having been requested by Mrs. Lincoln to do what I could for him I assumed the charge until the Surgeon Genl. & Dr. Stone his family physician arrived, which was about twenty-minutes after we had placed him in bed in the house of Mr. Peterson opposite the Theatre; & as I remained with him until his death I humbly submit the following brief account.

I arrived at Fords Theatre about 8¼ P.M. April 14th 1865, & procured a seat in the dress circle about 40 feet from the Presidents box; the play was then progressing & in a few minutes I saw the President; Mrs. Lincoln, Major Rathbone & Miss Harris enter, while proceeding to the box they were seen by the audience, who cheered, which was reciprocated by the President & Mrs. Lincoln by a smile & bow, the party was preceded by an attendant who after opening the door of the box & closing it after they had all entered took a seat near by for himself.

The theatre was well filled & the play of "Our American Cousin" progressed very pleasantly until about ½ past ten, when the report of a pistol was distinctly heard.

fire surge in the national economy, and vast cities would take shape.

In this explosion of creativity and productivity, America exhibited both an admirable energy and a disgraceful greed. She welcomed millions of immigrants, but on arrival conditions were harsh and assimilation rough. Factories grew, but hunger was everywhere, and the dazzling opulence of the Gilded Age could barely conceal the meaner realities that obtained on America's farms and in her mines and factories. And yet, in these times that were indeed both the "best and worst," a national identity was forged, and rich and poor alike became disputatiously but indisputably Americans. Though many raised their voices in dissent, Americans by and large entered World War I with an overwhelming show of patriotism, little dreaming that that conflict would banish forever their innocence and usher in a new and terrifying era of world power.

Contemplating these developments, one is at a loss to distill their origins and their effects into individual objects or particular items that stand out above the mass of documentary material dealing with the modern United States. There is no Columbus Letter to announce the dawn of a new day, no one diary that elucidates its complexities. For a sense of what our national experience has been in this century we must look to the archival collections of the Library. In them, neatly arranged in their dull gray acid-free boxes, is the raw material of our history. It requires the skill of the professional historian to make these dry bones live, and we can only hint at the eloquence they may convey in the hands of an accomplished narrator.

From among the archives in the Rare Books and Manuscripts Division, the personal papers of three modern American men suggest the crucial activities of the recent past, whose documentation the Library is preserving for the enlightenment of the future. These are the papers of Norman Thomas, Chester Carlson, and Robert Moses.

Norman Thomas was a leader of the Socialist Party of the United States and a perennial political candidate; he ran for president in six elections from 1928 to 1948. His papers document his participation in numerous organizations dedicated to socialism, civil liberties, racial equality, conscientious objection, universal disarmament, the labor movement, and the fight against Communism. Thomas's reaction to the pervasive corruption in politics, labor, and business in the United States in the early part of this century was individual activism in the context of the democratic process. There seems to be no area of protest and reform that escaped his notice or failed to capture his support, right down to the last years of his life when he was a leading objector to the war in Vietnam.

Chester Carlson, the inventor of the photocopying process that we usually call "Xeroxing," tried to solve some of the problems of the modern world through technical means. It is not generally known that he used the Science and Technology Research Center of The New York Public Library for the background reading that led him to his first successful experiment in electrophotography, which was conducted in Astoria, in the borough of Queens, in 1938. The patent he then filed for this process was met, as he reported, with "an enthusiastic lack of interest." It was not until 1950 that the first commercial application of xerography was achieved; but it is safe to say that since then our lives have been changed.

In the Carlson papers presented to the Library by his widow we find the twenty-three notebooks in which he recorded his various laboratory experiments from 1921 until 1961. Their appearance belies their significance, for in these plain little books lie the origins of much of the simplified communication we take so much for granted. The Xerox machine and its many imitators are omnipresent in our lives. We may sometimes think that they have always been there. Carlson's note-

8–24. Baseball Cards. *Late 19th and early 20th century. Rare Books and Manuscripts Division*

The most distinctively American sport is documented by a variety of materials in the Library's holdings, most evocatively by its collection of baseball cards.

books remind us that they are relatively recent and are here now only because of one individual's determination and genius.

The papers of Robert Moses are in some ways as monumental as some of the structures he erected in New York City. They take up 146 linear feet of shelving in the Library's manuscript-storage area. Through them the historian can exhaustively document the career of a man who changed the face of New York.

Moses was a public official, and from 1934 when he was appointed city parks commissioner, he was responsible for the construction of an enormous number of major projects in the state and city of New York, including bridges, tunnels, power plants, dams, public housing, and parks. Though never elected to public office, Moses was a master politician, skilled in the use of power, purposeful and dedicated to his vision of progress and the common good. Through this vast archive historians can document how the state and city of New York dealt with

urban problems in the years just preceding and following the Second World War. Retrospective assessments of Moses's achievements have sometimes been harsh, but libraries do not pass judgments on the historical figures whose records they preserve. It is left to the scholars and the public to deliver the verdicts.

If one were to attempt to characterize the rationale behind the Library's collecting of Americana, it might be done by comparing this institution to the combined efforts of the prosecution and defense in a court of law: the Library does not judge the past; instead, it provides all the pertinent evidence to the jury of researchers. Together, the vast and varied holdings of The New York Public Library form a panorama made from many discrete pictures of the nation's past — a panorama in which we see what we are, where we came from, and what we have done. It is not always a flattering image, nor is it invariably saddening. It is a mirror reflecting the achievements of a great and diverse people.

8–25. World War I Ephemera, 1914–1918. General Research Division

The Library made a great effort to document the first European war in which Americans were directly involved. To this end it collected not only books and documents about the conflict but also pamphlets, scrapbooks, and periodicals, all of which form one of the strongest collections anywhere on the subject.

CHAPTER NINE

BLACK HISTORY AND CULTURE

When Arthur Alfonso Schomburg was a young man, he asked a teacher for information about the history of black people. He was told that there was none worth recording. This was the traditional response in the late nineteenth century and would remain so until black activists, researchers, and collectors, of whom Schomburg was to become one of the most important, demon-strated its patent untruth. Increased awareness of and respect for the history of blacks is not merely a matter of academic interest, it also is an important aspect of the black struggle to achieve the rights and dignity due all people in a democratic society. The story of the development of the Schomburg Center—a unit of The New York Public Library's Research Libraries—is in some measure also the story of the awakening of black consciousness and of the struggle for liberation in the United States, the Caribbean, and Africa.

Let us begin with the story of the man: Arthur (baptized "Arturo") Alfonso Schomburg was born in Cangrejos, Puerto Rico, on January 24, 1874. His mother, Mary Joseph, was a black woman from St. Croix in the Virgin Islands; his father, Carlos Féderico Schomburg, was a Puerto Rican of German and Hispanic parentage.

Arthur Schomburg was educated in Puerto Rican schools and, perhaps more importantly in terms of his future activities, through his contacts with the *tabaqueros*, the cigar makers of San Juan who were among the most militant supporters of Puerto Rican independence. He continued to work for this cause when he came to New York in 1891, taking part in the organization of the political club Las Dos Antillas (The Two Antilles) in 1892. Out of this interest in the independence of his birthplace were to grow his consuming passions: the liberation of black people and the vehicle for that liberation, self-knowledge and self-respect based on the historical and cultural achievements of blacks wherever they dwelt.

Being without independent means, Schomburg found employment at various jobs in New York, ultimately becoming, in 1906, an employee of the Bankers Trust Company on Wall Street, from which he was to retire in 1929. In addition to holding down a full-time job, he continued his political and cultural organizational activities and developed his collections of books, manuscripts, and art-

work. He was an active Mason. In 1911, he helped to found the Negro Society
for Historical Research. He was elected president of the American Negro Academy
in 1920. He counted among his colleagues and friends leading scholars and literary
figures such as W. E. B. Du Bois and Countee Cullen. And, by 1926, he had
gathered together one of the most important collections ever assembled to be devoted to the black experience. It consisted of five thousand books, three thousand
manuscripts, two thousand prints and drawings, and several thousand pamphlets.

In 1926, the Carnegie Corporation, at the urging of the Urban League, provided
a grant to The New York Public Library to purchase the collection from Schomburg,
with the understanding that it would be housed in the 135th Street Branch as
a reference collection. In the early 1920s, the 135th Street Branch had become
a cultural center for the growing black population of Harlem, and with the help
of a local citizens' committee, the branch developed a reference collection of materials related to black literature, art, and music. Schomburg had been among
those members of the community who had encouraged the efforts of Ernestine

9–1. ALBERT SMITH.
Portrait of Arthur A.
Schomburg. *Etching, 1928.*
Schomburg Center
   Albert Alexander Smith was
a printmaker and cabaret musi-
cian. Two years before he made
this portrait, he had accom-
panied Schomburg on a re-
search and collecting trip
through France.

9–2. The Schomburg Center
Reading Room, ca. 1932

Rose, the branch librarian, in forming this collection. The community's efforts
led, in 1925, to the formation of the Division of Negro History, Literature, and
Prints in the 135th Street Branch, and it was thus appropriate that Schomburg's
own collection should be housed there.

From these beginnings, the collection has grown to contain some 3,500,000
items. In 1972 it became a major component of The Research Libraries, with
whose profile of collecting it was seen to have more in common than with The
Branch Libraries. Though a public collection for more than sixty years, the collection has remained true to the purposes that fired Schomburg's enthusiasm. It
does not merely collect and house materials in a passive way, it is also a focus
for community activities, education, and cultural life. The research carried on
in its reading rooms is of more than academic interest; it touches on contemporary
issues of great importance to our society. A list of recently published books that
contain acknowledgments to the Schomburg Center for the use of its collections include Gail Lumet Buckley's *The Hornes: An American Family*, David J. Garrow's
*Bearing the Cross: Martin Luther King, Jr. and the Southern Christian Leadership
Conference*, and Albert Murray's *Good Morning Blues: The Autobiography of Count
Basie*.

Not only have its users published works based on the Center's resources, but since its inception, the staff of Schomburg has been active in writing about black issues in particular. A bibliography of the publications of the staff runs to one thousand entries and covers subjects as diverse as black dance, black children's literature, and black photographers. The variety and scope of these publications suggest the breadth of Schomburg's holdings, which have grown to become the world's largest collection of materials related to the black experience. Schomburg himself remained actively associated with the collection after its purchase by the Library, serving as its curator from 1932 until his death in 1938.

Schomburg's particular interest in the achievements of black people in the Hispanic world is reflected in the earliest book by a black author in the Center's collections, Juan Latino's *Ad Catholicum* published in Granada in 1573. Latino was a full-blooded African. In 1528, at the age of twelve, he was sold (along with his mother) to General Fernando Gonzalo of Cordova, Spain, who appointed him a companion to his grandson. The two youths attended the University of Granada where they received an ecclesiastical education. Latino earned a Master of Arts degree in 1557 and went on to become a lecturer in Latin and Greek and to occupy the chair of poetry at the university during the reign of Philip II. He was acknowledged as Spain's leading Latinist, a reputation amply justified by *Ad Catholicum*, the Latin epic poem that he composed in praise of Don Juan of Austria, the illegitimate son of Charles V and the victor of the Battle of Lepanto.

Schomburg's interest in contemporary political movements in the Caribbean was complemented by his enthusiasm for documents that placed those activities in an historical perspective. To this end, he began the collections of Haitian materials recording the revolution that established the first independent black

9–3. Ernest Kaiser shown compiling his index of periodicals housed at the Schomburg Center

This index of 200,000 entries documents references to blacks in magazines and newspapers.

9–4. Juan Latino. Ad
Catholicum. . . . *Granada,
Hugo de Mena, 1573. Schomburg Center*
  *Considered one of the rarest
books in the world,* Ad Catholicum *is the earliest imprint by a
black author owned by the
Schomburg Center.*

9–5. A military order by
Toussaint Louverture issued
while he was chief of the French
Army in Haiti; a hostile
biography of Toussaint by Louis
Dubroca, published in Paris in
1802; shackles from the period.
Schomburg Center

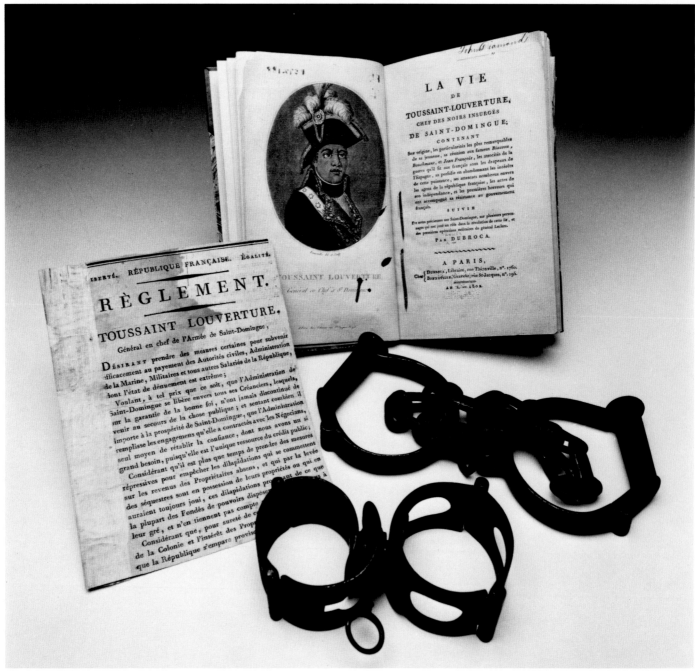

nation in the Western Hemisphere. This has grown to become the foremost archive devoted to Haitian history in the country.

The Haitian revolutionary materials are important for the light they throw on the attempts of enslaved blacks to free themselves and to acquire political self-determination. The leader of this revolt was Pierre Dominique Toussaint, known as Toussaint Louverture, who was born a slave in Santo Domingo in 1743. He was a descendant of Gaon Guinou, king of the Arada nation in central Africa. Under his leadership the British and Spanish armies were driven from Santo Domingo and an alliance formed with republican France. This alliance turned sour as Napoleon I attempted to reestablish the system of slavery that Toussaint, as master of the island, had abolished. The French forces defeated him, and he died in a French prison. Among the Center's materials relating to Toussaint is a manuscript letter from the Haitian leader to the French Minister of Marine and Colonies and dated July 13, 1801. In this letter he speaks of the French as a people "whose principles of freedom coincide with our system of government."

Schomburg's collection of works by and about North American blacks included the works of Jupiter Hammon, the first black poet in America, as well as early editions of the work of Phillis Wheatley, the slave of a Boston tailor who educated her and encouraged her creative efforts. Lady Huntington, who once entertained Wheatley, wondered that a born "savage" "could have by the grace of God and the good will of her white master learned to turn an ode as well as any of the school of Alexander Pope." Wheatley herself rejoiced that "young in life by seeming cruel fate [she] was snatched from Africa's fancy'd happy state" and taken to a land where, although under bondage, her talents could develop and win her recognition in a predominantly white world.

When the originality of Wheatley's poetry was questioned, Thomas Jefferson vouched for her credibility. Jefferson was also quick to appreciate the quite different genius of Benjamin Banneker, America's first and only black almanac

9–6. PHILLIS WHEATLEY. Poems on Various Subjects, Religious and Moral. *London, A. Bell, 1773. Schomburg Center*

Phillis Wheatley's first publication, On the Death of the Reverend George Whitefield, *was printed in 1770; she also wrote a poem in praise of George Washington. Her* Poems *is the first book by an American black.*

9–7. CHARLES HENRI
JOSEPH CORDIER. Bust of
an African Man *and* Bust of an
African Woman. *Both: bronze,
1852. Schomburg Center*
*These pieces were among the
first in the Schomburg Art and
Artifacts Collection. They were
probably purchased by Schomburg
himself in Paris in 1926.*

maker, whose works were collected by Schomburg. Indeed, many highly distinguished American contemporaries were as impressed as Jefferson when Banneker's first efforts were published in 1792. David Rittenhouse, the new republic's most eminent astronomer and president of the prestigious American Philosophical Society, wrote a testimonial for this "very extraordinary performance." That a virtually self-taught "celestial mechanic" of African descent could produce astronomical calculations that were beyond any reasonable criticism was to Rittenhouse an encouraging sign. "Every instance of genius amongst the Negroes," he wrote, "is worthy of attention, because their oppressors seem to lay great stress on their supposed inferior mental abilities." Banneker was skilled in clock making and related crafts. By selling property he had acquired, he negotiated a term annuity

9–8. Daguerreotypes of a master and his slave *and* A reward notice for a runaway slave. *Schomburg Center*

The history of a people can be found not only in the written record but also in the artifacts, some poignant, some harrowing, in which that history is encapsulated. Here are pictured rare daguerreotype portraits of a master and his slave and a "wanted" poster for a runaway slave, a reminder of the fundamental brutality of America's "peculiar institution."

9–9. Glass slides illustrating *Uncle Tom's Cabin. Schomburg Center*

Harriet Beecher Stowe's novel Uncle Tom's Cabin *helped fuel Abolitionist sentiment at home and the antislavery movement abroad. The novel remained, even after the Civil War, an important and much-read book whose story was told in every medium. It is pictured here in a "magic lantern" show popular in the decades before the invention of the moving picture.*

9–10. PIETRO CALVI. Ira Aldridge as Othello. *Marble and bronze bust, 1860s. Schomburg Center*

Although the exact date for this sculpture is not known, legend maintains that it was inspired by Calvi's witnessing Aldridge's famous portrayal of Shakespeare's Moor during Aldridge's triumphal tour of Europe in the 1860s. The bust was apparently shown at the Royal Academy Exhibition in London in 1873. From then until 1936 its whereabouts remain uncertain. It came to the Schomburg Center in 1936 through the efforts of Arthur Spingarn and Schomburg, who sought to secure subscription funds for its acquisition. Since then it has been one of the most popular works in the collection and is an unofficial symbol of the Center.

but outlived it by eight years; after his death it was remarked that this was the only miscalculation he ever made.

The scope of Schomburg's collecting was not limited to books and manuscripts. His holdings ranged from bills of sale for the purchase of slaves and posters for the capture of runaways to photographs. Among the ephemera he acquired was the scrapbook of Ira Aldridge, the nineteenth-century black Shakespearean actor who won fame in Europe for his performances. In 1936 the Library acquired the superb marble-and-bronze bust of Aldridge in the role of Othello by the Italian sculptor Pietro Calvi, a likeness that became one of the most popular works in the collection and an unofficial symbol of the Schomburg Center.

Like other great collectors of the nineteenth and twentieth centuries, Schomburg conceived of his library as a collection of both books and artworks. To his personal collection of some two thousand prints were added, over the years, works of art by black American artists such as Romare Bearden and Jacob Lawrence. Works of art were also added from Africa, including several hundred artifacts and sculptures. One collection came to the Center thanks to the efforts of Alain Locke. These were supplemented by Florence Bruce's collection of Nigerian art and, in the early 1940s, by Eric de Kolb's collection of African arms and armor. Through these and later acquisitions, such as the Oxmantown collection of Yoruba art, the Center has formed important collections of art created by black people throughout the world. They form a crucial part in documenting the black experience, for they relate in a more immediate fashion than can a book or manuscript the variety of that experience. They remind us that the history of blacks is not just the history of oppression and exploitation, it is also the story of accomplishments in the arts that have been made in spite of the onslaughts against them. These works of art are a stirring reminder to all peoples of the strength of the human spirit in the face of adversity. They also serve to recall the fact that the black experience is not only an American experience nor do the history and achievements of black people have meaning only when they represent a presence in American or European history. Juan Latino and Phillis Wheatley were indeed remarkable people, but their works and the works of other blacks active in Europe and the Americas do not provide a complete picture of the black experience.

As the Center's collections of art objects has grown over the years, the space available to display them properly has proven inadequate. To remedy this, ground was broken, on September 20, 1987, for a major addition to the Center's facility. The Center's original home, the old 135th Street Branch (which was closed in 1980 when a new building was opened), will be restored, and with adjacent structures it will provide the proper environment in which to view much of the Center's holdings.

This addition will also provide more space for two collections that have grown tremendously in the last two decades: photographs and film and recordings. The photograph collections now comprise approximately two hundred thousand items, up from the few hundred that were in Schomburg's own collection. The importance of these images both as artworks and documentation cannot be overstated. They offer us an impression of black life and of black individuals in the United States and abroad that not only allows us to put faces to well-known names, but also gives us a glimpse of ordinary people, whose lives may not be otherwise documented. A studio portrait of a black family from the 1920s not only shows us a group of people, it also suggests their self-image, their hopes, and their ambitions.

The earliest photograph in the collection is an 1842 daguerreotype of an unidentified black man. There are stereographs and cartes de visite depicting scenes

9–11. JACOB LAWRENCE. From *The Legend of John Brown* series. *Silkscreen after gouache originals, series of 22 prints, 1977. Schomburg Center*

Jacob Lawrence was born in 1917 in Atlantic City, New Jersey. He was a student of Charles Alston at the Harlem Art Center from 1937 to 1939 and at the American Artists School. He was employed by the WPA from 1938 to 1940 and had his first one-man exhibit at the Downtown Gallery in New York in 1941. Throughout his career, he has worked primarily in long print series dealing with black history and social issues.

from the slave era through the Civil War. For the twentieth century, holdings include the archives of important black photographers such as Austin Hausen and Morgan and Marvin Smith.

The film and recordings (or audiovisual) collections at the Center encompass musical documentation, oral-history recordings, motion pictures, and videotapes. Recordings of early radio broadcasts date from the late 1920s; there are also early recordings of statements by George Washington Carver, Booker T. Washington, and Marcus Garvey. Recorded music holdings include classics by artists such as Marian Anderson, Roland Hayes, Leontyne Price, Ulysses Kay, and William Grant Still, and blues by Mamie Smith, Alberta Hunter, and Bessie Smith. Jazz, gospel, reggae, and other contemporary forms are also represented. In addition to music by black Americans, materials document the music of Africa, the Caribbean, and other areas of the world where there are people of African descent.

Among the film and video holdings are early film classics such as *Scar of Shame* and *The Emperor Jones*, along with documentaries like *The Streets of Greenwood*, which portrays the Student Non-Violent Coordinating Committee (SNCC) in 1962.

9–12. Gadla Estifanos e Abakerazun [The Gospels of Stephen and Abakerazun]. *Tigre, Ethiopia, 15th century, in Ge'ez (Ethiopic). Manuscript on vellum, illuminated at the monastery of Gundé Gundié. Spencer Collection*

Important items relating to the black experience both in America and in Africa are housed not only at the Schomburg Center but throughout the Library. Here, from the Spencer Collection, is a fifteenth-century illuminated manuscript from Ethiopia—a beautiful example of Ge'ez, the literary and ecclesiastical language whose calligraphy is derived from South Semitic script.

9–13. Masks and figures from Nigeria.

The art of the Yoruba people of southwestern Nigeria is represented by a number of works in the Schomburg Center's collections. Among them are these Gelede cap masks and the pair of twin figures (ibeji) with their cowrie-shell coat.

9–14. Weapons from the Eric de Kolb Collection of African Arms. *Schomburg Center*

This collection was offered to the Schomburg Center for public display, probably in 1944, by Eric de Kolb. It consists of sixty-one objects of weaponry of all types. Among the African ethnic groups represented are the Kuba, Songye, Fang, Mangbetu, and Zande, as well as the Zulu and Matabele of South Africa and the Ashanti of Ghana.

9–15. The 135th Street Branch Library opened in May, 1925 to house the Division of Negro Literature, History and Prints

9–16. Woman and Small Boy. *Hand-colored ambrotype, ca. 1850s. Schomburg Center*
   Through the enormous collection of photographs at the Schomburg Center, the day-to-day experience of blacks in America is made immediate and visible.

9–17. Sheet music and African stringed instrument. *Schomburg Center*

The black contribution to American and, indeed, world music has been widely studied, and the tremendous impact of that contribution is nowhere more evident than at the Schomburg Center, where documents and artifacts relating to black artists and entertainers are collected and preserved. Juxtaposed with selections from the Center's collection of sheet music is a stringed instrument from Zaire, part of the Blondian Theatre Arts Collection.

There is early footage of Noble Sissle, Lena Horne, Kid Ory, Paul Robeson, Count Basie, Ethel Waters, Thelonious Monk, and Billie Holiday, and more recent footage documenting a diverse group of artists, performers, political figures, and civil-rights activists. To supplement its holdings, the Center has established an Oral History/Video Documentation Project that videotapes in-house interviews.

The Schomburg Center will draw upon resources from its special collections as well as outside sources for exhibitions in its expanded facilities. Live performances in the new auditorium will add another dimension to the Center's black cultural offerings. Along with the renovated adjacent Countee Cullen Branch Library, the Schomburg Center for Research in Black Culture, with its expansion, will form an unprecedented learning and activities complex. With its contemporary technology and facilities geared to accommodate future growth, the Schomburg

Center will be fully equipped to carry on Schomburg's proud legacy, for here, indeed, "is the evidence."

The evidence supplied by the Center's collections of recorded music helps us to recall that the field of the arts was one into which blacks in this country had an early entrée. In music, literature, and painting, American blacks have produced a tremendous body of important work, which the Center has in the past supported and which it continues to document and encourage.

The most conspicuous expression of black culture in America over the last century has been jazz. It has been called "America's classical music" and this country's "outstanding contribution to the art of music." Certainly it has influenced just about all twentieth-century music throughout the world. It developed from the work songs of slaves, from the spirituals sung in black churches, and from the chants of itinerant blacks along the Mississippi, but its roots may go much farther back, to the rhythms of music as it was made in Africa long before its inhabitants were forcibly transported to these shores.

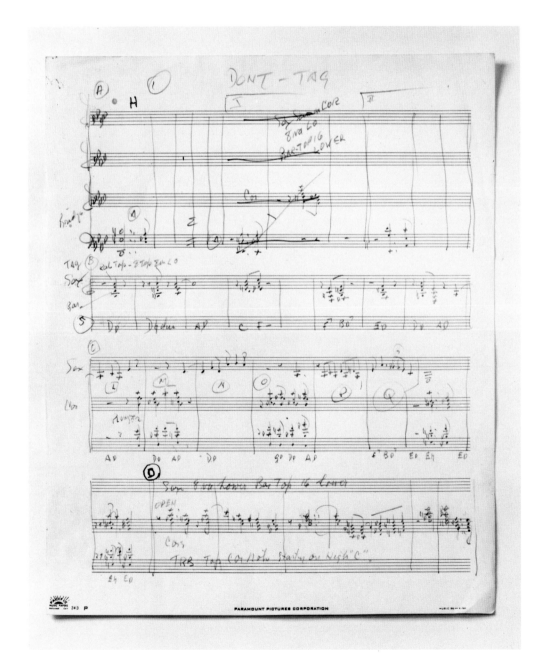

9–18. EDWARD KENNEDY [DUKE] ELLINGTON. Sacred Music. *Autograph score, 1968. Performing Arts Research Center, Music Division*

Presented by Duke Ellington—one of the most prolific and influential American composers of the twentieth century—this score is one of many unique documents by which the development of American music can be traced.

While the roots of jazz are still being explored and debated, what is certain is that by the time it took the form by which we know it today—at around the turn of the century, and probably first in New Orleans and along the lower Mississippi—it had become a distinctly American creation. As it traveled up the Mississippi and into the North, it captured the imagination of blacks and whites alike and soon was being heard and played by both populations, an early and profound instance of the blurring of the color bar in America. For years jazz was played as black and white Americans lived, separately and differently, but by the 1930s the overwhelming importance of the continuing black contribution to jazz could no longer be ignored, and when the white musician Benny Goodman conducted a racially mixed group in a jazz concert in Carnegie Hall on January 16, 1938, it marked a turning point in the history of blacks and whites together in America.

The New York Public Library is the repository of many important archives in the history of jazz, and in at least one important instance it has used those archives to make its own contribution to our understanding and enjoyment of this musical form. Recently, the Library published *The Complete Works of Scott Joplin*, a second, enlarged edition of the compositions of that great early master of ragtime music. The press called these volumes a "landmark in American musical history." What must be considered another milestone in American music—from the same roots, though of a distinctly different character—is *Sacred Music* by Edward Kennedy "Duke" Ellington, another celebrated jazz composer. The score of this solemn music was produced by invitation of the Protestant Episcopal Bishop of New York, and the piece itself was first performed in 1968 at the Cathedral Church of St. John the Divine in New York. The manuscript was presented to the Library by the composer.

Jazz music covers a broad and colorful spectrum. To the uninitiated, the varieties of seemingly ever-changing hues can be bewildering. However it is called—ragtime, Dixieland, blues, swing, bop, cool, boogie-woogie, punk—it can all be found in the Center's collections.

The very word "jazz" has worked its way into all corners of our vocabulary, in contexts that are far from its original usage—matters of dress, behavior, or other forms of art—to suggest the spirited innovation and compelling rhythms that

9–19. Manuscript page and reviews of Richard Wright's Native Son. *Schomburg Center*

For modern American literature generally, and certainly for relating the black experience in America, Richard Wright's Native Son *stands as a seminal work. The Schomburg Center has Wright's original manuscript, as well as extensive documents relating to the novel's publication and reception.*

9–20. CARL VAN VECHTEN. Portrait of Richard Wright. *Photograph. n.d. Schomburg Center*

animate the music itself. If we were to select just one example to indicate how that spirit has stimulated the other arts, it might very well be the book *Jazz* created in 1947 by Henri Matisse. In this work the vibrance and seemingly random qualities of the music are translated into forms that almost dance across the printed page.

A poignant archive in the Center's music collections is that of the late composer Philippa Schuyler. She was a prodigy who began composing and performing her own piano works at the age of four. She became one of the leading musicians of her day, performing throughout Europe as well as in the United States. Her career, still full of increasing promise, was tragically cut short when, in 1967, she died in a helicopter crash in Vietnam while on a concert tour for the U.S.O.

Literature written by American blacks had won some appreciative notice as early as the eighteenth century. In the next century, the short stories of Charles W. Chesnutt of Ohio were being printed in the pages of the august *Atlantic Monthly*. His novels continued to be published into the present century. He was a better novelist than many who followed him. Paul Laurence Dunbar (also from Ohio), Chesnutt's contemporary, sought the attention of William Dean Howells, then editor in chief of the *Atlantic,* who admired the "refined and delicate art" of Dunbar's work in which he voiced his conviction that there was an essential unity among human beings that crossed all color lines.

Since that time, such writers as Langston Hughes, W.E.B. Du Bois, Countee Cullen, James Weldon Johnson, Richard Wright, James Baldwin, Ralph Ellison, Toni Morrison, and Gwendolyn Brooks, to list but a few of many more examples that could be cited, have written novels and other works that are read and admired by all Americans. When Wright's *Native Son* was published in 1940, he was widely thought of as the leading black writer of the time. (The manuscript is preserved at the Schomburg Center.) Following the appearance of his first novel, *Go Tell It on the Mountain,* in 1953, Baldwin was hailed as a true spokesman of his people, and his portrait appeared on the cover of *Time* magazine. Ellison's *The Invisible Man,* published in 1952, won a National Book Award and thirteen years later was nominated by a large and impressive body of critics and authors as the one work of American fiction of all those issued since 1945 that was most likely to endure. Ellison pointed out that the "image of the American" must be an amalgam of black and white. Like other forms of black expression, black literature is, in the end, an inseparable element of American society.

The Center's involvement with the visual arts dates back over sixty years to the days when community members organized annual art exhibitions in the 135th Street Branch Library. Starting in 1921, committees that included cultural leaders such as W.E.B. Du Bois, James Weldon Johnson, and Arthur Schomburg were involved in planning these shows.

The groundwork for a permanent collection of works of art was laid by Schomburg when he traveled to Europe in 1926 to hunt for books and manuscripts to add to the collections that the Carnegie Corporation had helped the Library to purchase. On this trip he purchased works that included bronze busts of an African man and woman by the nineteenth-century French sculptor Charles Cordier. During the late 1920s, and while he served as curator of the collection, he was successful in securing additional works because of his personal role as a long-standing patron of black artists. Works were acquired from, among others, Augusta Savage, William Edouard Scott, William Ernest Braxton, Albert Alexander Smith, and Lois Mailou Jones. Caribbean black artists were also included in the collection, among them Pastor Argudin y Pedroso and Teodoro Ramos Blanco.

During the Great Depression the Works Progress Administration (WPA) commissioned works from black artists through the Harlem Art Center. These were given to the Schomburg Center in the early 1940s after the WPA was abolished. The artists represented in this collection included Palmer Hayden, Earle Richardson, Selma Burke, and Malvin Gray Johnson. Over the last forty years, important works by prominent black artists have been added to the Center's holdings. These acquisitions include works by Norman Lewis, Jacob Lawrence, Romare Bearden, Vivian Browne, Ed Clark, Emma Amos, and Herbert Gentry.

The collection of works of art serves several purposes. On the one hand, the works themselves are of aesthetic importance and impact. A collage by Romare Bearden, for example, has a strong visual presence, but beyond that, however, it is a statement about black achievement, which adds to the work's significance. The subject matter of a work may provide a further level of meaning. Elizabeth Catlett's sculpture entitled "Political Prisoner" (1971) reminds us that the history of black political and social movements occupies an important place in the collections.

As always, Schomburg led the way through his personal involvement in organizations like the Masons. Through his contacts with his fellow Mason Harry A. Williamson, he was able to obtain the latter's collection devoted to the black Prince Hall lodges as a gift. Williamson's collection represented over thirty years of research and included such records as the proceedings of fifty-nine Grand Lodges of Prince Hall dating back to 1860, the proceedings of Masonic conferences, lodge constitutions, and periodicals. Until his death in 1965, Williamson continued to add to his collection, keeping it current and developing it into the most important archive in the country for the study of this black organization. As with so many of the Library's holdings, the archives relating to the black Masonic movement offers researchers a glimpse into a microcosm of the past, which in turn provides a way of understanding how a people lived from day to day, organizing itself and coping with the need to participate in the often hostile culture in which it lived.

The Prince Hall lodges were examples of what might be called "parallel" organizations, formed by blacks excluded from participation in white fraternal societies. While these groups played an important role in the development of black pride and

9–21. A portion of the collection of buttons relating to black political activity in the United States. Schomburg Center

As in every department of the Library, acquiring "ephemera" is as important as discovering the rare and unique. In this collection of political buttons, an important part of the history of black activism can be traced.

political power, they were essentially reflections of the majority's attitudes and modes of behavior. A rather different sort of group was the Universal Negro Improvement Association (UNIA) founded by Marcus Garvey in Jamaica in 1914. The Center holds an important archive of material relating to this group's Central Division, which was headquartered in Harlem. The UNIA grew to become the most powerful organization of black people in the world, with over a million card-carrying members and an estimated two to three times that number of active sympathizers. Garvey was the leader of this, the first and largest organized mass movement of black people in the twentieth century.

Garvey emigrated from Jamaica to New York in 1916. After spending a year traveling and lecturing in several states, he settled in Harlem in 1917. There he organized a branch of the UNIA and launched what would become a multi-faceted economic, political, and cultural organization with an international scope. In January 1918, he began publishing the *Negro World,* a newspaper that quickly became one of the leading black weeklies and a highly effective vehicle for the advancement of his black-nationalist ideas.

The response to Garvey's vivid exhortations for racial pride and solidarity was electric: by 1920 he had many thousands of followers, and there were scores of UNIA divisions chartered throughout the United States and abroad. Liberty Hall, a large auditorium on West 138th Street in Harlem, which the UNIA purchased in 1919, almost overnight became the headquarters of a genuine mass movement of international scope.

9–22. Arthur Schomburg *[far right]* with fellow Prince Hall Masons, *1920. Schomburg Center*

The Schomburg Center's extensive documentation of the black Masonic movement records an important phenomenon in the history of blacks in America.

9–23. Marcus Garvey at Liberty Hall in Harlem, presiding over a meeting of the Universal Negro Improvement Association (UNIA) in 1920. *Schomburg Center*

While the black Masonic movement was essentially an attempt by blacks to "reflect" in their own organizations the white society from which they were excluded, the UNIA movement, started by Marcus Garvey in 1914, asserted black nationalist ideals. It grew to be the largest organized mass movement of black people in this century. The Schomburg Center has extensive documentation of this vitally important organization.

In August 1920, in New York, Garvey presided over the first international convention of the flourishing UNIA, a spectacular affair that more than lived up to the *Negro World*'s promise that it would be the largest gathering of its kind in the history of the race. Several thousand delegates came from all forty-eight states and more than a score of foreign countries on three continents. An exhilarating sense of racial pride accompanied the fervent black nationalism that pervaded every aspect of the month-long convention: the working sessions of the delegates and the mass meetings and parades of the UNIA divisions and auxiliaries, such as the paramilitary African Legion and the Black Cross Nurses. The delegates adopted a sweeping Declaration of Rights of the Negro Peoples of the World and also called for the liberation of Africa. In addition, the delegates named Garvey the Provisional President of the Republic of Africa—a kind of government in exile. When the convention adjourned, it was clear that Marcus Garvey, as no other black leader before him, had captured the attention of masses of blacks throughout the United States and the world, inspiring them to take pride in their color, their past, and their future. "Garveyism," a heady mixture of racial pride and black nationalism, became a potent force in race relations.

While Garvey's activities helped give blacks a sense of political and economic importance, efforts were being made by anthropologists and sociologists to explore the attributes and structures of black cultures. Through the combination of agitation on the part of blacks here and abroad, and the growth of awareness on the part of sympathetic whites of the profound and remediable injustices suffered by blacks, there grew the modern civil-rights movement in the United States and the movements for self-determination and against colonialism in Africa and the Caribbean.

The work and achievements of two of the most important twentieth-century social scientists active in the field of black studies can be examined in depth in the Center's Myrdal and Herskovits archives. In 1944, Gunnar Myrdal, a Swedish sociologist, wrote a work on the status of black Americans, *An American Dilemma*, which had a tremendous impact on the consciousness of whites both here and abroad. In this carefully researched and coolly written academic work, he laid bare, as perhaps only a non-American might, the systematic and pervasive racism of American society. The Center has eighty-one manuscript volumes of field notes and memoranda Myrdal accumulated for his work, a mine of information about the lives and experiences of ordinary black Americans in the twentieth century.

Melville J. Herskovits was an anthropologist who did ground-breaking work in the study of black cultures in North and South America. In 1948, he founded the first program of African studies in the United States at Northwestern University. He brought the insights and techniques of contemporary anthropology into play in order to answer, in a different way, the same question that Schomburg answered with his collection: Is there a past of any note for American blacks? Like Schomburg, Herskovits accumulated the evidence for an affirmative answer. It is thus fitting that the Center should now house his archive, which deals with subjects as diverse as Haitian Creole proverbs, traditional African architecture, and the black people of Brazil.

Important as these academic activities were in demolishing any of the "scientific" pretensions racists might have to support their opinions, more than study was needed to break the back of, if not racist opinion, at least racist practices in the United States. This was achieved through the works of black individuals whose actions helped spark the American civil-rights movement of the 1950s and 1960s, whose symbolic culmination was the 1963 March on Washington for Jobs and Freedom at which Martin Luther King, Jr. stirred the nation with his speech with its unforgettable refrain, "I have a dream." The records of the organizing committee of this march are housed in the Schomburg Center, and although they are not, as artifacts, prepossessing, they are, it seems to us, a great treasure. For what reverberates from these records is a spirit and energy directed toward the common good that few historical records can match. They suggest that Dr. King's dream had its source in the dream of Schomburg and others like him. They also remind us that, some twenty-five years later, the dream has yet to become a reality. What blacks have said and done has had some impact on American society, but much remains to be changed for the better. The Schomburg Center has had a role to play in providing this impact. It has, as we have suggested, many things to say about the black experience and black achievement. But a great deal more can and needs to be said until the dream of Dr. King and many others can be realized. Through its collections, the Schomburg Center will continue to say what needs to be said.

WAR KNOWS NO
COLOR LINE

9–24. ELMER SIMS
CAMPBELL. War Knows No
Color Line. *Oil on canvas, n.d.
Schomburg Center*
*Elmer Sims Campbell is
widely known for his cartoons
in* The New Yorker *and Es-
quire. He received his formal
art training at the School of the
Art Institute of Chicago.*

CHAPTER TEN

THE PERFORMING ARTS

Tucked away between the Metropolitan Opera House and the Vivian Beaumont Theater at the Lincoln Center for the Performing Arts there is a rather modest building with the name of The New York Public Library over its door. It seems somewhat out of proportion to the rest of the structures in that glittering complex, lacking as it does any grand ceremonial entrance or impressive physical presence. This building's unprepossessiveness belies its importance, however, for it houses one of the most important centers for research in the performing arts anywhere in the world.

Behind the curtain walls of this building lie the Library and Museum of the Performing Arts. Its circulating collections of books, records, and videos, its exhibition galleries, and the Bruno Walter Auditorium are administered by The Branch Libraries and funded by the City of New York. These facilities for the general public are complemented by the Performing Arts Research Center (PARC), a unit of The Research Libraries, encompassing the Dance Collection, the Music Division, the Billy Rose Theatre Collection, and the Rodgers and Hammerstein Archives of Recorded Sound.

The position of the Library's building has a kind of inadvertent symbolic meaning. For the institutions that seem to lean against it on either side in a literal sense also lean on it in a metaphorical one. The professionals who perform in the other buildings at Lincoln Center and many more who aspire to, depend upon the Library as an indispensable source of reference in pursuit of their particular interests. So, indeed, do producers, directors, stage and costume designers, composers, choreographers, critics, radio and television producers, and still others who come here in search of helpful information—often enough, information they might find nowhere else. The roster of those who take advantage of the Library's services and facilities is studded with the names of eminent practitioners of all the performing arts. And the experience has often had an important influence on their careers. As Hal Prince, the Broadway producer, has written, "I suppose I was bitten by the theater bug as much by the Library as in the theater!" Such professionals come here not only from just across the plaza at the Center or up from Broadway, but from the whole wide world of entertainment. The Library is an international and encyclopedic center for information concerning anything and everything related to the stage or recital hall.

Those who cannot visit the place in person phone or write in their requests for information from every corner of the globe concerning every conceivable matter relating to the performing arts. Since, as in other divisions, the Lincoln Center staff considers nothing too trivial, almost all the questions will merit and be given a thoughtful answer. A curator of a London museum asks for the identification of a bronze figure in his institution's custody that has been simply labeled as "Mlle Nattova." A clipping from the Library's files advises him that the subject was Natacha Nattova, then dancing in the Greenwich Village Follies, "who has achieved immortality at the age of 19." A letter from New Zealand asks for information about the "Castle Walk," made popular by Irene and Vernon Castle early in the century. That was an easy one, for the Castles made headlines year after year in the early 1900s, and the Library's archives tell that whole story.

Some years ago, a more unusual request came from a man who had been reared in an orphanage. He had been told that he resembled both an actor and an actress who had enjoyed considerable success in the late 1800s. He wondered whether he might be the illegitimate child of this couple and asked where each of them had been during a critical month in 1886. The Library's files revealed that the lady was acting in Philadelphia at that time and the gentleman in New York, but the librarian drew no conclusions from that evidence.

Here as everywhere else in the institution, the remarkable expertise of the staff members in their separate divisions is matched only by their willingness to share it with the public, at every level. Some years ago the long-time and distinguished drama critic of *The New York Times* Brooks Atkinson paid eloquent tribute to those indispensable and talented persons:

> The busy staff of the Library of the Performing Arts accepted me as a permanent resident amid the silent uproar of their many duties. They are modest people with a mission. Nearly everyone else engaged in public service in the city is bored, surly, and inefficient and regards the citizens as intruders. The Library of the Performing Arts is not only hospitable but efficient, knowledgeable and obliging.

But that is just one more indication of the nature of the Library's resources and the informed staff that tends them; there are very few questions, however unexpected, that do not receive ample consideration. (The Library does admit that it could not help the man who wanted to trace the diamond-encrusted bicycle that, legend says, Jim Brady gave to Lillian Russell.)

Although the building at Lincoln Center provides the greatest concentration of facilities and services related to the performing arts, other divisions of the Library have rare and important supplementary material that adds substantially to the full story of these arts. As has already been explained, and might well be repeatedly emphasized, the numerous departments of the Library as a whole are not sealed containers of special fields of interest. Rather, they form a mosaic of interdependent parts. A thorough study of any subject may lead from one room or building to another as the search for information continues. In this case, statistics offer the quickest method of initially grasping the encyclopedic nature of PARC's holdings: the Dance Collection includes 37,300 books; 800,000 press clippings; more than half a million manuscripts; 517,000 photographs; and 8,620 reels of film and videotape. The Music Division has 360,000 printed books and scores; 60,000 letters and documents; 10,836 autograph musical manuscripts; 394,000 pieces of sheet music (of which 145,000 are American); and 4,001,000 clippings and programs. The Rodgers and Hammerstein Archives of Recorded Sound contain 466,000 audiovisual items. And the Billy Rose Theatre Collection numbers among its holdings some 34,000 typescripts and promptbooks;

2,000,000 programs and playbills; 31,000 scrapbooks; 790,000 letters, contracts, and business papers; 2,000,000 prints and photographs; and 20,000,000 newspaper and magazine clippings—not to mention their 24,000 posters!

These statistics are even more striking than they may at first appear when one realizes that PARC is essentially a creation of the last fifty years. Only music was represented in the original institutions that came together in 1895 to form The New York Public Library. Dance, theater, and recorded sound have all grown up with the century. And it is only since 1965 that they have had a building (or part of one) to themselves. Prior to the opening of the Lincoln Center facility, these departments' holdings were crammed into the Central Research Library. And now they have doubled and even tripled in size since that move and are in need of yet more space.

These massive and important holdings may broadly trace their lineage to 1888 when Joseph W. Drexel, the Philadelphia philanthropist, bequeathed his music collection of six thousand items to the Lenox Library, not yet incorporated into The New York Public Library. Among the treasured rarities Drexel had brought together were a book on the theory of music by Franchino Gaffurio, published in 1492, and *Parthenia In-Violata; or, Mayden-Musicke for the Virginalls and Bass-Viol*, a title that was a pun upon the Greek "Parthenos" (virgin) and "In Violata" (set for the viol to accompany the virginal). The book, published about 1625, contains twenty duets, selected by one Robert Hole, that may have been intended as a wedding present for the marriage of Prince Charles (later King Charles I) and his bride, Henrietta of France.

During the sixteenth and seventeenth centuries, sumptuous entertainments in which music, dance, and theater intermingled enjoyed great popularity in the courtly circles of Europe. Here were the beginnings of opera. Such extravaganzas were not staged in theaters by professional actors, but in palatial homes and carefully manicured gardens by and for royalty and the nobility. The great Sun King himself, Louis XIV, took part in such performances until, after fifty years of such activity, he became too fat to dance, and without his royal participation, interest in that form of amusement dwindled.

One of the most precious items in the Drexel Collection, *Le balet comique de la royne* by Baltazarini da Belgiojoso, was presented in 1581 at the court of Catherine de' Medici, the queen of France. This, the first *ballet de cour*, ancestor of the modern ballet, was organized to celebrate the wedding of the duc de Joyeux to Mlle de Vaudemont, sister to the queen. Just one further indication of the interest this book has attracted is the fact that, before it came into Drexel's hands, it had been owned in turn by Ben Jonson and Horace Walpole.

Another early festival book, *La magnifica et triumphale entrata del christianis (imo) re di Francia*, is from the Spencer Collection. Printed in 1549, it celebrates a state visit to Lyons by Henry II and Catherine de' Medici in 1548, the year after Henry had ascended the throne. When the two were married, Catherine was only fourteen years of age, but Francis I had chosen her as his son's bride for reasons of state—and she brought with her a very handsome dowry.

Almost half the bound volumes in the Music Division are scores. Many of the earlier ones have never been published and can be found only in these manuscript copies. To make these unique records available to performers and scholars who can bring them back to life is an important mission of the Library. Some years ago, for example, the Library published *The First Book of Consort Lessons* collected by Thomas Morley, one of the greatest of secular Elizabethan composers who, among other accomplishments, put a number of Shakespeare's songs to music. To recreate this long-lost repertory of the Elizabethan theater and to listen to music

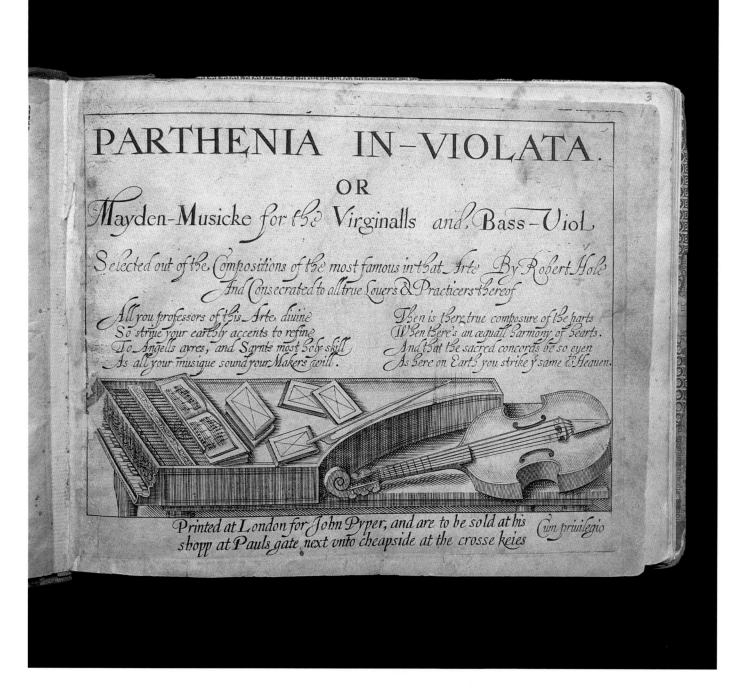

PARTHENIA IN-VIOLATA.

OR

Mayden-Musicke for the Virginalls and Bass-Viol

Selected out of the Compositions of the most famous in that Arte By Robert Hole
And Consecrated to all true Louers & Practicers thereof

All you professors of this Arte, diuine
So striue your earthly accents to refine
To Angells ayres, and Saynts most holy skill
As all your musique sound your Makers will.

Then is there true composure of the parts
When there's an æquall harmony of hearts.
And that the sacred concords be so euen
As here on Earth you strike y same in Heauen.

Printed at London for John Pyper, and are to be sold at his
shopp at Pauls gate next vnto cheapside at the crosse keies   Cum priuilegio

10–1. Parthenia In-violata; or, Mayden-Musicke for the Virginalls and Bass-Viol. *Selected by Robert Hole. London, J. Pyper, ca. 1620. Music Division*

Only one copy of a single issue of this collection of music for the virginalls (a type of harpsichord) and bass viol has survived. The pages were printed from engraved copperplates.

10–2. OTTAVIANO DEI PETRUCCI. Harmonice Musices Odhecaton A. *Venice, Petrucci, 1504. Music Division*
    This work contains ninety-six songs for three and four voices. Petrucci was the first to print polyphonic music with movable type.

that has not been heard since Shakespeare's day provides us with a fresh appreciation of our musical heritage as it was taking shape some four hundred years ago.

It is through references to such available sources that important programs like those produced by the New York Pro Musica, the Waverly Consort, and other groups both here and abroad devoted to the revival of ancient music are made possible. This recent and current recovery of audible evidence from earlier times might be compared with archaeological rediscoveries of tangible art objects whose original character had previously been known—if at all—merely by hearsay. The analogy may not be precise, but it serves to suggest how important—and fascinating—it is to be able to fill the gaps in our cultural history.

There are in the Music Division many original autograph scores of later composers whose works have been repeatedly performed over the years by musical groups around the world. Here again, the archives provide an important service. As edition after edition of these scores have been printed, omissions, alterations, and misinterpretations made by more or less scholarly editors have been perpetuated, often obscuring the composer's intentions. These can be detected only by reference to an original holograph copy (written and signed in the same hand). Even this does not always provide easy answers. Perhaps the composer himself made changes as he hastily recorded his notations. These may cause confusion enough, as they certainly do to an untutored layman who may find the resulting page utterly indecipherable.

There are rewards in studying these documents, however. To a knowing eye, the composer's musical handwriting reveals significant aspects of his temperament and personality, or at least his style. One of the Library's most highly valued manuscript scores is a twenty-two-page holograph of Mozart's G-major Symphony, K. 318, which he composed in 1779. Characteristically, the young genius (he was twenty-three at the time) swiftly produced an orderly script that was clearly readable. Beethoven's sketch for his so-called *Archduke* Trio, on the other hand, was scribbled with feverish tension, constantly reworked until he ended with a barely readable jumble of quill marks. The scores of Johann Sebastian Bach, as might be expected, show little of the strain of the creative process, but rather condensed, economical results of a thoroughly considered concept.

A close, inside look at what was going on in European musical circles during the first half of the nineteenth century can be had from some seven hundred autograph letters of Felix Mendelssohn-Bartholdy in the Library's archives. (The composer added "Bartholdy" to his name after he was converted from Judiasm to Christianity when he was a youth.) This collection, which narrowly escaped destruction in the bombing of Dresden during World War II, includes Mendelssohn's correspondence with his family as well as delightful pen-and-ink sketches of places he visited during his travels throughout Europe.

The performing arts differ from all the other arts by their very nature. We can admire a Classical sculpture, a Renaissance painting, or a Gutenberg Bible

10–3. WOLFGANG AMADEUS MOZART. Symphony in G-Major (K. 318). Manuscript, 1779. Music Division

In musical as in literary manuscripts the artist's original composition in his own hand provides scholars with the essential element of their research. It also offers the layman who reveres the work a proximity to the act of creation that no copy can achieve.

with the assurance that we can always return to them and find them unchanged. A performance on stage is a different matter; every presentation is a thing unto itself. It is a passing experience we may witness only for the time required for it to reach its end and the stage to be emptied.

With the development of the phonograph, the motion picture, and a constantly increasing and improving variety of audio-visual instruments, ways have been found to capture those fleeting moments in time and preserve them as invaluable, fixed references for the present and future. We take such devices as an essential birthright. Yet, an autograph book in the Rodgers and Hammerstein Archives of Recorded Sound reveals that only a century ago, after tours throughout Europe, an Edison representative returned with handwritten tributes to the "miracle" of the phonograph from such personages as Tchaikovsky, Rimsky-Korsakov, and Tolstoy, among many others.

The testimonials of the 1890s were evidently taken at face value, for sound recordings have become one of the omnipresent features of twentieth-century life, and a major aspect of collecting and research in the field of the performing arts. The Rodgers and Hammerstein Archives had their start in 1937 when Columbia Records began donating copies of their latest releases to the Music Division. This good example was soon followed by other record companies and private collectors. In 1962, the Rodgers and Hammerstein Foundation gave the Library a grant to organize and catalogue for public use the tens of thousands of records that had accumulated since the initial Columbia gift. After the opening of the Lincoln Center building in 1965, the Rodgers and Hammerstein Archives remained a separate part of the Music Division until they became a full-fledged unit of PARC in 1980.

Among its some 460,000 recordings the Archives count historically significant items such as "The Mapleson Cylinders," a set of recordings of live performances at the Metropolitan Opera House in 1901–1904. Originally recorded on wax cylinders, these have now been transferred to tape. They provide us with an invaluable record of the past when such greats as the DeReszke brothers starred at the Met. To avoid distracting audiences completely unused to the primitive process of recording sound, the operator at one point retreated to the catwalk to do his job. In addition to recordings of opera and classical music, the Rodgers and Hammerstein Archives collects records of popular music, from jazz to rap, plays, poetry readings, political speeches, and radio, television, and film soundtracks.

10–4. FELIX MENDELSSOHN-BARTHOLDY. Letter. Manuscript. Music Division

The collection of 742 letters from which this example has been chosen was written to members of his family during the years 1821–1847. They include delightful pen-and-ink sketches of places the composer visited during his travels throughout Europe.

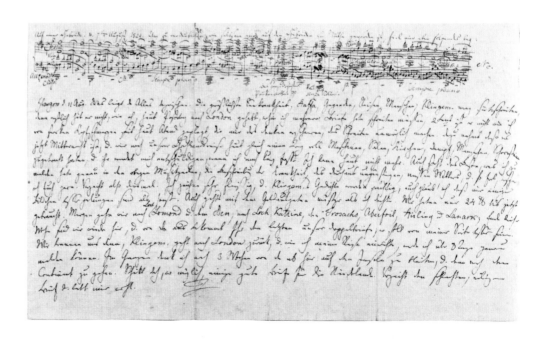

The popular recordings, together with the Library's 145,000 pieces of American sheet music from the eighteenth through the twentieth centuries, is a treasure trove for performers and composers in search of whatever may shed light on their professional undertakings. Beyond that, these collections are a reflection of the changing tastes of the American public and, as well, reminders of our social life and customs over the years. They offer a lyrical indication of what was on people's minds during hard times and good. The most memorable in the Library's collections is a copy of the first edition of "The Star-Spangled Banner" by Francis Scott Key. That precious document, celebrating the American flag as an enduring emblem of national pride, was written during the War of 1812, aptly enough called

10–5. Mapleson Cylinders. Recordings. 1901–1904. Rodgers and Hammerstein Archives of Recorded Sound

Mapleson was the librarian of the Metropolitan Opera. During the years 1901–1904, he made live recordings of performances at the Opera House on these wax cylinders.

our "second war of independence." The song was officially proclaimed the national anthem in 1931.

In the archives devoted to the theater, among many other things, will be found more than a million playbills going back almost two hundred years and the programs of virtually every Broadway play staged over the past century or so. (Included in these is the earliest American example, printed in Philadelphia in 1767 to announce a performance of *Romeo and Juliet*.) At the Library the word "theater" is very broadly construed. It includes not only the legitimate stage, but vaudeville, the circus, motion pictures, radio, television, and almost every other kind of performance that has been contrived to entertain in the past and present. There are thousands of books and pamphlets in various languages from the seventeenth century to our own day dealing with stage magic and magicians.

For earlier generations of children there was nothing in the world of entertainment comparable to the circus. In *A Son of the Middle Border* (1917) Hamlin Garland wrote:

> To rob me of my memories of the circus would leave me as poor as those to whom life was a drab and hopeless round of toil. It was our brief season of imaginative life. In one day — in a part of one day — we gained a thousand new conceptions of the world and of human nature. It was an embodiment of all that was skillful and beautiful in manly action. It was a compendium of biologic research but more important still, it brought to our ears the latest band pieces and taught us the most popular songs. It furnished us with jokes. We relieved our dullness. It gave us something to talk about.

Very few of us outlive the excitement engendered by the variety of performances in the sawdust rings. For the aging circus buff and for serious students of this phenomenal kind of theater, the Library has documentation dating back to the eighteenth century. There are books and periodicals devoted to the subject and files of contemporary clippings that can bring us very close to the lives and activities of the clowns, equestrians, jokesters, and others who are fondly remembered from past performances. Sensational posters, broadsides, and other promotional devices bear witness to the forgivable exaggerations that made great heroes of such figures as Buffalo Bill, Tom Mix, Emmett Kelly, and others. Complementing these holdings are seventeen letters by P. T. Barnum in the Rare Books and Manuscripts Division of the Central Research Library.

The cornerstone of the Theatre Collection was laid in 1931, when the executors of the estate of David Belasco, the renowned theatrical manager and producer, gave to the Library his lifetime gatherings of documents relating to the American stage — with the proviso that it be made fully available to the public. The Theatre Collection was one of the earliest models for many subsequent archives in other parts of the nation. In practice, this quickly became a laboratory where professionals came daily to inform and refine their crafts. In preparing her uncut version of *Hamlet,* in which Maurice Evans would play the title role, the eminent director Margaret Webster spent five months of hard labor at the Library studying earlier productions of the play, mainly from promptbooks. From its thousands of such books the Library could produce more than four hundred for productions of Shakespearean plays, ranging in date from the late eighteenth to the twentieth century. A promptbook of the original production of *Camille* in 1853, complete with scene plots and music, helped Lillian Gish plan her revival of that work. When he was undertaking the set and costume research for *My Fair Lady,* Cecil

10–6. Playbill for a performance
of *Romeo and Juliet*, 1767.
Billy Rose Theatre Collection
   This is the earliest playbill in
the Billy Rose Theatre Collection, and it highlights the central role of the collection in
documenting the American
theater.

By Authority.

By the AMERICAN COMPANY,
At the *NEW THEATRE* in SOUTHWARK; On *TUESDAY*,
The *Seventh* of *April*, will be prefented, *BY PARTICULAR DESIRE*,
A *TRAGEDY* called

ROMEO AND JULIET,

Romeo by Mr. HALLAM,
Mercutio by Mr. DOUGLASS,
Capulet by Mr. MORRIS,
Fryar Lawrence by Mr. ALLYN,
Mountague by Mr. TOMLINSON,
Efcalus by Mr. BROADBELT,
Tibalt by Mr WALL,
Paris by Mr. WOOLLS,---*Benvolio* by Mr. GODWIN,
Balthazer by Mr. GREVILLE,---*Fryar John* by Mr. PLATT,
Lady Capulet by Mrs. DOUGLASS,
Nurfe by Mrs. HARMAN,
Juliet by Mifs CHEER.

With the Funeral Proceffion of *Juliet*,

To the Monument of the *Capulets*;
And a SOLEMN DIRGE:
The *VOCAL PARTS* by Mr. WOOLLS, Mr. WALL, Mifs WAINWRIGHT,
Mifs HALLAM, Mrs. HARMAN, Mrs. MORRIS, &c.
With DANCES incident to the *PLAY, Viz.*
A *COMIC DANCE* by Mr. GODWIN;
A *MASQUERADE DANCE*;
And a *MINUET* by Mr. HALLAM and Mifs CHEER.
To which will be added, A *DRAMATIC SATIRE* called

LETHE, or *Æfop in the Shades.*

Drunken-Man by Mr. HALLAM,
Frenchman by Mr. ALLYN,
Old Man by Mr. MORRIS,
Mercury (with Songs) by Mr. WOOLLS,
Fine Gentleman by Mr. WALL,---*Charon* by Mr. TOMLINSON,
Æfop by Mr. DOUGLASS,
Mrs. *Tattoo* by Mifs HALLAM,
Mrs. *Riot* (with a Song in Character) by Mifs WAINWRIGHT.
To begin exactly at Half an Hour after SIX *o'Clock.*----Vivant Rex & Regina.
No Perfons can, on any Pretence whatfoever, be admitted behind the Scenes.
TICKETS are fold at the *London Coffee-Houfe*, at Mr. *Hawkins's* in *Walnut-Street*, and at
Mrs. *Scott's* in *Lombard-Street*; at which laft *Office*, PLACES in the BOXES are to be had.
BOXES *Seven Shillings and Sixpence.* PIT *Five Shillings.* GALLERY *Three Shillings.*

1767

Beaton looked to these collections for the information he needed, as did José
Ferrer in gathering material for *Cyrano de Bergerac*, and so on down a long list
of theatrical folk who have worked on and in memorable productions with promptbooks as their points of reference.

For those who want a closer look at the playwright's work in its original stages,
the collections can provide manuscripts and significant early published editions
of dramas created by such distinguished figures as George Bernard Shaw, Eugene
O'Neill, and other English and American writers.

In 1979 the Theatre Collection was named after Billy Rose, theatrical producer,
impresario, and songwriter, when the foundation named after him provided an
endowment for the support of the collection.

The Library's holdings of movie material practically grew up with that industry
and is now probably the greatest source of information relating to that "modern"
art in any public institution in the world. A constantly mounting attendance at
movie theaters showed that nothing so appealing had ever before served for public
entertainment. Considered as an art form, it is the only one that those still living

10–7. Costume and scene designs by Claude Bragdon for a production of Rostand's *Cyrano de Bergerac. Drawings and watercolors, 1923. Billy Rose Theatre Collection*

Original designs for theatrical productions such as these form one of the major elements in providing researchers with the fullest documentation of theatrical productions from the days before film and videotape.

have witnessed from its beginnings. In fairly short order, it became obvious that the spirit, the language, the dress, the gadgetry, the behavior, and even the physical appearance of a wide public was being conditioned by Hollywood standards. The effects were apparent far beyond American borders in all directions. In many parts of the world, Hollywood's picture of American habits and manners was serving as the main version of life in the United States—with questionable results!

Virtually every phase of that phenomenal development, from the technique of writing for films and the engineering and photographic aspects to reviews of the latest hits, can be explored in the Library's resources. Movie buffs can turn to a generous sampling of such fan magazines as *Photoplay, Picture Play,* and *Motion Picture Classics,* as well as fifty years of movie stills.

The rocketing rise of the Library in the past century to its present eminence is nowhere more dramatically demonstrated than in the growth of the resources dealing with the dance. When the Astor and Lenox libraries and the Tilden Trust were consolidated in 1895, these resources consisted of a few rare books and some contemporary newspaper accounts. Today, the Dance Collection is without peer in its field. The public services this wealth of material provides are an increasingly important influence in shaping today's dance world. There is hardly a significant book on the dance published in recent years that does not give generous credit to this division of the Library for the research help it has provided. Many of them have been illustrated almost entirely from the Library's copious picture files, the largest of their kind in the world.

The Dance Collection has grown tremendously in the last generation or two as America's interest in the dance in all its forms awakened with a relatively sudden start; and it has been sustained in a generous measure through gifts of private donors. Probably no other division of the Library has benefited so greatly from such support.

As one very important example, in 1955 the distinguished bibliophile Walter Toscanini gave the Library his matchless collection of historical materials in memory of his wife, the ballerina Cia Fornaroli. With that one incomparable gift, the Dance Collection gained international importance as an archive. Among much other material, the Cia Fornaroli collection includes more than a thousand books dealing with the history, theory, and technique of theatrical and social dancing—books of which no duplicate copies are known to be in any other library in the United States. The few rare books of 1895 have multiplied wondrously!

One of the rarest of all is a manuscript written about 1460 by a Jewish dancing master in Italy who called himself Guglielmo Ebreo. In Guglielmo's time, Italy led the world in the art of dancing, and the recorded history of European dancing begins with the writings of such Italian dancing masters. His collection of twenty-three choreographed dances for ballet and social dancing—a few attributed to Lorenzo de' Medici—is one of the earliest and richest manuscripts of its kind from the Renaissance to have survived. Some of the examples he presents are to be found in no other known document. To add to the interest Guglielmo's manuscript commands, this is not a presentation piece but a working copy made for himself and for his own use—the only existing one known from this period to have served this workaday purpose.

In the many other rarities in the Cia Fornaroli collection we can trace the shifting attitudes and varying practices that highlight the history of the art over four centuries. With the sixteenth century, France became the capital of the dancing world. Here with the vigorous and lavish patronage of the Italian-born queen Catherine de' Medici, the beginning of modern theatrical dancing took place and the first significant French work on dancing was published. In the next century, Louis XIV

Cyrano Act II
Roxane's Coach

Cyrano Act I Cyrano

Cyrano Act I Jodelet

ACT II: RAGUENEAU'S SHOP

CYRANO DE BERGERAC

WALTER HAMPDEN'S PRODUCTION OF CYRANO

10–8. ROBERT EDMOND
JONES. Costume design.
*Watercolor, ca. 1943. Billy Rose
Theatre Collection*
   *Jones prepared this design for
Margaret Webster's production of*
Othello *with Paul Robeson in
the title role, Uta Hagen as
Desdemona, and Jose Ferrer as
Iago.*

established the Académie Royale de la Dance. During the eighteenth century, the Age of Reason, contemporary dance along with just about everything else fell under criticism for its superficiality. "On our stage," wrote one critic, "we have excellent feet, brilliant legs, and admirable arms. What a pity that we lack the art of dance!" About the same time Jean Georges Noverre, whom David Garrick called "the Shakespeare of the dance," published his angry, analytical essays, which many, if not most, authorities consider still the best introduction to the concept of theatrical dancing. Noverre boasted that he had achieved a revolution in dancing, and if he did not do such a thing single-handedly, he was nonetheless an influential innovator who left a firm imprint on the art.

Even earlier in the century, a German reformer had questioned the propriety of mixed dancing. If it were to take place, he admonished his readers, it should be in the presence of respectable chaperones and, in any case, it is improper to approach a lady partner closer than one pace.

He was not alone in his reactionary stand against "modern" ballroom dancing. Another contemporary critic spoke out about "the abomination of permitting a man who is neither your lover nor your husband to encircle you with his arms, and slightly press the contour of your waist." However, such warnings against licentiousness did very little to discourage such exciting new diversions as the waltz and the polka.

A century later an Italian, Carlo Blasis, wrote a more understanding treatise on private dancing that was so popular it lived on in edition after edition. This was originally part of Blasis's larger and most important work, *The Code of Terpsichore*. Blasis was famous in his day as a dancer and a composer of ballets. He was also a teacher and a polymath of sorts. In one translation or another, his *Code* has long been a standard text in ballet schools. A recently acquired treasure of the collection is his manuscript scrapbook from around 1855, containing 191 drawings of ballet technique.

Such cursory references to books in the library of the Dance Collection barely begin to suggest the wealth of information available in its collections. In spite of that abundance, the books constitute a relatively small part of the resources that are housed in this division of the Library. As the importance and effectiveness of the division's function become increasingly manifest, men and women who have dedicated their lives to the dance and have made vital contributions to the art have turned over to the Library their personal papers and records, as have outstanding collectors of relevant material. The list of such donors is long and impressive. It is virtually a Who's Who of the dance world.

A great gift from Ted Shawn and Ruth St. Denis of documents relating to their illustrious joint careers on stage is a prominent landmark in the history of the Dance Collection. No recounting of twentieth-century dance in America could be adequately prepared without reference to the Humphrey-Weidman Collection and that of Hanya Holm given to the Library about the same time. The family and associates of Isadora Duncan have added a memorable collection of papers to the archives. They start with her own personal journals written in Paris in 1901 and continue with reviews of her performances in Russia, which had an important influence on Michel Fokine, the Russian-born American choreographer and dancer. Fokine in turn helped shape the careers of such rising luminaries as Nijinsky and Pavlova. He is considered the founder of modern ballet.

For centuries, efforts have been made to devise a system of notation to preserve the structure of dance comparable to that used for music. Once dismissed as a scholarly folly, the idea has become a working reality. The Labanotation method proposed in 1928 by Rudolf Laban, the most successful of the methods that have

10–9. Charlie Chaplin as "The Little Tramp." *Poster, ca. 1925. Billy Rose Theatre Collection*
   The universal appeal of some aspects of American popular culture is evident in this poster where Charlie Chaplin appears described in Greek as "The Clown of Life."

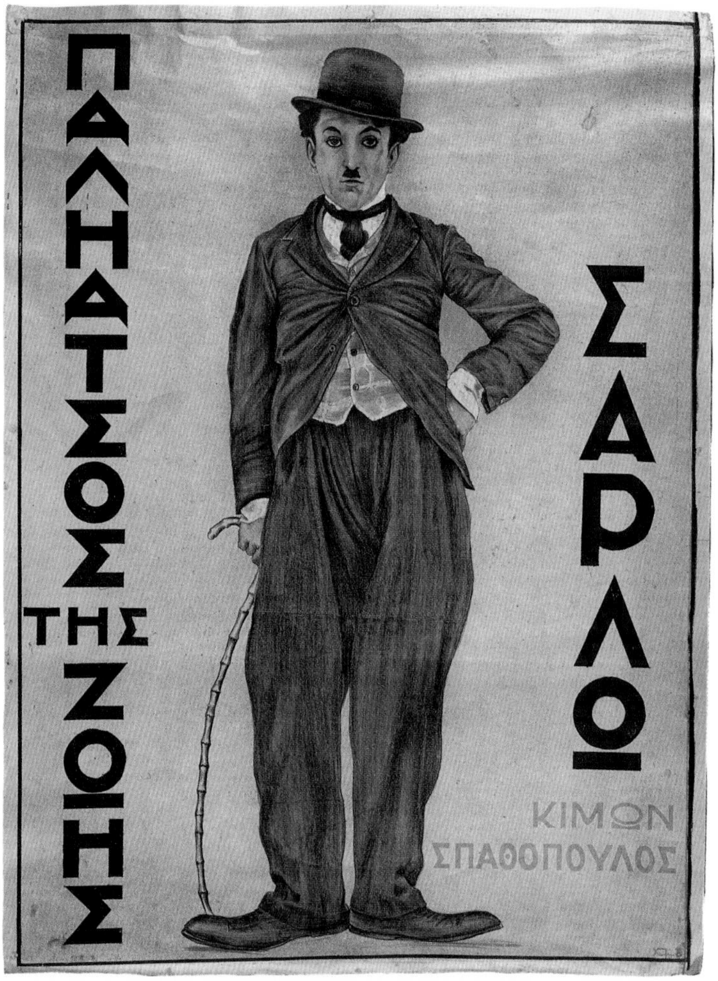

10–10. Cole Bros. Circus Poster, *ca. 1930. Billy Rose Theatre Collection*
   Among the activities that the Library includes in its definition of "theater" is the circus.

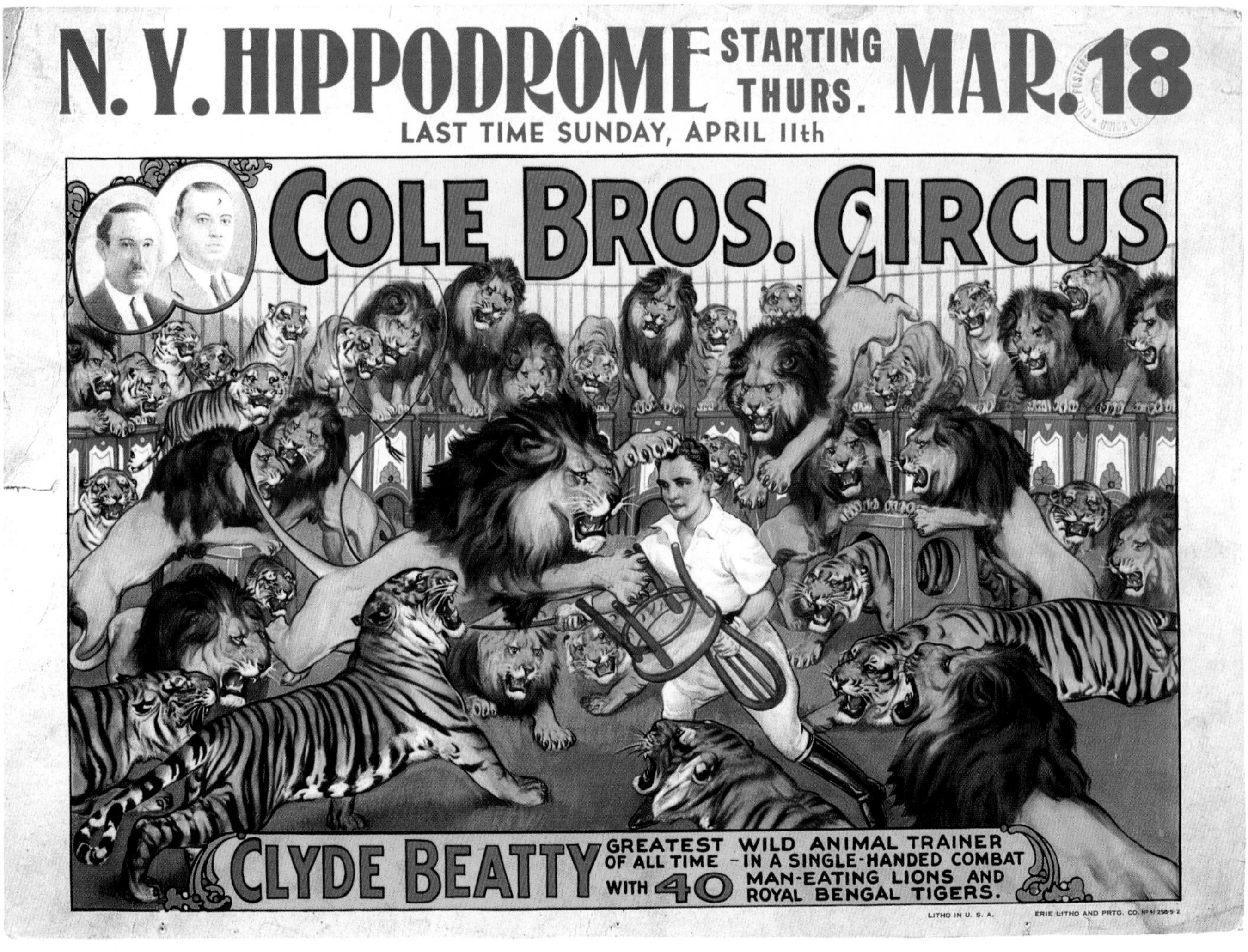

ΠΑΛΗΑΤΣΟΣ ΤΗΣ ΖΩΗΣ

ΣΑΡΛΟ

ΚΙΜΩΝ ΣΠΑΘΟΠΟΥΛΟΣ

N. Y. HIPPODROME STARTING THURS. MAR. 18
LAST TIME SUNDAY, APRIL 11th

COLE BROS. CIRCUS

CLYDE BEATTY GREATEST WILD ANIMAL TRAINER OF ALL TIME – IN A SINGLE-HANDED COMBAT WITH 40 MAN-EATING LIONS AND ROYAL BENGAL TIGERS.

LITHO IN U. S. A.   ERIE LITHO AND PRTG. CO. Nº 41-258-5-2

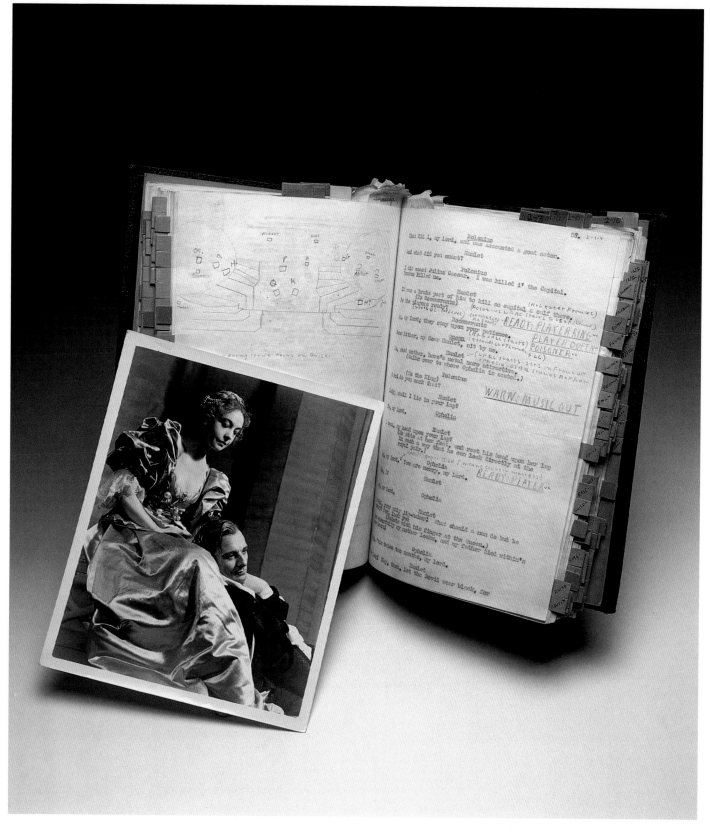

10–11. Photograph of Sir John Gielgud as Hamlet, together with the stage manager's copy of the production in which he starred, *1936. Billy Rose Theatre Collection*

Sir John's Hamlet shared the stage with Lillian Gish as Ophelia and Dame Judith Anderson as Gertrude. The production was designed by Jo Mielziner.

10–12. Trattato dell'Arte del Ballo. *Manuscript. Italy, ca. 1460. Shown with* Guerra d'Amore *by Jacques Callot. Etching, 1615. Dance Collection*

This work by the Italian dancing master Guglielmo Ebreo is one of the earliest extant descriptions of specific dances.

been tried, is applicable to sports and the theater, recording by symbols the movement of human bodies. In 1983, a Balanchine work, "Symphonie Concertante," was danced for the first time in more than thirty years thanks to a Labanotation score discovered in the files of City Ballet.

However, as the American choreographer and dancer (and generous contributor to the Library's archives) Jerome Robbins has pointed out: "We must be able to observe works in their original state and be able to watch the specific, subtle and elusive qualities of performance and performers which are outside of the actual choreography itself, and which no system of dance notation or verbal description is ever able to realize." And here the motion picture camera has served,

10–13. Dance Cards. *English and American, 19th century. Dance Collection*

The Dance Collection is concerned not just with the ballet or classical dance but also with dance in its popular forms and its social aspects.

10–14. CARLO BLASIS. Scrapbook. *Manuscript, 1855. Dance Collection*

Carlo Blasis wrote a treatise on private dancing that was so popular it was constantly reprinted in the nineteenth century. He was a dancer, composer of ballets, and teacher. In this scrapbook he preserved 191 of his drawings of ballet technique.

10–15. Denishawn costume, ca. 1925. Dance Collection
    Ted Shawn and his wife, Ruth St. Denis, were among the pioneers of American dance in the twentieth century. This costume from one of their ballet productions reflects the oriental richness of effect that fascinated them.

as the phonograph has done for music. To achieve this in significant fashion, in the past twenty-odd years the Dance Collection has filmed more than three hundred major dance works by twenty choreographers performed by ten leading companies, in addition to acquiring many thousands of running feet of other performances by gift or purchase.

To many of us, the word "research" brings to mind scholars (usually old and often dowdy) delving into musty tomes and manuscripts in quest of obscure facts with which they will be able to confront other scholars. An updated understanding of the word can be gathered by visiting the Library at Lincoln Center and witnessing performing artists actively engaged in their own lines of research. One

10–16. Photograph of Isadora Duncan *by Edward Steichen, 1920. Shown with Duncan memorabilia. Dance Collection*

In her concert dances Isadora Duncan fused an American attitude of freedom with "Greek Revival" attitudes and costumes.

10–17. JULES GRANDJOUAN. Pastel Drawings of Isadora Duncan, *1912. Dance Collection*

Duncan's European vogue is reflected in these drawings (from a series of twenty-five) that were published in France in 1912.

10–18. Archival material from the Martha Graham Collection. *Dance Collection*

Martha Graham's original and often stark balletic vision helped to give American dance an international interest and impact.

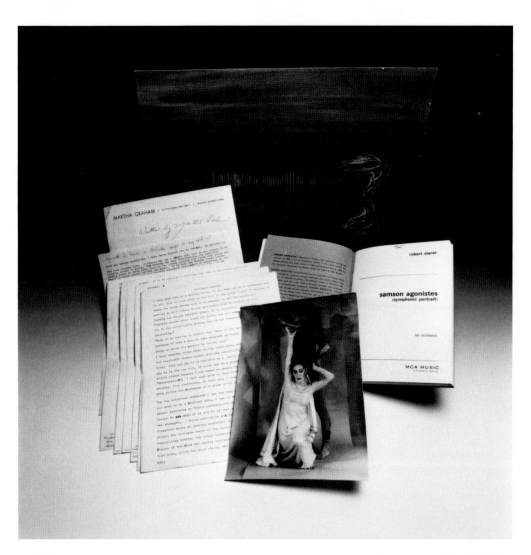

10–19. ENRICO CECCHETTI. Manual of Ballet Exercises and Technique. *Manuscript, 1904. Dance Collection*

Cecchetti came from a family that had been important in European ballet in the nineteenth century. This manuscript was written while he was in St. Petersburg.

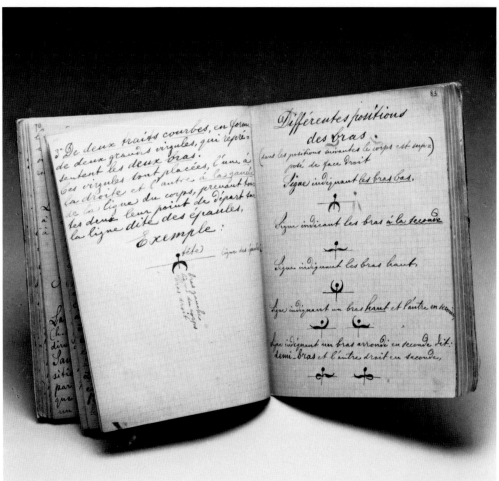

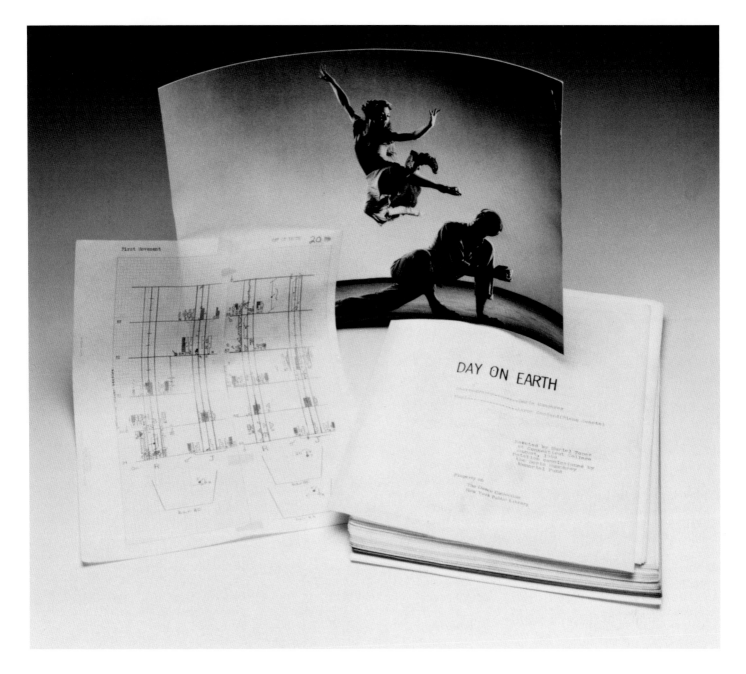

might well spy a dancer attentively practicing steps before a video screen to find in some earlier, classic performance a long-overlooked passage that might spur her own innovative talents. Having this "live" libretto is an advantage to professional careers never enjoyed by earlier generations of students of this art.

In this dancer's use of the collection we may see a paradigm of the significance of the whole of the Performing Arts Research Center and, indeed, The New York Public Library as a whole: through its vast and varied mass of material it documents the past in order to inform the present and inspire the future.

10–20. DORIS HUMPHREY. Day on Earth. *Photograph and Labanotation. Dance Collection*

Doris Humphrey's Day on Earth *was one of the major works of postwar American dance. It was first performed in 1947.*

INDEX

PHOTOGRAPH CREDITS

ALL PHOTOGRAPHS BY JONATHAN WALLEN EXCEPT AS NOTED BELOW:

Introduction: Pages 8, 12, 13, 14, 16–19 The New York Public Library; pages 24, 25 Adam Bartos.

Chapter I: Plate 18 Robert D. Rubic.

Chapter II: Plates 8, 11, 15, 19, 20, 32 The New York Public Library; plate 28 Philip Pocock; plates 2, 3, 4 Robert D. Rubic.

Chapter III: Plate 25 The New York Public Library.

Chapter IV: Plates 1, 2, 4–9, 11–16 The New York Public Library.

Chapter V: Plates 1, 3, 5, 7, 9, 12, 13, 15, 18, 20, 21, 23, 25 The New York Public Library; plates 16, 17 Philip Pocock.

Chapter VI: Plates 3, 8, 9, 10, 17 The New York Public Library.

Chapter VII: Plate 25 The New York

Public Library; plates 4, 8, 17, 19, 20 Stephen L. Senigo.

Chapter VIII: Plates 1, 2, 4, 6, 7, 10, 13, 15, 16, 20 The New York Public Library; plate 17 Philip Pocock.

Chapter IX: Plates 2, 7, 15, 16, 20, 22, 23 The New York Public Library; plate 18 Peter Bittner; plate 19 Bob Serating.

Chapter X: Plate 6 The New York Public Library.